— NEW —
Saint Joseph
ANNOTATED
Catechism

JESUS IS THE LIGHT OF THE WORLD
"I am the light of the world. No follower of mine shall ever walk in darkness; no, he shall have the light of life" (Jn 8:12).

New ... Saint 'Joseph

Annotated
Catechism

A CLEAR AND FULL EXPLANATION
OF THE CATHOLIC FAITH
IN QUESTION-AND-ANSWER FORM
WITH COPIOUS INFORMATIVE AND
HISTORICAL NOTES

With Many Citations from the Bible,
the Second Vatican Council,
and the Papal Documents

In complete Accord with "Sharing the Light of Faith"
— the National Catholic Directory
Approved by the Bishops of the United States

●

BY REV. ANTHONY SCHRANER

CATHOLIC BOOK PUBLISHING CO.
NEW YORK

NIHIL OBSTAT: Michael J. Wrenn, M.A., M.S.
Thomas M. O'Hagan, S.L.L.
Censores Deputati

IMPRIMATUR: Joseph T. O'Keefe
Vicar General, Archdiocese of New York

The nihil obstat and imprimatur are official declarations that a book or pamphlet is free of doctrinal or moral error. No implication is contained therein that those who have granted the nihil obstat and imprimatur agree with the contents, opinions or statements expressed.

ACKNOWLEDGMENTS

We are grateful for permission to quote from the following copyrighted works:

Official Documents:

LITURGICAL TEXTS: Excerpts from the English translation of the *Rite of Baptism for Children* © 1969, International Committee on English in the Liturgy, Inc. (ICEL); excerpts from the English translation of *Rite of Anointing and Pastoral Care of the Sick* © 1973, ICEL; excerpts from the English translation of *The Roman Missal* © 1973, excerpts from the English translation of *Holy Communion and Worship of the Eucharist Outside Mass* ©1974, ICEL; excerpts from the English translation of *Rite of Penance* © 1974, ICEL; excerpts from the English translation of *Rite of Confirmation* ©1975, ICEL. All rights reserved.

BIBLICAL TEXTS: Excerpts from *The New American Bible* ©1970 by the Confraternity of Christian Doctrine, Washington, D.C. All rights reserved.

COUNCIL TEXTS: Excerpts from NCWC Council Texts, USCC Publications, altered and adapted for discriminatory language and using NAB version for Bible citations.

Other Citations:

Excerpts from *A New Catechism: Catholic Faith for Adults* ©1967 and 1969 Herder & Herder, Inc. Used by permission of the Crossroad Publishing Company.

Excerpts from *The Roman Ritual* ©1954 by Bruce Publishing Co. Used by permission of the author, Rev. Philip T. Weller.

Note: The material contained in Questions 163, 165-169, 171-172, 174, 178, 184-187 is taken from *Spotlight on Liturgy* © 1981 by Catholic Book Publishing Co.

(T-545)

CONTENTS

PART THREE: THE COMMANDMENTS

FOREWORD

THIS new *Annotated Catechism* is a happy blend of the old and the new. It gives the teachings of the Catholic Church in the format of the Question-and-Answer Method and appends copious notes from the teachings of Vatican II as well as postconciliar documents.

The legacy of the Second Vatican Council makes it advisable, indeed necessary, to state some things in a way that may depart somewhat from older formulations —though basically it is always the same truth of faith that is expressed. This Catechism takes into account the deposit of the Council. Specifically, it incorporates in the answers numerous excerpts from Conciliar documents. At the same time, it also includes citations from postconciliar documents and practices. Thus, this Catechism is an effort to present the truths of the Catholic faith as they ought to be presented in the light of the Second Vatican Council.

This work is the fruit of over thirty years experience in catechetics. On every page it offers clear instruction on the fundamentals of Catholic doctrine concerning faith, grace, and morality. And it does so with special reference, in numerous cases, to the actual problems of our time. Hence, it is a real help to individual believers as well as parents, teachers, and students.

Special care has been taken with every phase of the production to make this Catechism an invaluable aid for all who want to have the teachings of the Church ready at hand and in a form that is easy to understand. The time-tested Question-and-Answer Method allows the reader to get the substance of each teaching very quickly.

Furthermore, the many helpful *Notes* provide wonderful supplementary material that facilitates studying the teaching in greater depth. The *Council Summaries* in the Appendix give at a glance the main teachings and circumstances of each of the twenty-one Ecumenical Councils of the Church. They constitute an ideal way to learn the history of the Church. The *Analytical Index* constitutes an ideal means of getting the most out of the massive amount of information in the book. Finally, the superb *Illustrations* serve to keep Christ ever before the reader—for it is His teaching and His Person that are spoken about throughout the text.

We wish to extend special thanks to Reverend John A. Otto for his many invaluable suggestions and general editorial help. His contributions, together with those of the Editorial Staff of the Catholic Book Publishing Co., assisted greatly in putting final shape to this Catechism.

It is the sincere hope of the Publisher that this new Catechism will help spread the teaching of the Church and inculcate true devotion to Jesus Who is the Savior and the Light of the world.

The Publisher

INTRODUCTION

1. *Why are we on earth?*

We are on earth to serve God and by serving Him to gain eternal happiness in heaven.

"Life is short but of everlasting value; it contains the seed of eternity"— St. Francis de Sales (d. 1662).

"You have made us for Yourself, O Lord, and our hearts are restless until they rest in You" — St. Augustine (d. 430).

"The Church holds that the recognition of God is in no way hostile to human dignity, since this dignity is rooted and perfected in God. For human beings were made intelligent and free members of society by God Who created them; but even more important, they are called as children to commune with God and share in His happiness. She further teaches that a hope related to the end of time [i.e., hope of the next life] does not diminish the importance of intervening duties but rather undergirds the acquittal of them with fresh incentives" *(Pastoral Constitution on the Church in the Modern World,* no. 21).

2. *What must we do to serve God?*

To serve God we must
1. have faith,
2. keep the Commandments
3. and receive the holy Sacraments and pray.

This answer, with its three parts, introduces the three major divisions of the present Catechism: Faith, Sacraments, Commandments. The Catechism develops and explains each division in detail.

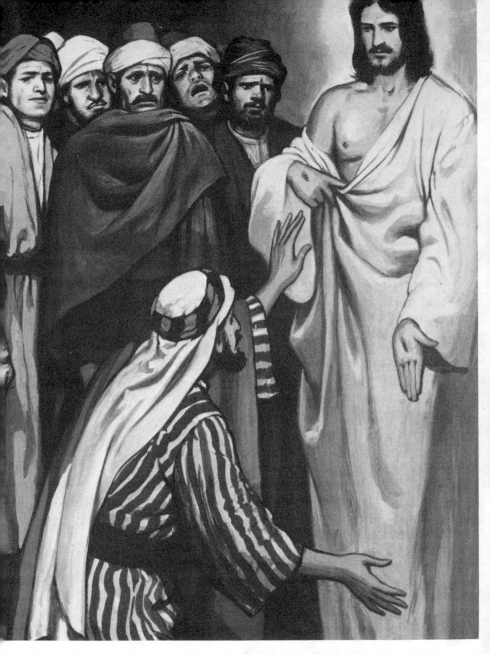

JESUS ASKED FOR FAITH AND BLESSED THOSE WHO BELIEVE
"Jesus then said to [Thomas]: 'You became a believer because you saw me. Blest are they who have not seen and have believed'" (Jn 20:29).

PART ONE: FAITH

FAITH

3. *What is meant by faith?*

By faith is meant accepting and holding as true all that God has revealed and through His Church teaches us to believe.

To reveal means to make known truths that were unknown. Even in purely human affairs we must often rely on faith, i.e., the word of another. Many Europeans have never been in America, and many Americans have never been in Europe. But they take it on the word of another, perhaps a teacher, that there is a land mass called Europe or America. For historical events of the past we are similarly dependent on the word or testimony of others.

It is not enough, however, to "hold as true" the truths of faith. For faith to be complete, its truths must bring us into a more personal relationship with God. In other words, we must live according to what we believe. Every religious truth should bind us more closely to God. Faith then becomes our response to God's call to follow Him.

4. *Through whom did God reveal what we must believe?*

What we must believe God revealed:
1) **through the Prophets and Patriarchs in the Old Testament;**
2) **through His Son Jesus Christ and the Apostles in the New Testament.**

God's Revelation began with the very first man, Adam. After him revelations were made to Noah, Abraham, Moses, and various Prophets like Isaiah, Jeremiah, Daniel, etc.

"In times past, God spoke in fragmentary and varied ways to our fathers through the prophets; in this, the final age, he has spoken to us through his Son" (Heb 1:1-2).

5. Why must we believe what God has revealed?

We must believe what God has revealed because God cannot err or lead us into error.

"God is not man that he should speak falsely, nor human, that he should change his mind" (Nm 23:19).

6. Where is God's Revelation contained?

God's Revelation is contained in the Bible and in Sacred tradition.

On this twofold source the Second Vatican Council (Vatican II, for short) said the following in the *Dogmatic Constitution on Divine Revelation* (no. 9): "There exist a close connection and communication between sacred tradition and Sacred Scripture. For both of them, flowing from the same divine wellspring, in a certain way merge into a unity and tend toward the same end.

"Sacred Scripture is the word of God inasmuch as it is consigned to writing under the inspiration of the divine Spirit. Sacred tradition takes the word of God entrusted by Christ the Lord and the Holy Spirit to the Apostles, and hands it on to their successors in its full purity, so that led by the light of the Spirit of truth, they may in proclaiming it preserve this word of God faithfully, explain it, and make it more widely known.

"Consequently it is not from Sacred Scripture alone that the Church draws her certainty about everything which has been revealed. Hence, both sacred tradition and Sacred Scripture are to be accepted and venerated with the same sense of loyalty and reverence."

Oral tradition, a handing on by word of mouth, came first. Christ and His Apostles spoke the word of God in public discourse and informally with individuals and groups. There were Christians before any book of the New Testament was written.

Christ commanded the Apostles to preach His teaching: "Go into the whole world and proclaim the good news to all creation" (Mk 16:15).

St. John ends his Gospel with this statement: "There are still many other things that Jesus did, yet if they were written about in detail, I doubt there would be room enough in the entire world to hold the books to record them" (Jn 21:25). And Paul admonishes the Christians of Thessalonica: "Brothers, stand firm. Hold fast to the traditions you received from us, either by our word or by letter" (2 Thes 2:15).

The Bible

7. What is the Bible?

The Bible is a collection of sacred books, which were composed under the positive influence of the Holy Spirit by men chosen by God, and which have been accepted by the Church as inspired. It is the most authorized, most admirable, and most important book in the world because it is the only "divine book," the word of God in the language of man.

The Bible is composed of many books (it is really a "library" of books), some by unknown authors, written over the course of more than a thousand years—from about 950 B.C. to 100 A.D.

The Bible is incomparable as far as all other "sacred" literature is concerned because (1) it is the unique revelation of God; (2) it is inspired by God in a unique way (2 Tm

3:16); (3) it discloses God's saving plan for time and eternity; and (4) it centers on God incarnate in Jesus Christ, Savior of the world (Heb 1:1-2).

Other names for the Bible are: Holy or Sacred Scripture(s), Holy Writ, the Sacred Writings, the Good Book, and the Word of God.

"The Bible is the most perfect of all books, the most certain of all sciences, the most august, the most effectual, the most wise, the most useful, the most solid, the most necessary, the most fundamental and elevated. It is the only thing necessary because it is the word of God. It is not Moses who speaks in it but God. It is not the Patriarchs and Prophets who speak in it but God. It is not the Evangelists Matthew, Mark, Luke, and John who speak; it is God. And it is evident that God possesses all knowledge and possesses it without error" (Cornelius à Lapide).

The word Bible comes from the Greek term *biblia* which means "books." The Book of Daniel (9:2) refers to the writings of the Prophets as *ta biblia* in Greek, translated as "Scriptures." The sacred writer of the First Book of Maccabees (12:9) calls them the "sacred books." This usage was accepted by the Christians and by the 5th century A.D. came to be applied to all the sacred writings. St. Jerome (d. 400) called the Bible "the Divine Library." By the 13th century *the books* became *the book*—stressing the unity of all the books contained therein.

8.   *What are the two main parts of the Bible?*

The two main parts of the Bible are the Old Testament and the New Testament.

The word "testament" is used here in the sense of "agreement" or "covenant." The Old Testament is a record of the *old agreement* between God (Yahweh) and His chosen people, the Hebrews. It describes the remote preparation for the coming of the Messiah.

The New Testament is a record of the *new agreement* made by God with the whole human race through the Life, Death, and Resurrection of Jesus Christ, the Son of God made Man.

Jesus Himself usually referred to the Old Testament books (there were not yet any New Testament books) as "the Scriptures" or "Scripture" (Mt 21:42; Mk 14:49; Jn 5:39). His followers do the same (Lk 24:32; Acts 18:24; Rom 15:4). St. Paul also calls them "the sacred Scriptures" (2 Tm 3:15), "the holy Scriptures" (Rom 1:2), and "the words of God" (Rom 3:2).

Jesus also calls the Old Testament "the law of Moses and the prophets and the psalms" (Lk 24:44), citing the order in which the books of the Old Testament were arranged. The Old Testament is also called "the law and the prophets" (Mt 5:17; Acts 13:15), or "the law" (Jn 10:34; 12:34).

The writer of the Second Letter of Peter (3:16) refers to St. Paul's writings as "Scripture" at a time when the New Testament was just beginning to take shape.

9. *How many books are in the Bible?*

In the Bible as we know it, there are seventy-three books: forty-six in the Old Testament and twenty-seven in the New.

There are numerous citations from the Bible in this Catechism. Given below, as a help to the reader, is the system of abbreviations used in citing the books of the Bible together with the location of the books, Old Testament (OT) or New (NT). In citations, the first number after the name of the book indicates the chapter; the number after the colon indicates the verse. For example, Nm 23:19 means that the citation is from the Book of Numbers, chapter 23, verse 19.

Acts — Acts of the Apostles (NT)
Am — Amos (OT)
Bar — Baruch (OT)
1 Chr — 1 Chronicles (OT)
2 Chr — 2 Chronicles (OT)
Col — Colossians (NT)
1 Cor — 1 Corinthians (NT)
2 Cor — 2 Corinthians (NT)
Dn — Daniel (OT)
Dt — Deuteronomy (OT)
Eccl — Ecclesiastes (OT)
Eph — Ephesians (NT)
Est — Esther (OT)
Ex — Exodus (OT)
Ez — Ezekiel (OT)
Ezr — Ezra (OT)
Gal — Galatians (NT)
Gn — Genesis (OT)
Hb — Habakkuk (OT)
Heb — Hebrews (NT)
Hg — Haggai (OT)
Hos — Hosea (OT)
Is — Isaiah (OT)
Jas — James (NT)
Jb — Job (OT)
Jdt — Judith (OT)
Jer —Jeremiah (OT)
Jgs — Judges (OT)
Jl — Joel (OT)
Jn — John (NT)
1 Jn — 1 John (NT)
2 Jn — 2 John (NT)
3 Jn — 3 John (NT)
Jon — Jonah (OT)
Jos — Joshua (OT)
Jude — Jude (NT)
1 Kgs — 1 Kings (OT)

2 Kgs — 2 Kings (OT)
Lam — Lamentations (OT)
Lk — Luke (NT)
Lv — Leviticus (OT)
Mal — Malachi (OT)
1 Mc — 1 Maccabees (OT)
2 Mc — 2 Maccabees (OT)
Mi — Micah (OT)
Mk — Mark (NT)
Mt — Matthew (NT)
Na — Nahum (OT)
Neh — Nehemiah (OT)
Nm — Numbers (OT)
Ob — Obadiah (OT)
Phil — Philippians (NT)
Phlm — Philemon (NT)
Prv — Proverbs (OT)
Ps(s) — Psalms (OT)
1 Pt — 1 Peter (NT)
2 Pt — 2 Peter (NT)
Rom — Romans (NT)
Ru — Ruth (OT)
Rv — Revelation (NT)
Sir — Sirach (OT)
1 Sm — 1 Samuel (OT)
2 Sm — 2 Samuel (OT)
Song — Song of Songs (OT)
Tb — Tobit (OT)
1 Thes — 1 Thessalonians (NT)
2 Thes — 2 Thessalonians (NT)
Ti — Titus (NT)
1 Tm — 1 Timothy (NT)
2 Tm — 2 Timothy (NT)
Wis — Wisdom (OT)
Zec — Zechariah (OT)
Zep — Zephaniah (OT)

10. *Who is the principal author of the Bible?*

The principal author of the Bible is God.

God *revealed himself* in time. He intervened in history and communicated to human beings His merciful plans. The Bible (Word of God) is the record of this self-revelation of God which was set forth in a *message* as well as in *events*. God spoke and acted—word and event went together.

Human beings left to themselves cannot discover all the mysteries of God or His creatures. In His goodness, God has revealed to us many truths which He wants us to know. "God has given us the wisdom to understand fully the mystery, the plan he was pleased to decree in Christ, to be carried out in the fullness of time: namely, to bring all things in the heavens and on earth into one under Christ's headship" (Eph 1:9-11).

In the *Dogmatic Constitution on Divine Revelation,* Vatican II says: "Holy Mother Church, relying on the belief of the Apostles, holds that the books of both the Old and the New Testaments in their entirety, with all their parts, are sacred and canonical because written under the inspiration of the Holy Spirit, they have God as their Author" (no. 11).

However, this does not mean that God used the sacred author as a secretary to whom He dictated. Nor did He simply reveal to the human author the contents of the book and the way in which this should be expressed. Rather, the human author is a living instrument endowed with reason who under the divine impulse brings his faculties and powers into play in such a way that all can easily gather from the book produced by his work his distinctive genius and his individual characteristics and features. In other words, the sacred author, like every author, makes use of all his faculties—intellect, imagination, and will.

By virtue of the *divine condescension,* things are presented to us in the Bible in a manner which is in common use among human beings. For as the substantial Word of God made Himself like human beings in all things except sin

(Heb 4:15), so God's words, spoken by human tongues, have taken on all the qualities of human language except error.

11. What is Biblical inspiration?

Biblical inspiration is a divine action or supernatural influence of the Holy Spirit on the sacred writers, moving and impelling them to write in such a manner that they first rightly understood, then willed faithfully to write down, and fully expressed in apt words and with infallible truth all the things, and those only, which He ordered.

The Israelites believed in the inspiration of Moses, the Prophets, and the authors of the Wisdom literature, the priests in giving instruction. They ascribed the highest type of inspiration to the *Pentateuch* or Five Books attributed to Moses (also known as the "Torah" or Law), a lower type to the *Prophets,* and an even lower one to the *Writings.*

The sacred writers of the New Testament cited the Old Testament about 350 times in such a way as to show that Christians shared the belief of the Israelites in the divine origin of the sacred books. In addition, the New Testament speaks of inspiration of the Old Testament Scriptures explicitly in 2 Tm 3:15-17 and 2 Pt 1:19-21, and of the New Testament writings implicitly in 2 Pt 3:14-16:

"From your infancy you have known the sacred Scriptures, the source of the wisdom which through faith in Jesus Christ leads to salvation. All Scripture is inspired of God and is useful for teaching—for reproof, correction, and training in holiness so that the man of God may be fully competent and equipped for every good work" (2 Tm 3:15-17).

"Paul, our beloved brother, wrote you this in the spirit of wisdom that is his [that was given him by God], dealing with these matters as he does in all his letters. There are certain passages in them hard to understand. The ignorant and the unstable distort them (just as they do the *rest of Scripture . . ."* (2 Pt 3:15-16, italics added).

The *Fathers of the Church* accepted the divine origin of the Bible. They see God as the Author of the Bible and the human author as His instrument; thus the Bible is the word of God. In the 2nd century, they begin to equate the New Testament with the Old Testament as Scripture and Word of God.

"The Bible is a letter from Almighty God to His creatures" (St. Gregory the Great, d. 604). — It "was dictated by the Holy Spirit" (St. Irenaeus, d. 202). — "The authors of the sacred books wrote what God inspired them to do and they chose the manner of expression, that is, the style or form of expressing the thoughts" (St. Justin, d. 165).

Criterion of inspiration. *Inspiration does not follow from the religious enthusiasm produced in the reader, nor from the matter or form of the books themselves, nor from the prophetic or apostolic origin of a book, nor from a writer's own witness to the inspiration of his book. The criterion of inspiration follows solely from the Catholic Tradition by which the formal witness of God to the inspiration of the Sacred Scriptures was revealed to the Apostles and handed down to the whole Church.*

12.   *What is Biblical inerrancy?*

Biblical inerrancy is the quality flowing from inspiration by which the Scriptures are—both in theory and in fact—free from all error in the message they intend to convey.

The words of the Bible are always true in the sense intended by their human authors. Though these authors may have erroneous beliefs that are at times perceptible in the text, such erroneous beliefs are not affirmed.

The sacred writers made use of customary linguistic practices. They say, as we do, that the sun sets whereas the sun does so only in appearance and not in actual fact. Inerrancy must take such ways of speaking into consideration.

The Church has always held the inerrancy of the Bible, and this quality is not extended solely to what concerns faith or morals.

However, the sacred text must be *rightly understood* (which is the role of the professional exegetes under the guidance of the Church), in particular with respect to the natural sciences, historical events, implicit citations of the Bible, certain apparent contradictions, and even certain passages in the Old Testament concerning faith, morals, and worship.

What is exempt from error is the word of God contained in the Bible, but not the manner in which anyone interprets it. Three principles must be utilized for a *wise interpretation:* (1) To determine what God reveals to us in His written word, we must first determine the exact thought of the sacred writer. (2) Error is possible only where there is a judgment or an affirmation, and not for example a simple reproduction of the thought of someone else or a literary ornament. (3) Account must be taken of the psychology proper to the sacred writer in terms of literary styles of his time. And dominating the whole is the fact that the affirmation of the sacred writer—and hence of God Himself—*depends on his intention.*

13. *What are literary forms?*

Literary forms are types or genres of literature that are distinguished from one another by distinct form and structure adapted to content. In order to understand the Bible correctly, we must know the specific literary forms it contains.

Distinctions of form and structure appear in all human speech and writing. The most basic distinction, for example, is the one between *prose* and *poetry.* These are then broken down into more specific forms, such as epic, lyric, and dramatic poetry and narrative, rhetorical, and expository prose. In turn, the latter can give rise to subspecies of their own, for example satiric poems, travelogue narratives, or fictitious lawsuits.

Literary form is part of the communication of meaning. Diverse literary forms are fashioned by cultures because of a desire to cover different subjects more meaningfully and to express different aspects of truth which cannot be imparted by a single form. Thus, we can treat an event in a prose narrative, or a ballad or an epic poem as well as in a tragedy, or an oration, or a philosophical meditation, or a prayer of lamentation or thanksgiving.

There can also be diversity of forms based on *content* of a work. A writer of a chronicle thinks, speaks, and expresses ideas in a different way from the writer of a play, or a poem, or a religious treatise.

The "truth" of an event or a subject is presented in a different fashion in each literary form—*but it is still the truth.* Thus, the whole Bible is true, absolutely true, every part of it, but it is true in the sense in which each kind of literary form bears witness to it. "Truth is proposed and expressed in a variety of ways, depending on whether a text is history of one kind or another or whether its form is that of prophecy, poetry, or another type of speech" (Vatican II: *Dogmatic Constitution on Divine Revelation,* no. 12).

Ultimately, it is society that creates literary forms, for every work is a dialogue between the author and his society. Even when a writer single-handedly creates a new form, that form will not endure unless society accepts it.

Pope Pius XII in his ground-breaking encyclical Divino Afflante Spiritu, *which revolutionized Bible studies in the Church, declared: "Let the interpreter then endeavor with all care and without neglecting any light derived from recent research to determine the distinctive genius of the sacred writer, his condition in life, the age in which he lived, the written or oral sources he may have used, and the literary forms he employed. He will then be better able to discover who the sacred writer was and what he meant by what he wrote" (nos. 33-34).*

Vatican II mentioned other factors that must be taken into consideration in the identification of literary forms: "The interpreter must investigate what meaning the sacred writer intended to express and actually expressed in particular circumstances as he used contemporary literary forms in accordance with the situation of his own time and culture. For the correct understanding of what the sacred writer wanted to assert, due attention must be paid to the customary and characteristic styles of perceiving, speaking, and narrating which prevailed at the time of the sacred writer, and to the customs people normally followed at that period in their daily dealings with one another" (Dogmatic Constitution on Divine Revelation, *no. 12*).

Indeed, even preliterary forms *of feeling, thinking, and speaking which affected the author's choice of form are to be considered since the sacred writers were more than mere instruments—they were "true authors" with all that this entails (Vatican II:* Dogmatic Constitution on Divine Revelation, *no. 11).*

14. *What is the Canon of the Bible?*

The Canon of the Bible is the list of books which the Church has declared to be inspired by God and which she regards as the Rule (Canon) of Truth, Faith, and Life by reason of their divine origin.

The Greek word "canon" means a rod or reed, and so came to connote a "measuring rod" or a "a measure." Since the books of Scripture were regarded as a Rule of Truth, Faith, and Life, the word "Canon" was used to designate that Rule as written. Thus, the adjective "Canonical" came to be applied to a book included in the Canon of the Bible.

Canon of the Old Testament

The formation of the Old Testament Canon was an historical process over the course of many years. The *Law* (First Five Books) was canonized about the 5th century B.C., the *Prophets* about the 3rd century, and the *Writings* about the 2nd century. In addition, there were two sets of Canons—one held by the Palestinian Jews and the other by the Alexandrian Jews or those outside Palestine. The Palestinians accepted 22 books, really 24 if Ruth-Judges and Jeremiah-Lamentations were split. These are known as the *Proto-canonical Books* (that is, books that were early included in the group and universally received without doubts). The Alexandrians accepted 46 books, but because of the enumeration used in the Protocanonical books (Twelve Prophets are numbered as one), these number only seven more books and parts of two others: Tobit, Judith, Sirach, Wisdom, 1 and 2 Maccabees, and parts of Esther and Daniel. The latter are called *Deuterocanonical Books* (that is, those that were included in the group later).

Canon of the New Testament

The formation of the New Testament Canon also had its problems. The four Gospels and the thirteen Epistles of St. Paul were accepted by 130 A.D. and placed on the same level as the Old Testament writings as God's word between 170 and 220. These are called *Protocanonical Books* of the New Testament. The others were accepted later and are called *Deuterocanonical Books:* Hebrews, James, 2 Peter, 2 and 3 John, Jude, and the Book of Revelation.

The complete list of the Canonical Books of both the New and the Old Testaments was given by the Fourth Council of Rome (382) under Pope Damasus, the Council of Hippo (393), the Third Council of Carthage (419), and the Gelasian Decree (Pope Gelasius, 494-496). The Ecumenical Council of Florence (1438-1445) also mentioned the complete canon, and finally the Ecumenical Council of Trent put an end to all doubts by defining the complete Canon of both Testaments on April 8, 1546.

The Apocrypha

Non-Catholic Christians usually call the Deuterocanonical Books of the Old Testament the *Apocrypha.* Traditionally, they have regarded these books as not forming part of the Canon but as worthy of veneration. In recent times, however, they have added these books to editions of the Bible.

Apocryphal Books

Apocryphal books properly so-called are those which the Church has not accepted into the Canon of seventy-three books and did not consider as inspired. For example, the Book of Enoch, the Assumption of Moses, The Gospel of Thomas, and the Acts of Paul. These are commonly termed *Pseudepigrapha* by non-Catholics.

15. *In what languages were the books of the Bible originally written?*

The books of the Bible were originally written some in Hebrew, some in Greek, and some parts in Aramaic.

The Old Testament was written almost entirely in *Hebrew,* a Semitic dialect akin to Phoenician or Ugaritic. *Aramaic* is a branch of the Semitic and was the spoken language of the Jews at the time of Christ. It is related to Hebrew in the same way that modern English is related to Elizabethan English. Aramaic is used for all of the Book of Tobit, parts of the Books of Daniel (2:4—7:28), Ezra (4:8—6:18; 7:12-26), and Esther (chapters 10—16), and single verses in Genesis (31:47) and Jeremiah (10:11), as well as the original Gospel of Matthew (of which we do not have a copy).

Greek, the common everyday language of the Greco-Roman world, was used for the Book of Wisdom, the Second

Book of Maccabees, and the whole New Testament except the original Gospel of Matthew.

Manuscripts of the Bible

No *autograph* or original editions of the books of the Bible exist. The reason for this is partly the perishable writing material (papyrus) used and partly the decree of the Roman emperors calling for the destruction of the Christian holy books. The Bible has thus been transmitted through *ancient copies* called *manuscripts* and through *translations* or *versions.* However, the copies we do possess are more ancient and far more numerous than copies of any other ancient books of the same period. This means that the Bible is more perfectly authenticated than any other book of that time.

For example, we have copies of the works of the Latin poet Horace that go back to only 900 years after his death, the Greek philosopher Plato, only 1,300 years, and the Greek dramatist Sophocles, 1,400. For the New Testament, however, we have complete copies of the Gospels dated 250 years after their writing, an almost complete copy within 150 years after their writing, and fragments within 50 years. As far as the Old Testament is concerned, the Dead Sea Scrolls found in 1947, and still being studied, have yielded an astonishing amount of material. Scholars have recovered manuscripts for almost every Protocanonical Book of the Old Testament except Esther and some of the Deuterocanonical Books as well. These copies dated around 100 B.C have been shown to jibe remarkably well with existing copies. This brings us within seven or eight hundred years from the time that the *Law* was written and within three or four hundred years from the time of the codification of the *Prophets* and the *Writings.*

The most famous Biblical Manuscripts or Codexes are: (1) *Sinaitic MS,* 4th century: complete New Testament and fragments of the Old in Greek. (2) *Alexandrine MS,* 5th century: most of Old and New Testament. (3) *Vatican MS,* 4th century: almost all Old Testament and New Testament.

Early Translations of the Bible

We do have very early witnesses to the Bible text from the Versions or Translations into other languages. When Hebrew became a dead language and was no longer intelligible to the ordinary people, the Palestinian Jews required an Aramaic version and the Hellenistic Jews required a Greek version. Thus, the first Christians became acquainted with the Old Testament Bible through the *Targums* (Aramaic), *Septuagint* (Greek), and *Vulgate* (Latin) Versions.

The Targums

These were translations made in the synagogue services from Hebrew into Aramaic so that the people could understand what had just been read. In this way the entire Old Testament (Protocanonical Books) was translated into Aramaic.

The Septuagint

This is a translation into Greek of the Hebrew and Aramaic Old Testament (including the Deuterocanonical Books) made in Egypt by various authors during the period between 250 B.C. and 100 B.C. Its name comes from the fact that legend ascribes the work to a group of seventy-two scholars and it is designated by the Roman numerals LXX. It is by far the most important ancient Version of the Old Testament and until recently was our sole witness for the state of the original text of the Hebrew Old Testament before the Christian era. The Septuagint was the Version used by the Hebrews in Christ's time, by the Apostles and New Testament writers, and by the Greek Fathers of the Church; it is still the official text of the Greek Church.

The Vulgate

This is the official Latin translation of the Bible which was prepared almost entirely by St. Jerome from 382 to 405 A.D.

JESUS QUOTED THE JEWISH SCRIPTURES AS GOD'S WORD
"[Jesus] stood up to do the reading [in the synagogue]. When
the book of the prophet Isaiah was handed him, he unrolled the
scroll and found the passage . . . : 'The spirit of the Lord is upon
me. . . .' 'Today this Scripture is fulfilled' " (Lk 4:16-21).

Jerome borrowed heavily from Origen in translating the Psalter and took Sirach, Baruch and both books of Maccabees from Old Latin texts. He translated everything else from the existing Hebrew, Aramaic, or Greek manuscripts. The Council of Trent declared the Vulgate to be "authentic in public readings, disputations, preachings, and exposition" because it conforms to the original texts and contains no errors in faith or morals.

Vernacular Versions of the Bible

History tells us that there were popular translations of the entire Bible as well as the Gospels in the vernacular before the days of printing: Spanish, Italian, French, Polish, Danish, Norwegian, Hungarian, and Bohemian.

In English, too, there were numerous editions at least of parts of the Bible in the vernacular. There was, for example, a work by Caedmon (a monk of Whitby) in the 7th century. St. Bede the Venerable also translated much of the Scriptures in the 8th century. But it is usually claimed that John Wycliffe was the first to put a complete English translation of the Bible in the hands of the people (in 1382), although St. Thomas More declared that there were other English editions before it.

Modern English Translations

In recent years there has been a tremendous increase in new Bible translations into English—the result of the providential Biblical Movement and the steadily-increasing emphasis on the Bible. For Catholics, unquestionably the best is the version known as the *New American Bible*. It was produced over a twenty-five year span by scholars of the Catholic Biblical Association of America (45 Catholic and 5 non-Catholic) and sponsored by the Bishops of the United States through the Confraternity of Christian Doctrine. It is translated from the original texts, makes use of all the latest Biblical scholarship and techniques, and is governed by reverence for the inspired text.

Some other versions approved for Catholic use include: the *Jerusalem Bible* (a translation of the Bible originally done in French by the Dominicans at Jerusalem), the *Revised Standard Version,* Catholic Edition, (a revision of the famous *King James Version* done in the 16th century by Protestant scholars in England), and the *Douay-Rheims Bible* done in the 16th and 17th century.

Division into Chapters and Verses

In 1226 Stephen Langton, a professor at the University of Paris who later became Archbishop of Canterbury, divided the text of the Bible into *chapters.* He did remarkably well considering the state of Bible studies in his day, and his work has held up. In 1551, the famous printer Robert Stephen (also called Estienne or Stephanus) inserted into the Bible text the *numbering of verses* that had been formulated by Santes Pagnini in 1528.

This division of the text into chapters and verses has proved invaluable by providing a universal system for citations from the Bible. (The way of reading the Bible references has already been mentioned in Question 9.)

16. *What are the divisions of the Old Testament?*

The divisions of the Old Testament are:

1. the Historical Books,
2. the Didactic (Wisdom or Sapiential) Books,
3. and the Prophetic Books.

The threefold division of the Old Testament comprises 46 books and corresponds roughly to the division of the Hebrew Old Testament into (1) the Torah or Law, (2) the Prophets (Former and Latter), and (3) the Writings. It included thirty-nine books that were numbered as 24 or 22 as already noted. See the chart below for differences between the Hebrew and Christian Old Testament and between the Catholic and Protestant Old Testament.

JEWISH O.T.	PROTESTANT O.T.	CATHOLIC O.T.
(24 books = 39)	(39 books)	(46 books)
The Torah (Law) (5)	*Historical Books* (17) (The Law)	*Historical Books* (21) (The Law)
Genesis	Genesis	Genesis
Exodus	Exodus	Exodus
Leviticus	Leviticus	Leviticus
Numbers	Numbers	Numbers
Deuteronomy	Deuteronomy	Deuteronomy
	Joshua	Joshua
The Prophets (8) (Former)	Judges	Judges
	Ruth	Ruth
	1 Samuel	1 Samuel
Joshua	2 Samuel	2 Samuel
Judges	1 Kings	1 Kings
Samuel (1 & 2)	2 Kings	2 Kings
Kings (1 & 2)	1 Chronicles	1 Chronicles
	2 Chronicles	2 Chronicles
(Latter)	Ezra	Ezra
Isaiah	Nehemiah	Nehemiah
Jeremiah	Esther	*Tobit**
Ezekiel		*Judith**
Prophets		Esther *(parts)**
Hosea		*1 Maccabees**
Joel		*2 Maccabees**
Amos		
Obadiah	*Wisdom Books (5)*	*Wisdom Books (7)*
Micah	(The Writings)	(The Writings)
Jonah	Job	Job
Nahum	Psalms	Psalms
Habakkuk	Proverbs	Proverbs
Zephaniah	Qoheleth	Qoheleth
Haggai	Song of Songs	Song of Songs
Zechariah		*Wisdom**
Malachi		*Sirach**

* Deuterocanonical Book (or parts)

JEWISH O.T.	PROTESTANT O.T.	CATHOLIC O.T.
The Writings (11)	*Prophetic Books* (17) (The Prophets)	*Prophetic Books* (18) (The Prophets)
Chronicles (1 & 2)	Isaiah	Isaiah
Ezra-Nehemiah	Jeremiah	Jeremiah
Esther	Lamentations	Lamentations
Ruth		Baruch*
Psalms	Ezekiel	Ezekiel
Proverbs	Daniel	Daniel *(parts)**
Job	Hosea	Hosea
Lamentations	Joel	Joel
Qoheleth	Amos	Amos
Song of Songs	Obadiah	Obadiah
Daniel	Jonah	Jonah
	Micah	Micah
	Nahum	Nahum
	Habakkuk	Habakkuk
	Zephaniah	Zephaniah
	Haggai	Haggai
	Zechariah	Zechariah
	Malachi	Malachi

17. *What is the Pentateuch?*

The Pentateuch is the name given to the First Five Books of the Bible: Genesis, Exodus, Numbers, Leviticus, and Deuteronomy. They narrate the primitive history of mankind and the actual history of God's chosen people and His laws.

The Historical Books of the Bible (of which the Pentateuch is the first part) begin with the divine origin of the universe, mankind, the Hebrew race under Abraham and the Hebrew nation under Moses. Then the various inspired writers portray for over a thousand years the religious and historical development of their nation, bringing the picture to a close—not long before the advent of Jesus Christ—with the Books of Maccabees (43 B.C.).

"The grandeur of this historic sweep is the result of a careful and complex joining of several historical traditions, or sources. These are primarily four: the so-called *Yahwist, Elohist, Priestly,* and *Deuteronomic* strands that run through the Pentateuch. (They are conveniently abbreviated as Y, E, P, and D.) Each brings to the Torah its own characteristics, its own theological viewpoint—a rich variety of interpretation that the sensitive reader will take pains to appreciate. A superficial difference between two of these sources is responsible for their names: the Yahwist prefers the name *Yahweh* (represented in translation as *Lord)* by which God revealed Himself to Israel; the Elohist prefers the generic name for God, *Elohim.* The Yahwist is concrete, imaginative, using many anthropomorphisms in its theological approach, as seen, e.g., in the narrative of creation in Gn 2, compared with the Priestly version in Gn 1. The Elohist is more sober, moralistic. The Priestly strand, which emphasizes genealogies, is more severely theological in tone. The Deuteronomic approach is characterized by the intense hortatory style of Dt 5—11, and by certain principles from which it works, such as the centralization of worship in the Jerusalem temple.

"This is not to deny the role of Moses in the development of the Pentateuch. It is true we do not conceive of him as the author of the books in the modern sense. But there is no reason to doubt that, in the events described in those traditions, he had a uniquely important role, especially as lawgiver. Even the later laws which have been added in P and D are presented as a Mosaic heritage. Moses is the lawgiver *par excellence,* and all later legislation is conceived in his spirit, and therefore attributed to him" *(New American Bible,* "The Pentateuch").

The composition of the various strands is assigned as follows: the Yahwist to United Kingdom in the 9th century B.C. or even earlier by some; the Elohist to the Northern Kingdom in the 8th century B.C.; the Priestly to the Kingdom after the Exile in the 5th century; and the

Deuteronomic partly to the Southern Kingdom at the time of Josiah (7th century) and after the Exile (6th century).

Genesis is the book of beginnings, the beginnings of the people of God and those of the world. The first eleven chapters paint in broad strokes the history of the world, from its beginning to Abraham, and form the setting for the history of salvation. They give two different pictures of creation; followed by the traditions about the life of the first human beings and the beginning of civilization, the flood, the repeopling of the earth and the dispersion of mankind, manifesting at the same time God's merciful love and humanity's sin.

The remaining chapters deal with the pre-history of the chosen people through the great patriarchs Abraham, Isaac, and Jacob and his twelve sons. They illustrate the fact that the God of the chosen people is not a far-off deity conceived by some philosopher. He is the God Who had manifested Himself to Abraham, Isaac, and Jacob, the God Who made a Covenant with them and made promises to them among which is the promise of the Messiah.

The next four books concern the exodus from Egypt which was an exceptional period in the history of the people of God. After the patriarchal history followed by the long obscurity of the sojourn in Egypt, the time of the exodus is one in which Israel becomes a people under Moses, the leader chosen by God.

Exodus is the book about the exodus from Egypt and the sojourn in Sinai, with the giving of the Law and the construction of the Ark of the Covenant and the Dwelling in which it is housed.

Leviticus is the collection of Laws governing the various areas of human existence.

Numbers is the narrative of the numbering of the people (whence the title) and the long trek through the desert up to the borders of the promised land.

Deuteronomy is the testament of Moses and a backward look at the events and includes a series of laws.

18. *What are the other Historical Books of the Old Testament?*

The other Historical Books of the Old Testament are: Joshua, Judges, Ruth, 1 and 2 Samuel, 1 and 2 Kings, 1 and 2 Chronicles, Ezra, Nehemiah, 1 and 2 Maccabees, Tobit, Judith, and Esther. They deal with the history of Israel beginning with the entry into the promised land and narrating in turn the grandeur under David and Solomon, the division of the Kingdom into North and South, the Babylonian Exile and Return, and culminating in the glorious struggle for freedom under the Maccabees.

These Historical Books provide a great amount of factual information. However, their main purpose in doing so is *to interpret it in the manner of the Deuteronomic strand*—that is, in its primary relation to the Covenant. They include (1) history of the conquest of the promised land (Joshua, Judges); (2) history of the royalty (1 and 2 Samuel, 1 and 2 Kings with Ruth as an appendix in the form of a religious novel); (3) theology of this history (1 and 2 Chronicles); (4) history of the community upon return from the Exile (Ezra and Nehemiah); (5) underground or persecution literature (1 and 2 Maccabees, Tobit, Judith, and Esther).

It is important to note that Ruth, Tobit, Judith, and Esther are not properly historical but examples of free compositions—the religious novel used for purposes of edification and instruction. *Ruth* contains true history in dramatic form, giving the story of an ancestress of David and Christ, and thus foreshadows the universality of the Messianic salvation.

Judith is a lesson in Providence: a pious reflection on the annual Passover observance to convey the reassurance that God is still the master of history who saves Israel from her enemies. *Esther's* purpose is the glorification of the Jewish people and the explanation of the origin, significance, and date of the feast of Purim. *Tobit* teaches the providential guidance of the lives of the righteous.

The Historical Books demonstrate that before as well as during the millennium of history with which they are concerned, Israel was a covenanted people, bound to Yahweh, Lord of the universe, by the ties of faith and obedience. This required the observance of the Law and worship in His Temple, the consequent rewards of which were divine favor and protection. In this way these books anticipate and prepare for the coming of Him Who would bring type and prophecy to fulfillment, history to term, and holiness to perfection: Christ, the Son of David and the promised Messiah. (See *New American Bible,* Introduction to Historical Books.)

19. *What are the Seven Wisdom Books of the Old Testament?*

The Seven Wisdom Books of the Old Testament are: Job, Psalms, Proverbs, Ecclesiastes (or Qoheleth), Song of Songs, Wisdom, and Sirach (or Ecclesiasticus).

"The Books of Job, Psalms, Proverbs, Ecclesiastes, the Song of Songs, Wisdom, and Sirach are all versified by the skillful use of parallelism, that is, of the balanced and symmetrical phrases peculiar to Hebrew poetry. With the exception of the *Psalms,* the majority of which are devotional lyrics, and the *Song of Songs,* a nuptial hymn, these books belong to the general class of wisdom or didactic literature, strictly so called because their chief purpose is instruction. . . .

"The *Book of Proverbs* is a collection of sentences or practical norms for moral conduct. The *Book of Job* is an artistic dialogue skillfully handling the problem of suffering though only from the standpoint of temporal life. *Ecclesiastes* examines a wide range of human experience only to conclude that all things are vanity except the fear of the Lord and observance of His commandments, and that God requites man in His own good time. *Sirach* gathers and presents the fruits of past experience, thus preparing for the *Book of Wisdom*, which sees for the just man seeking happiness the full hope of immortality (Wis 3:4)....

"The limitations of Old Testament wisdom served to crystallize the problems of human life and destiny, thus preparing for their solution through New Testament revelation. *Ecclesiastes'* vain search for success and happiness on earth ends when the Savior assures these things for His followers, not in this world but in the bliss of heaven. The anxiety in the *Book of Job* over reconciling God's justice and wisdom with the suffering of the innocent is relieved by the account of the crucified and risen Redeemer in the Gospel. By fulfilling all that the *Psalms* foretold concerning Him, Jesus makes the Psalter His prayer book and that of the Church for all time. The love of God for all people which underlies the *Song of Songs* is perfected in the union of Christ with His Church. The personification of the wisdom of *Proverbs, Wisdom,* and *Sirach* shines forth in resplendent reality in the Word Who was with God, and Who was God, and Who became incarnate to dwell among us; cf. Jn 1:2, 14" *(New American Bible,* introduction to Wisdom Books).

The *Psalms* are Hebrew poems (many attributed to David) composed over a 700-year span but they are also a *school of Christian prayer.* These sacred songs cover a wide range of human experiences; they bring out our strengths and weaknesses, faith and wonderment, joys and sorrows.

Among the many different types of Psalms are Royal Psalms as well as Psalms of Individual Lament, Communal Lament, and Praise.

Written under God's inspiration, these sacred texts have God's plan showing through. More specifically, the Psalms are Christological—they keep repeating and fostering the Hope of the Promised Redeemer. They show forth the prophesied glory of Jesus Christ: His lowly coming to earth, His Kingly dignity and priestly power, and finally His beneficent labors and the shedding of His Blood for our Redemption. So true is this, that they have fittingly been designated "The Gospel accoring to the Holy Spirit."

Possibly their most attractive feature for us is that—in the words of St. Athanasius—"the Psalms have a unique value; most Scripture speaks to us, whereas the Psalms speak *for us.*" They are the prayers of Christ which we also can use.

20. *What are the Eighteen Prophetic Books of the Old Testament?*

The Eighteen Prophetic Books of the Old Testament are: Isaiah, Jeremiah, Lamentations, Baruch, Ezekiel, and Daniel (known as the Major Prophets), and Hosea, Joel, Amos, Obadiah, Jonah, Micah, Nahum, Habakkuk, Zephaniah, Haggai, Zechariah, and Malachi (known as the Minor Prophets).

"The Prophetic Books bear the names of the four Major and twelve Minor Prophets, besides *Lamentations* and *Baruch.* The terms "Major" and "Minor" refer merely to the length of the respective compositions and not to any distinction in the prophetic office. *Jonah* is a story of the mission of the prophet rather than a collection of prophecies. *Lamentations* and *Daniel* are listed among the Hagiographa in the Hebrew Bible, not among the Prophetic Books. The former contains a series of elegies on the fate of Jerusalem; the latter is apocalyptic in character. Daniel, who lived far removed from Palestine, was not called by God to preach; yet the book is counted as prophecy. *Baruch,* though excluded from the Hebrew canon, is found in the Septuagint version, and the Church has always acknowledged it to be sacred and inspired.

"The Prophetic Books, together with the oral preaching of the Prophets, were the result of the institution of prophetism, in which a succession of Israelites chosen by God and appointed by Him to be Prophets received communications from Him and transmitted them to the people in His name (Dt 18:15-20). The Prophets were spokesmen of God, intermediaries between Him and His people. The communications they received from God came through visions, dreams, and ecstasies and were transmitted to the people through sermons, writings, and symbolic actions. . . .

"The prophetic literature . . . contains the substance of the Prophets' authentic preaching, resumes, and genuine samples of such preaching. Some parts were recorded by the Prophets themselves, some by persons other than the Prophets who uttered them. . . .

"Thus the universal blessing for mankind, often promised by God through the mouths of his Prophets in figures and types, was in time to become personalized and to confer its full benefit on us through the Word made flesh, Who became for us the New Covenant through His Life, Death, and Resurrection, as the Prophets had foretold" *(New American Bible,* introduction to Prophetic Books).

Isaiah is named for the greatest of the Prophets who lived in a period of high economic prosperity (8th century) but with idolatry rampant amid low moral standards. After the destruction of the Northern Kingdom (722 B.C.), he influenced King Hezekiah of Judah to inaugurate religious and social reforms. This Book contains many Messianic prophecies. Chapters 40-55 are attributed to one of his followers called *Deutero-Isaiah,* and chapters 56-66 are attributed to another writer called *Trito-Isaiah.*

Jeremiah is named for the "Prophet of the Eleventh Hour" who lived in the 7th-6th century and had the unpleasant task of predicting the destruction of the Holy City and the Southern Kingdom as well as seeing this come to pass. Because of his many sufferings for his divine mission, he is regarded as a symbol of Jesus Christ. *Lamentations* gives his meditations over Jerusalem's destruction. *Baruch* is attributed to Jeremiah's secretary.

Ezekiel is named for the 6th century exilic Prophet who predicted the same fate for Jerusalem but also described the New Covenant and New Kingdom of God. He had great influence on the religion of Israel after the Exile.

Daniel is named after a young Jew in Exile, but it is more apocalyptic than prophetic. It may be classed as persecution or underground literature written during the Maccabean struggle in the 2nd century. It envisions Israel in glory to come and conveys the message that people of faith can resist temptation and overcome adversity.

Hosea, the longest of the Minor Prophets, preached in the Northern Kingdom against social injustices some time before the Assyrian Exile in 722 B.C. He was the first to describe the "marriage" of God with His people.

Joel preached in the Southern Kingdom before the Babylonian Exile and called for penance to avert the Day of the Lord.

Amos, the Prophet of the Divine Judgment, prophesied in the Northern Kingdom at Bethel in the 8th century.

Obadiah is the shortest book of the Bible. Written in the 5th century it emphasizes that the "Kingdom is the Lord's.'

Jonah, written in the 5th century B.C., is a didactic story with an important theological message: the universality of God's salvation.

Micah, a contemporary of Isaiah, predicted the birthplace of Christ and the universality of the Messianic salvation.

Nahum, dating from the 7th century, passes judgment on Nineveh and asserts God's moral government of the world.

Habakkuk (605-597) inveighs against the enemies of Judah and calls for confidence in God.

Zephaniah denounced the religious degradation in Judah before the reforms of Josiah (in the 7th century) and announced that a remnant would remain.

Haggai, one of the first postexilic prophets of the 6th century, encouraged the returning exiles to reestablish the community and rebuild the second Temple.

Zechariah, a contemporary of Haggai, encouraged the exiles and prophesied about a coming Prince of Peace.

Malachi, last of the Minor Prophets, prophesied after the Exile and spoke of a perpetual, clean, and universal sacrifice (i.e., the Mass).

21. *What are the divisions of the New Testament?*

The divisions of the New Testament parallel those of the Old Testament. They are:

1. Five Historical Books,
2. Twenty-one Didactic Books,
3. and One Prophetic Book.

Like the divisions for the Old Testament Books, this division is an artificial one and does not really fit some of the Books. However, it is used because it can be a good aid to memory and a fine rule of thumb.

The New Testament is the reflection of the history of the primitive Church. It is a collection of twenty-seven books written during the hundred years or so following the crucifixion of Jesus (30 A.D.). It was written in the Church, for members of the Church, and for use by the Church. Hence, the Church is the historical reality that explains the existence of this literature.

All twenty-seven books are about Jesus Christ, and together they make up the New Testament. But they are strongly influenced by the Old Testament, by Hebrew history and religion. So it is difficult to understand the New Testament unless we are familiar with the history, religious practices, and sacred books of the Hebrew tradition within which Christ and Christianity were born.

Around the central figure of Christ revolve the mysteries of time, the world, and human beings in the plan of salvation, because He is the protagonist (as the eternal Word) of Creation and (as the Word made flesh) of the Redemption and the goal of everything. The books of the New Testament reflect the expectation of the coming of Christ in all His glory to put an end to human history.

22. *What are the Five Historical Books of the New Testament?*

The Five Historical Books of the New Testament are: the Four Gospels and the Acts of the Apostles. These provide a record of the Life, Death, and Resurrection of Jesus Christ, the Savior of the world, and the beginning of the Church He founded.

The word *Gospel* means "good news," the good news of salvation proclaimed by Christ and the Church. It also refers to the four forms in which this good news has come down to us in written form: Matthew, Mark, Luke, and John.

Jesus Himself proclaimed the good news of God's Kingdom through His Person, teachings, and deeds—especially His Passion, Death, and Resurrection. In turn, the Apostles preached this good news of the Gospel after His Ascension and only some thirty years later was it set down in writing.

The sacred writers of the Gospels had before them the oral Gospel tradition together with collections of sayings of Jesus and eyewitness accounts. They used these sources to weave a coherent account for those people for whom their Gospel was intended and for the purpose they had in mind —liturgical, catechetical, or missionary.

They did not write biography alone. What they wrote were faith documents based on historical principles. The Evangelists presented the true sayings of Jesus in the light of the better understanding they had after being enlightened by the Holy Spirit.

The heart of the Gospels is the Passion Narratives— Jesus' sufferings, Death, and Resurrection. These are the central events in establishing the New Covenant. To these are added the Public Life of Jesus and the Infancy accounts (in Matthew and Luke).

The first three Gospels are very similar and are called *Synoptic*—because their contents can be encompassed in a single glance if they are placed in three adjacent columns. In their composition the Evangelists used the identical sources or used one another as sources. But each author has his own distinctive arrangement.

The *Gospel According to Matthew* is known as the first Gospel because there is a tradition that it was written in Aramaic first, but this version is lost. The Greek version extant was written in the 70's or 80's and thus preceded by Mark. It is characterized by clarity, pedagogical direction, and remarkable balance in narrative sections and the five magnificent discourses in chapters 6—7, 10, 13, 18, and 24—25.

While Mark probably addresses himself to the Romans and Luke to the Greeks, Matthew, who is a Jew, writes for the Jews. It is the most Jewish of the Gospels in its style, its methods of composition, and its way of arguing. Matthew wants to convince his countrymen that Jesus is indeed the Messiah Who was expected by the Prophets, and thus he seeks to show that Jesus has fulfilled the Scriptures.

Matthew is the Gospel of the Church but also the Gospel of Jesus. It constantly seeks to bring out the majesty of Jesus, His superhuman greatness, and His power. For Matthew, Jesus is the Lord, the Messiah, and above all the Son of God.

The *Gospel According to Mark* was written about 70 A.D. by Mark, a companion of St. Paul and later a co-worker of St. Peter. This Gospel is short, vivid, concrete, and gives the impression of immediate contact with Jesus. It makes use of a familiar style that is occasionally awkward but always direct, and might almost be called photographic in its handling of details.

Mark desires to establish a close bond between the Passion of Jesus and His Lordship, showing that the Son of Man had to endure the Cross before attaining His glory and that His destiny is one of the Suffering Servant prophesied by Isaiah (ch. 53). It is also his design to teach us that if we want to encounter the living Christ, we must follow His

JESUS PROCLAIMED THE GOOD NEWS OF GOD TO THE PEOPLE
"After John's arrest, Jesus appeared in Galilee proclaiming the good news of God: 'This is the time of fulfillment. The reign of God is at hand! Reform your lives and believe in the gospel'" (Mk 1:14f).

Way. We will deserve the name of His disciple only if we accept the same destiny as the Master.

The *Gospel According to Luke* was written in the 70's for Gentile Christians by a physician and companion of St. Paul. The Evangelist portrays Christianity not as a political movement nor as a sect organized for an initiated few but as a religious faith open to all human beings. His portrait of Jesus, drawn from the Gospel Tradition, manifests the Savior's concern for humanity, and His identification with the poor, the outcast, and the criminal.

Luke wants to present the History of Salvation from the beginnings of the world until the return of Christ. For Luke, this history comprises three great periods: (1) the time of the Law and the Prophets; (2) the time of Christ from His coming on earth until His Ascension; and (3) the time of the Church, whose foundations were laid in the preceding period, and which has been unfolding fully from that time on.

In this History it is the coming of Christ that marks the truly decisive turning point; it constitutes the "middle of the times." During the time of expectation people had their eyes fixed on the "middle of the times" that was to come. During the time of the Church, people look backward with their eyes on Jesus. We must fulfill from day to day what Jesus has lived and what He has taught until His final return.

The *Gospel According to John* is the last Gospel written (about 90 A.D.) by John the beloved disciple. It is the most sublime and theological of the Gospels and very different from the Synoptics in plan and content. It was written for Christians of Asia Minor, probably at Ephesus, and seeks to complement the Synoptics which it presupposes are known to its readers. It makes use of accounts of signs and long reflective discourses to reveal Christ's present mission as Word, Way, Truth, Life, and Light. Its purpose is to inspire belief in Jesus as the Messiah, the Son of God (Jn 20:31).

Finally, the fourth Gospel is the Gospel of love. No other Evangelist has so clearly emphasized the love of the Father: "God has so loved the world that He has given his only Son"; nor has any other so brought out the love of the Son for His own: "He loved them unto the end," that is, to the very limit. And no other Gospel has so insistently reduced the new law to the one precept of fraternal love: "As I have loved you, so must you love one another" (Jn 13:34; 15:12).

The *Acts of the Apostles* is the last Historical Book of the New Testament. It was also written by Luke as part of a two-volume work. It describes the origin and spread of the Church through the help of the Holy Spirit from the time of Christ's Ascension to the time of Paul's first Roman imprisonment in the early 60's.

23. *What are the twenty-one Didactic Books of the New Testament?*

The twenty-one Didactic Books of the New Testament are:

1. **the Thirteen Epistles of Paul (Romans, 1 and 2 Corinthians, Galatians, Ephesians, Colossians, Philippians, Philemon, 1 and 2 Thessalonians, 1 and 2 Timothy, and Titus);**

2. **the Epistle to the Hebrews;**

3. **and the Seven Catholic Epistles (James, 1 and 2 Peter, 1, 2, and 3 John, and Jude).**

The Didactic or Wisdom Books consist of Epistles or Letters written to answer the concrete needs of the early Church. They are the first documents of the New Testament and contain doctrinal and moral instructions, disciplinary actions, practical advice, and exhortations.

Paul's Letters can be divided into four groups:

1) The *First Epistles:* 1 and 2 Thessalonians written about 51, after Paul's journey through Macedonia.

2) The *Major Epistles:* 1 and 2 Corinthians, Galatians, and Romans, written during his second missionary journey between 56 and 58. These are concerned with the great themes of the Christian life.

3) The *Captivity Epistles:* Ephesians, Colossians, Philippians, and Philemon, written during Paul's Roman Captivity (61-63). These are also called the Christological Epistles because they stress the central part played by Christ in the divine plan of salvation.

4) The *Pastoral Epistles:* 1 and 2 Timothy and Titus, written during Paul's last days. These are principally concerned with the pastoral duties of the men to whom they were addressed.

The *Epistle to the Hebrews* is a letter attributed to Paul which is really a complex theological treatise on Christology, the priesthood and sacrifice of Christ, the New Covenant, and the way of Christian life.

The *Seven Catholic Epistles* are so called because they were thought at one time to be addressed to the Church in general rather than to individual Churches or people. *James* (written between the 60's and 80's) is an exhortation to Christian living, stressing good works and citing the anointing of the sick. *1 Peter* (written in the mid 60's) stresses the joy of the baptized Christians and the unity of the faithful around Jesus. *2 Peter* (written about 100-125) is intended to refute false doctrines and exhort to faith and love of God. *Jude* (written between 70 and 90) is a brief treatise against false teachings and practices, and advocating authority and true Christian freedom. *1 John* (written about 90) stresses that God is Love and Light and is encountered through Jesus. *2 and 3 John* (written in the 90's) deal with specific questions, urging steadfastness in faith.

24. *What is the Prophetic Book of the New Testament?*

The Prophetic Book of the New Testament is the Book of Revelation.

The *Book of Revelation* (formerly known as the *Apocalypse)* is classified as a prophetic book but is more properly an apocalyptic book. This was a type of writing that can best be described as "underground literature." It lasted from 200 B.C. to 200 A.D. and was very popular among both Jews and Christians while in vogue.

Written about 95 A.D., this book is the most mysterious of all the books of the Bible. It cannot be adequately comprehended except against the historical background which occasioned its writing. Like the Book of Daniel and other apocalypses, it was composed as resistance literature to meet a crisis. The book itself suggests that the crisis was ruthless persecution of the early Church by the Roman authorities; the harlot Babylon symbolizes pagan Rome, the city on seven hills.

The book is, then, an exhortation and admonition to Christians to stand firm in the faith and to avoid compromise with paganism, despite the threat of adversity and martyrdom; they are to await patiently the fulfillment of God's mighty promises. The triumph of God in the world remains a mystery, to be accepted in faith and longed for in hope. It is a triumph that unfolded in the history of Jesus of Nazareth, and continues to unfold in the history of the individual Christian who follows the way of the cross, even, if necessary, to a martyr's death.

Though the perspective is eschatological—ultimate salvation and victory are said to take place at the end of the present age when Christ will come in glory at the parousia —the book presents the decisive struggle of Christ and his followers against Satan and his cohorts as already over. Christ's overwhelming defeat of the kingdom of Satan has ushered in the everlasting reign of God. Even the forces of evil unwittingly carry out the divine plan for God is the sovereign Lord of history.

Tradition

25. *What is Sacred Tradition?*

Sacred Tradition is the Word of God given to the Apostles by Christ and the Holy Spirit and handed down to their successors through the Church by means of prayer and Creeds, liturgical practices, and authoritative writings (Popes, bishops, and theologians).

Tradition can be defined as the way the Church understands and lives the teachings of Jesus *at any particular moment in time.* Tradition and Sacred Scripture form one deposit of the Word of God. Thus, Scripture, Traditon, and the Catholic Church combine to bring us God's revelation.

"Faith is expressed in words and deeds.

"What we are to believe is found in Tradition and Scripture, which together form one sacred deposit of the word of God which is committed to the Church. Scripture is the word of God inasmuch as it is consigned to writing under the inspiration of the divine Spirit. To the successors of the Apostles, Sacred Tradition hands on in its full purity God's word. Thus, led by the light of the Spirit of truth, these successors can in their preaching preserve this word of God faithfully, explain it, and make it more widely known.

"The Tradition which comes from the Apostles is unfolded in and by the Church with the help of the Holy Spirit. (Cf. 1 Cor 12:2f) Believers grow in insight through study and contemplation. Such growth comes about through the intimate understanding of spiritual things they experience, and through the preaching of those who have received through episcopal succession the sure gift of truth.

"As the community of believers grows in understanding, its faith is expressed in creeds, dogmas, and moral principles and teachings. The meaning of dogmatic formulas remains ever true and constant in the Church, even when it is expressed with greater clarity or more developed. Because they are expressed in the language of a particular time and place, however, these formulations sometimes give way to new ones, proposed and approved by the Magisterium of the Church, which express the same meaning more clearly or completely.

"What we believe is also expressed in the deeds of the Church community. The 'deeds' in question are worship—especially the celebration of the Eucharist, in which the risen Christ speaks to His Church and continues His saving work—and acts performed to build up Christ's body through service to the community of faith or voluntary service in the universal mission of the Church. (Cf. Eph 4:11f) While it is true that our actions establish the sincerity of our words, it is equally true that our words must be able to explain our actions. In catechesis Catholics are taught a facility in talking about their faith, lest they be silent when it comes to explaining what they are doing and why.

"Belief can also be expressed in the visual arts, in poetry and literature, in music and architecture, in philosophy, and scientific or technological achievements. These, too, can be signs of God's presence, continuations of His creative activity, instruments by which believers glorify Him and give witness to the world concerning the faith that is in them" (National Catechetical Directory, no. 59).

The Church's Use of the Bible in Worship

The Liturgy has fittingly been called "the Bible in action." For the Bible pervades every part of the liturgical rites of the Church. We find in this public worship biblical passages (Readings), biblical chants (Antiphons), biblical formulas (Greetings, Acclamations, and Institution Narrative), biblical allusions (Prayers), and biblical instruction (Homily.)

This is not very strange when we consider that the Bible is God's Word to us and that it was first written with worship in mind. Indeed, it was the Word of God which formed God's people and which continues to do so today.

By the same token, it is the Liturgy that provides the perfect forum for God's Word to be proclaimed, understood, and loved. The Liturgy presents the true background for the interpretation and appreciation of God's Word.

In the new Liturgy of the Mass, the Church has brought the Liturgy of the Word into closer relationship with the Liturgy of the Eucharist and has increased the number of Scripture readings contained therein. The Liturgy of the Word consists of the readings from the Bible and the songs occurring between them. The Homily, the Profession of Faith (Creed), and the Prayer of the Faithful develop and conclude it.

In the readings God speaks to His people, reveals to them the mysteries of redemption and salvation, and provides them with spiritual nourishment; and Christ Himself, in the form of His Word, is present in the midst of His faithful. The people appropriate this divine Word to themselves by their singing, and testify their fidelity to God's Word by their profession of faith. Strengthened by the Word of God they intercede, in the Prayer of the Faithful, for the needs of the entire Church and for the salvation of the whole world.

26. *How should we read the Bible?*

We should read the Bible with the mind of the Church for it is the Church who gave us the Bible and who interprets it for us. It will then become God's Word to us today.

The Catholic Church is the official interpreter of the Bible. As the people of God—both of the Old Covenant *in figure* and of the New Covenant *in reality*—she wrote the Sacred Scriptures. As the Church of Christ, she has interpreted them. And as the Church of Christians, she has always treasured them.

She encourages her members to study the Scriptures for she knows that they can discover nothing but what will make the Bible a greater force in her life and that of her members. And she knows that "ignorance of the Scriptures is ignorance of Christ."

"The Sacred Scriptures contain the Word of God and, since they are inspired, really are the Word of God. ... This Sacred Council urges all the Christian faithful to learn by frequent reading of the divine Scriptures the 'excelling knowledge of Jesus Christ.' 'For ignorance of the Scriptures is ignorance of Christ' (St. Jerome). Therefore, they should gladly put themselves in touch with the sacred text. ...

"And let them remember that prayer should accompany the reading of Sacred Scripture, so that God and man may talk together; for 'we speak to Him when we read the divine saying' (Vatican II: *Dogmatic Constitution on Divine Revelation,* no. 25).

The Senses of Scripture

There are three general senses of Scripture that have traditionally been utilized in the Church—two are real senses of Scripture and one is not.

1) The *literal or grammatical sense* is the meaning conveyed directly and immediately by the words of the text when they are interpreted in accord with the ordinary rules of language. It is also called the historical sense. Every text in the Bible has a literal sense.

2) The *spiritual or typical sense* is a meaning that goes beyond the literal sense but is based on it. Therefore, when

a text has a typical sense, it really has two meanings. For example the bronze serpent in the Old Testament was a prophetic figure of Christ on the Cross, and the Prophet Jonah in the belly of the fish was a figure of Christ in the tomb. The only way that we know that a text has a typical sense is through revelation.

3) The *accommodated sense* is not a biblical sense. It is an "accommodation" of the Scriptural text to a subject that neither the sacred writer nor the Holy Spirit meant to indicate. The Church uses the accommodated sense in her Liturgy for the edification of the faithful and to pray in the very words of Scripture, but it never sets forth these senses as true biblical senses. This sense of Scripture must be used with caution.

God's Word to Us Today

When reading the Bible, we should take pains to discover the literal sense of every passage. Reading introductions and footnotes in our Bible is very important in this respect. However, we should also realize that the Bible is God's Word to us today. We can therefore read it *existentially.*

The past is dead. *We* do not expect Christ's second coming as happening tonight; *we* are not in an occupied country, nor can we artificially create the situation of 2,000 years ago. Yet there is *something in common,* namely, *we* are captives in our odd and sorry human situation (as the Hebrews were in Egypt and in Palestine during the Roman occupation); *we* know about God's coming in Christ and wait for a brighter future through Christ's coming (as did the early Christians of 1 and 2 Thessalonians).

This something in common found in any Scripture is called *existential understanding.* This understanding, related to our existence or life-situation, is aided by faithful Bible reading. It is the very reason why Christians can read the same Bible time and again, since it is *our book!*

27. *Who teaches us what God has revealed?*

What God has revealed is taught to us by the Catholic Church.

Concerning this point, Vatican II says in the *Declaration on Religious Freedom:* "The Church is, by the will of Christ, the teacher of the truth. It is her duty to give utterance to, and authoritatively to teach, that truth which is Christ Himself, and also to declare and confirm by her authority those principles of the moral order which have their origins in human nature itself" (no. 14).

28. *Is faith necessary for salvation?*

Faith is absolutely necessary for salvation, because without faith no one can please God.

There always are people who say that it does not matter what we believe, just so we live right; that is the main thing. Such an attitude is an insult to God. God sent His own Son into the world to teach us the way to heaven. But if God went to such an extreme to teach us, it must have been very important to Him that we know and believe what He teaches, rather than whatever we please. To say, then, that it does not matter what we believe is not only to offend God but to imply that truth and error are the same, or are equally good.

Furthermore, in such a case, who would decide what is "right living"? The State? In that case execution without a just trial or arbitrary banishment to Siberia also would be "right." But if not the State, who then? The majority? But if the majority of those in power or control approved, the hijacking of planes or the taking of hostages also would be "right." Nor could we condemn what once was common practice in India, Hindu widows cremating themselves on their husband's funeral pile—it was "right." And the doctor who kills an unborn child also could say he is "living right"—he is helping a woman.

Clearly, without faith, without believing what God teaches, we cannot live right—right in the eyes of God.

29. Through which sign especially do Catholics profess their faith?

Catholics profess their faith especially through the holy Sign of the Cross.

Through the holy Sign of the Cross we profess our belief in the principal Mysteries of the Christian religion, namely, the Mystery of the Most Blessed Trinity and the Mystery of our Redemption through Christ's death on the Cross.

Hence, we should always make the Sign of the Cross with proper reverence, slowly, devoutly, and think of these Mysteries while making it. An old, commendable custom is for parents to make the Sign of the Cross on the forehead, the lips, and the breast of their children, first thing in the morning and last thing at night. And when children leave the house for school, etc., parents should bless them with the Sign of the Cross. There is great power in this sign.

St. Cyril, bishop of Jerusalem (d. 386), writes *(Catech. 13)*: "Let us make the Sign of the Cross with trust in its power. It is the great means of protection, a sign for believers and a dread to evil spirits." — That the early Christians had frequent recourse to the Sign of the Cross can be seen from these words of Tertullian (d. ca. 240): "At the beginning and in the course of any work, on coming in and going out, when we dress, when we go to bed, and in everything we do, we make the Sign of the Cross on the forehead."

Saints knew the power of this sign and drove off the devil by it, when he surprised them with temptation: saints like St. Meinrad (d. 861), whose struggle against the devil is the subject of a painting in the chapel of Etzel. But the Sign of the Cross is not only for times of temptation. St. Louis, king of France (d. 1270), signed himself before meals, before taking up affairs of state, before going into battle, etc.

30. *What is the wording of the Apostles' Creed?*

The Apostles' Creed reads as follows:

I believe in God, the Father almighty,
  Creator of heaven and earth.
And in Jesus Christ, His only Son, our Lord;
  Who was conceived by the Holy Spirit,
  born of the Virgin Mary,
  suffered under Pontius Pilate,
  was crucified, died, and was buried.
  He descended into hell;
  the third day he rose again from the dead;
  He ascended into heaven,
    and sits at the right hand of God,
    the Father almighty;
  from thence He shall come again to judge the
    living and the dead.
I believe in the Holy Spirit,
  the Holy Catholic Church,
  the communion of Saints,
  the forgiveness of sins,
  the resurrection of the body,
  and life everlasting. Amen.

This profession of faith is called the Apostles' Creed because according to ancient tradition it goes back to the Apostles themselves. Historical evidence places its first formulation in Rome, toward the end of the 2nd century. Candidates for Baptism were obliged to make this profession. In the course of time it acquired some additions. From the 6th century on, it was known in Gaul (kingdom of the Franks) in practically the same form that we have today. Its final formulation is traced to St. Firmin, bishop and abbot (d. 753), who founded a number of monasteries, the most noted being the Abbey of Reichenau, situated on an island in Lake Constance.

First Article of Faith

"I believe in God, the Father almighty, Creator of heaven and earth."

31. *Who is God?*

God is the eternal, infinite, perfect Spirit, Lord of heaven and earth.

"God is Spirit" (Jn 4:24). — "I am God, there is no other; I am God, there is none like me" (Is 46:9).

God is Spirit. As Spirit, He has intellect and free will but not a body, which is why we cannot see Him. Sometimes the Bible speaks of God's eyes and hands. This is figurative language, a means of making God's knowledge and action more understandable to us. The same is to be said for painters and sculptors who depict God in human form. They do not pretend that God actually is like that, but the only way they can tell us anything about God is through some form of imagery —that, or nothing at all.

"God is infinitely perfect" means that He possesses every good quality or attribute in the highest degree. He is eternal and unchanging, omnipresent, all-knowing, all-wise, all-powerful, infinitely holy and just, infinitely good and merciful, infinitely true and truthful, infinitely faithful.

Because of our limited minds we humans must speak of God's attributes as though they were separate and distinct. In God, however, they are all one.

32. *Can we know there is a God?*

We can know there is a God
1. from the visible world,
2. from the voice of conscience
3. and most especially from divine Revelation.

1) Reason tells us that the world did not always exist but must have had a beginning. It cannot have made itself. An almighty Maker or Creator must have called it into being. This maker of heaven and earth is God.

Reason also tells us that life did not always exist in the universe. But life cannot come from nonlife. A living Creator must have created it. This Creator of life is God.

Reason further tells us that in the world as a whole and in its minutest parts there exists a wonderful order. This order cannot be the result of chance. An all-wise Orderer must have ordered the universe and all things in it. This Orderer is God.

2) Not a day or hour goes by but that we hear within us the mysterious voice of conscience telling us what is good and what is evil, what to do and what not to do. But conscience is not something we gave to ourselves. A holy and just Judge planted it in our hearts. This Judge is God.

3) It remains true, of course, that in this life we cannot see God face to face. The Apostle John writes: "No one has ever seen God." He adds, however: "It is God the only Son, ever at the Father's side, who has revealed him" (Jn 1:18).

Our belief in God is reasonable, which means it is supported by human reason as well as being grounded in divine Revelation. God, in short, can be known to exist by arguing from things made to the Maker. "The fool says in his heart, 'There is no God' " (Ps 14:1). — "All men were by nature foolish who were in ignorance of God, and who from the good things seen did not succeed in knowing him who is, and from studying the works did not discern the artisan" (Wis 13:1).

The Second Vatican Council spoke along similar lines, in the *Dogmatic Constitution on Divine Revelation;* "God, the beginning and end of all things, can be known with certainty from created reality by the light of human reason (see Rom 1:20); but ... it is through His Revelation that those religious truths which are by their nature accessible to human reason can be known by all people with ease, with solid certitude and with no trace of error, even in this present state of the human race" (no. 6).

The next three Questions (33, 34, and 35) deal with three of God's attributes.

33. What does "God is all-wise" mean?

"God is all-wise" means that He knows all things, the past, the present, the future, even our most secret thoughts.

"O searcher of heart and soul—for you darkness itself is not dark, and night shines as the day, and darkness and light are the same" (Pss 7:10; 139:12).

Before God, even the greatest human minds are small and ignorant. Many of them acknowledged this, in one way or another. Among them, Copernicus, founder of modern astronomy and the heliocentric system (d. 1543); Kepler, inventor of the telescope (d. 1630); Sir Isaac Newton, perhaps the greatest scientific genius, who always uncovered his head at the name of God (d. 1727); Michael Faraday, chemist and physicist famous for his work in the field of electricity (d. 1867); Max Planck, Nobel Prize winner, one of the greatest pioneers in modern physics (d. 1947).

Even though God knows everything before it happens, this does not mean that God compels us to sin or that God, who knows what we are going to do, is to blame for the sins we commit. God's foreknowledge is a great mystery and, like every divine mystery, raises questions that the finite human mind cannot fully answer. What is beyond question, however, is that God cannot sin or be the cause of our sins.

The following illustration, while not perfect, may shed some light. A police helicopter monitoring city traffic may foresee that in the next moment two cars will meet head-on, because neither driver has stopped or slowed to yield the right of way. Though the police in the helicopter can foresee the collision, they are not to blame for it. In the same way, God is not to blame for our sins because He foresees them. See also Questions 39 and 40.

34. What does "God is all-powerful" mean?

"God is all-powerful" means that He can do all things, what He wills and as He wills.

"Nothing is impossible with God" (Lk 1:37). — "All that the Lord wills he does, in heaven and on earth, in the seas and in all the deeps" (Ps 135:6).

35. What does "God is just" mean?

"God is just" means that God rewards the good and punishes the wicked, according as each deserves.

"[He] judges each one justly on the basis of his actions" (1 Pt 1:17).

Sometimes God punishes or rewards already in this life. Examples of punishment are Adam and Eve (Gn 3:8), Cain (Gn 4:9), Eli (1 Sm 2:27; 4:13), Herod (Acts 12:23). Rewarded, among others in the Bible, were Mordecai (Est 9:20ff) and Tobit, father of Tobiah. Perfect punishment and reward, however, only comes after death. For this reason God often permits the wicked and the immoral to be well-off in this life; it is His way of rewarding them for whatever good they do and for which in consequence they can expect nothing further in the next life, as Christ indicates in the example of the rich man and Lazarus (Lk 16:19-31).

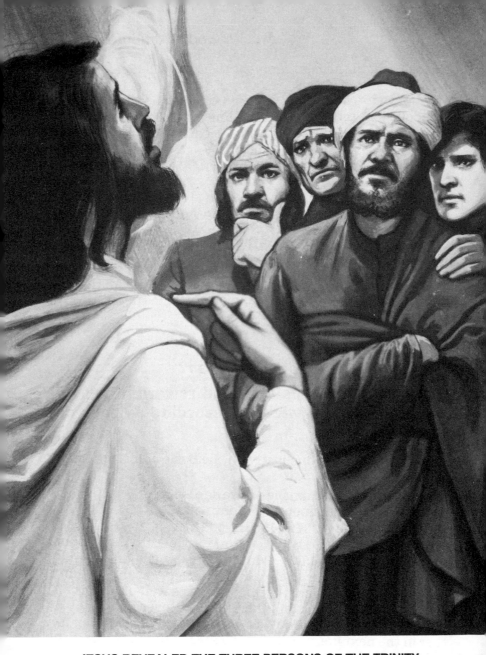

JESUS REVEALED THE THREE PERSONS OF THE TRINITY
"When the Paraclete comes, the Spirit of truth who comes from
the Father—and whom I myself will send from the Father—he
will bear witness on my behalf" (Jn 15:26f).

36. *How many Persons are there in God?*

In God there are three Persons: the Father, the Son, and the Holy Spirit, but these three Persons are only one God.

That there are three Persons in God, this we only know from divine Revelation. It is a Mystery that remained hidden to the Old Testament but was revealed to us through Jesus Christ. When our Lord was baptized in the Jordan, all three Persons were in evidence. In the river stood the Son of God. From the heavens the Father's voice was heard, and the Holy Spirit descended in the form of a dove (Mt 3:16-17).

The Mystery of one God in three Persons is one of the deepest and most incomprehensible Mysteries of our faith. We shall never be able to grasp it; we can only believe it. Illustrations are possible, but they do not explain it. The clover has three leaves yet is only one leaf. Water remains water, whether flowing, frozen, or in the form of dew. Fire in a way is three-in-one as flame, light, and heat.

Perhaps the "clearest" illustration is with three burning candles. Hold them close together and the three flames remain three. But join the three wicks and there is only one flame but still three candles.

In the name of the Blessed Trinity we were baptized, and through Baptism we became temples of the Blessed Trinity. We ought frequently to remind ourselves of this, and especially whenever we make the Sign of the Cross or renew our Baptismal Promises.

37. *Why do we call God the Creator of heaven and earth?*

We call God the creator of heaven and earth because it was from nothing that He made heaven and earth.

The first two chapters of Genesis, which is the first book of the Bible, recount the creation of the world. The Bible, however, does not intend to give what we could call a scientific description; its purpose here is to teach us that everything that exists was created by God. The creation account is a devotional narrative Oriental in form and character. Set forth, in expressive imagery, are important truths about God and the world.

In the *Dogmatic Constitution on the Church,* Vatican II says: "The eternal Father, by a free and hidden plan of His own wisdom and goodness, created the whole world" (no. 2). And in its *Pastoral Constitution on the Church in the Modern World* it makes this point: "God intended the earth with everything contained in it for the use of all human beings and peoples" (no. 69).

38. *Does God still watch over the world?*

God still watches over the world; He orders and directs everything for the best.

When we look at the world and all the evil and suffering that exists, we might wonder about the truth of this answer. Nevertheless, the words of the Bible which we read in St. Peter still hold: "Cast all your cares on him because he cares for you" (1 Pt 5:7).

39. *If God watches over everything, why does He permit sin?*

God permits sin
1. because He wants our choice of Him to be free;
2. because He knows how to turn evil, or sin, to good.

Joseph in the Old Testament is a perfect example. His brothers hated him and sold him into Egypt, hence committed a very grave sin. But through this evil Joseph came to high office in Egypt and was able to help his brothers at a time of severe famine: "Even though you meant harm to me, God meant it for good" (Gn 50:20).

Vatican II in its *Declaration on Religious Freedom* has this: "God calls human beings to serve Him in spirit and in truth; hence they are bound in conscience but they stand under no compulsion. God has regard for the dignity of the human persons whom He Himself has created and they are to be guided by their own judgment and they are to enjoy freedom" (no. 11).

40. If God governs everything, why does He permit suffering?

God permits suffering to punish and correct sinners, but also to test the righteous and prepare them for greater reward in heaven.

"I consider the sufferings of the present to be as nothing compared with the glory to be revealed in us. . . . We know that God makes all things work together for the good of those who have been called according to his decree" (Rom 8:18, 28). "Commit to the Lord your way; trust in him, and he will act" (Ps 37:5).

In the Dogmatic Constitution on the Church, *Vatican II declares: "On earth, still as pilgrims in a strange land, tracing in trial and in oppression the paths He trod, we are made one with His sufferings as the body is one with the Head, suffering with Him, that with Him we may be glorified" (no. 7). In the* Pastoral Constitution on the Church in the Modern World *the Council again points to Christ, in Whom alone this problem finds solution: "Through Christ and in Christ, the riddles of sorrow and death grow meaningful. Apart from His Gospel, they overwhelm us" (no. 22).*

41. What are angels?

Angels are perfect, spiritual beings, created by God to worship Him, to serve Him, and to carry out His commands.

The word "angel" derives from the Latin *angelus*, meaning messenger. The existence of angels is shown in many places of Sacred Scripture. In the New Testament angels appear particularly as messengers from heaven. They deliver God's instructions to people and usually appear as young men dressed in dazzling white garments (Mt 28:3; Mk 16:5; Lk 24:4; Jn 20:12; Acts 1:10). Their number is exceedingly large (Mt 26:53; Heb 12:22, and many other places in the Bible). Above all, they ministered to our Lord throughout His life on earth, from beginning to end.

The Church's teaching on angels was officially stated by the Fourth Lateran Council in 1215. The Council pronounced the existence of angels a doctrine of Catholic faith, part of its inviolable content. In 1870 the First Vatican Council put its own stamp of approval on this teaching.

That each person has a guardian angel, an angel that attends the individual from birth to the grave, is an age-old belief in the Church. The Fathers of the Church, from early on, testify to it. Biblical support can be found as well. In Ps 91:11 we read: "To his angels he has given command about you, that they guard you in all your ways."

Our Lord Himself said: "See that you never despise one of these little ones. I assure you, their angels in heaven constantly behold my heavenly Father's face" (Mt 18:10).

42. What are evil spirits?

Evil spirits are fallen angels who hate God and try to harm us in body and soul.

According to Old Testament teaching Satan, or the devil, is a personal power hostile to God (Jb 1:6; Zec 3:1; Wis 2:24). In the New Testament there are frequent manifestations of the devil and evil spirits. Even Christ was tempted (Mt 4:1-11). and St. Peter in his First Epistle puts us on guard against the devil: "Stay sober and alert. Your opponent the devil is prowling like a roaring lion looking for someone to devour. Resist him, solid in your faith" (1 Pt 5:8-9).

Vatican II took note of the devil and his work. In the *Decree on the Missionary Activity of the Church,* the Council said: "God [sent] His Son, clothed in our flesh, in order that through Him He might wrest human beings from the power of darkness and Satan and reconcile the world to Himself in Him" (no. 3).

The Council enlarges on this thought in the *Pastoral Constitution on the Church in the Modern World:* "A monumental struggle against the powers of darkness pervades the whole of human history. The battle was joined from the very origins of the world and will continue until the last day, as the Lord has attested. Caught in this conflict, human beings are obliged to wrestle constantly if they are to cling to what is good, nor can they achieve their own integrity without great efforts and the help of God's grace" (no. 37).

43. What do human beings consist of?

Human beings consist of body and soul.

"The Lord God formed man out of the clay of the ground and blew into his nostrils the breath of life, and so man became a living being" (Gn 2:7).

The first man and woman were called Adam and Eve; they are our first parents, the protogenitors of the human race.

The description of human creation in the Book of Genesis should not be taken literally, as St. Augustine already cautioned. It is simply an imaginative way of saying that human beings, like everything else, were created by God.

In the Pastoral Constitution on the Church in the Modern World, *Vatican II asks the question: "But what is humanity?" and goes on to say: "About itself the human race has expressed, and continues to express, many divergent and even contradictory opinions. In these humanity often exalts itself as the absolute measure of all things or debases itself to the point of despair. The result is doubt and anxiety. The Church certainly understands these problems. Endowed with light from God, she can offer solutions to them, so that the true human situation can be portrayed and its defects explained, while at the same time dignity and destiny are justly acknowledged.*

"*For Sacred Scripture teaches that human beings were created 'in the image of God,' are capable of knowing and loving their Creator, and were appointed by Him as masters of all earthly creatures that they might subdue creatures and use them for God's glory. . . .*

"*Though made of body and soul, a person is one. In bodily composition the person gathers together the elements of the material world; thus these elements reach their crown through the human person and raise their voice in free praise of the Creator. For this reason one is not allowed to despise bodily life, but is obliged to regard the body as good and honorable since God has created it and will raise it up on the last day. . . .*

"*Now, human beings are not wrong when they regard themselves as superior to bodily concerns, and as more than a speck of nature or a nameless constituent of the city of man. . . . Thus, in recognizing an inner spiritual and immortal soul, a person is not being mocked by a fantasy . . . but is rather laying hold of the proper truth of the matter. . . .*

"*Since all human beings possess a rational soul and are created in God's likeness, since they have the same nature and origin, have been redeemed by Christ and enjoy the same divine calling and destiny, the basic equality of all must receive increasingly greater recognition*" (nos. 12, 14, 20).

44. What was the most precious gift that God bestowed on the first man and woman?

The most precious gift that God bestowed on the first man and woman was the life of grace.

Hence from their beginning the first two human beings were children of God, holy and heirs of heaven. Their understanding was clear; their will was free and unweakened. They lived happily in Paradise and had neither to suffer nor to die.

Adam did not receive these gifts for himself alone. As head and progenitor of the human race, he received them both for himself and his wife and for all his posterity. We would have inherited them from him had he remained obedient to God.

On this topic Vatican II teaches in the *Dogmatic Constitution on the Church:* "The eternal Father, by a free and hidden plan of His own wisdom and goodness, created the whole world. His plan was to raise human beings to a participation in the divine life. After they had fallen in Adam, God the Father did not leave human beings to themselves, but ceaselessly offered helps to salvation, in view of Christ, the Redeemer" (no. 2)

45. *What does Sacred Scripture say in regard to the first sin?*

The first man and woman disobeyed God; they wanted to become like Him and so they ate of the forbidden fruit.

The expression "they ate of the forbidden fruit" is allegorical language to dramatize the fact that in their pride the first man and woman disobeyed God. The Bible does not give us the actual data of this sin, what exactly it was that God forbade or commanded and they ignored. In any event, it was a sin of pride and disobedience, as Sacred Scripture makes clear. To say, then, that because of a pilfered apple all mankind suffered ruin is simple nonsense.

The devil, "father of lies" (Jn 8:44), used a lie to lead the first human pair into sin. The consequences for Adam and Eve were very grave:

1) they lost sanctifying grace;
2) their understanding was clouded; their will was weakened and disposed to evil;
3) they had to suffer much and eventually to die.

"Cursed be the ground because of you! In toil shall you eat its yield all the days of your life. Thorns and thistles shall it bring forth to you. By the sweat of your face shall you get bread to eat, until you return to the ground, from which you were taken. For you are dirt, and to dirt you shall return" (Gn 3:17-19).

46. What misfortune did the first sin bring upon all human beings?

All human beings are burdened with fault in the eyes of God before they themselves have sinned.

Our original parents in Paradise represented and acted for the whole human race. God in His eternal wisdom willed it so. Therefore, just as they would have transmitted God's gifts to all human beings that came after them, so they transmitted to all human beings the first sin and its consequences. St. Paul speaks of this in the Epistle to the Romans (5:12-19):

"Through one man, sin entered the world and with sin death, death thus coming to all men inasmuch as all sinned. . . . But the gift is not the offense. For if by the offense of the one man all died, much more did the grace of God and the gracious gift of the one man, Jesus Christ, abound for all. . . . To sum up, then: just as a single offense brought condemnation to all men, a single righteous act brought all men acquittal and life."

On this question, Vatican II says in the *Pastoral Constitution on the Church in the Modern World:* "Although human beings were made by God in a state of holiness, from the very onset of their history they abused their liberty, at the urging of the Evil One. Human beings set themselves against God and sought to attain their goal apart from God. . . . Therefore they are split within themselves. As a result, all of human life . . . shows itself to be a dramatic struggle between good and evil, between light and darkness.

"Indeed, human beings find that by themselves they are incapable of battling the assaults of evil successfully, so that everyone feels as though bound by chains. But the Lord Himself came to free human beings. . . . The call to grandeur and the depths of misery, both of which are a part of human experience, find their ultimate and simultaneous explanation in the light of this revelation" (no. 13).

47. *In what does original sin consist?*

Primarily, original sin consists in the fact that human beings come into the world without the life of grace, hence without the state of righteousness required by God.

Original sin, therefore, is not a personal sin, one that we ourselves commit. It is rather a kind of privation, or an inherited defect which signifies that we lack the life of grace at birth and must receive it by being baptized.

In the *Decree on the Apostolate of the Laity,* Vatican II amplifies: "In the course of history, the use of temporal things has been marred by serious vices. Affected by original sin, people have frequently fallen into many errors concerning the true God, the nature of human beings, and the principles of the moral law. This has led to the corruption of morals and human institutions and not rarely to contempt for the human person" (no. 7). And in the *Decree on the Media of Social Communication,* the Council admonishes restraint in the reporting or portraying of moral evil because matters of this kind, "given the baneful effect of original sin in human beings, could quite readily arouse base desires in them" (no. 7).

At the closing of the Year of Faith (June 30, 1968), Pope Paul VI proclaimed the Creed of the People of God in which he affirmed the following in regard to original sin: "We believe that in Adam all have sinned, which means that the original offense committed by him caused human nature, common to all human beings, to fall to a state in which it bears the consequences of that offense, and which is not the state in which it was at first in our first parents, established as they were in holiness and justice, and in which they knew neither evil nor death. It is human nature, so fallen, stripped of the grace that clothed it, injured in its own natural powers and subjected to the dominion of death, that is transmitted to all human beings and it is in this sense that every person is born in sin."

48. *Who alone was preserved from original sin?*

The only person preserved from original sin was the Blessed Virgin Mary, the Mother of our Lord Jesus Christ.

Concerning this privilege Pope Paul VI stated in his Creed of June, 1968: "We believe that Mary, who remained ever a Virgin, is the Mother of the Incarnate Word, our God and Savior Jesus Christ, and that by reason of this singular election she was, in consideration of the merits of her Son, redeemed in a more eminent manner, preserved from all stain of original sin and filled with the gift of grace more than all other creatures."

This privilege of grace is celebrated on December 8, the feast of the Immaculate Conception. In the official liturgy of the Church the full name of the feast is "Solemnity of the Virgin and Mother of God, Mary conceived without original sin." The feast had its origin in the Eastern Church. It is mentioned in a Church calendar of Constantinople about the year 1000.

In the West the Franciscans were the first promoters of the feast, giving it a place in their liturgical calendar. In 1477 the Franciscan Pope Sixtus IV prescribed it for the diocese of Rome. In 1708 Clement XI prescribed it for the universal Church. Pope Pius IX, in 1854, defined the Immaculate Conception as a dogma of the Church and made the feast a holyday of obligation, which it had not been before. The Immaculate Conception is the patronal feast of the United States and, until now, a holyday of obligation for American Catholics.

Second and Third Articles of Faith

"I believe in Jesus Christ, His only Son, our Lord; Who was conceived by the Holy Spirit, born of the Virgin Mary."

49. Who is Jesus Christ?

Jesus Christ is the true Son of God, Who became man for our sake.

Human nature is composed of body and soul. The eternal Son of God always had a divine nature. At Bethlehem He was born a human being, with a human body and soul, i.e., a human nature. But He did not cease to be God. Hence He is God-Man, true God and true man. His two natures, the human and the divine, are inseparably united in the one Person of the Son of God.

The Epistle to the Hebrews states (1:1-4): "In times past, God spoke in fragmentary and varied ways to our fathers through the prophets; in this, the final age, he has spoken to us through his Son, whom he has made heir to all things and through whom he first created the universe. This Son is the reflection of the Father's glory, the exact representation of the Father's being, and he sustains all things by his powerful word. When he had cleansed us from our sins, he took his seat at the right hand of the Majesty in heaven, as far superior to the angels as the name he has inherited is superior to theirs."

Vatican II in the Pastoral Constitution on the Church in the Modern World, *remarks: "Since human nature as [Christ] assumed it was not annulled, by that very fact it has been raised up to a divine dignity in our respect too. For by His incarnation the Son of God has united Himself in some fashion with every human being. He worked with human hands, He thought with a human mind, acted by human choice, and loved with a human heart. Born of the Virgin*

71

Mary, He has truly been made one of us, like us in all things except sin" (no. 22).

The name of Jesus means Redeemer or Savior, as the angel indicated to Joseph: "You are to name him Jesus because he will save his people from their sins" (Mt 1:21). The name Christ, from the Greek *christos,* means Anointed. Messiah is the Hebrew word for Anointed. In Old Testament times prophets, high priests, and kings were solemnly anointed to consecrate and prepare them for their office.

Jesus Christ, our supreme prophet, priest, and king, was not anointed by human hand but by the power of the heavenly Father, Who poured the fullness of the Holy Spirit in the soul of Jesus. "The Spirit of the Lord is upon me; therefore he has anointed me. He has sent me to bring glad tidings to the poor" (Lk 4:18).

50.   Who is the mother of Jesus?

The mother of Jesus is the Most Blessed Virgin Mary. Since Jesus is God as well as man, she is also called Mother of God.

The archangel Gabriel announced to Mary that she had been chosen to be the mother of God's Son: "The angel went on to say to her: 'Do not fear, Mary. You have found favor with God. You shall conceive and bear a son and give him the name Jesus. . . .' Mary said to the angel, 'How can this be since I do not know man?' The angel answered her: 'The Holy Spirit will come upon you and the power of the Most High will overshadow you; hence, the holy offspring to be born will be called Son of God . . . for nothing is impossible with God.' Mary said: 'I am the servant of the Lord. Let it be done to me as you say' " (Lk 1:30-38).

In the *Dogmatic Constitution on the Church,* the Second Vatican Council says: "Predestined from eternity by, that decree of divine providence which determined the incarnation of the Word, to be the Mother of God, the Blessed Virgin was on this earth the virgin Mother of the Redeemer, and above all others and in a singular way the generous associate and humble handmaid of the Lord. She conceived, brought forth, and nourished Christ; she presented Him to the Father in the temple, and was united with Him by compassion as He died on the Cross.

"In this singular way she cooperated . . . in the work of the Savior in giving back supernatural life to souls. Wherefore she is our mother in the order of grace. . . . As St. Ambrose taught, the Mother of God is a type of [prefigured] the Church in the order of faith, charity, and perfect union with Christ.

"For in the mystery of the Church, which is itself rightly called mother and virgin, the Blessed Virgin stands out in eminent and singular fashion as exemplar of both virgin and mother. By her belief and obedience, not knowing man but overshadowed by the Holy Spirit, as the new Eve she brought forth on earth the very Son of the Father, showing an undefiled faith, not in the word of the ancient serpent, but in that of God's messenger" (nos. 61, 63).

Concerning the veneration of the Blessed Virgin in the Church the same Constitution says: "From earliest times the Blessed Virgin is honored under the title of Mother of God, under whose protection the faithful took refuge in all their dangers and necessities. . . . The various forms of piety toward the Mother of God which the Church . . . has approved bring it about that while the Mother is honored, the Son . . . is rightly known, loved, and glorified and that all His commands are observed.

"This most Holy Synod deliberately teaches this Catholic doctrine and at the same time admonishes all the children of the Church that the cult, especially the liturgical cult, of the Blessed Virgin be generously fostered, and the practices and exercises of piety, recommended by the magisterium of the Church toward her in the course of centuries, be made of great moment, and those decrees which have been given in the early days regarding the cult of images of Christ, the Blessed Virgin and the Saints, be religiously observed. . . .

"Let the faithful remember moreover that true devotion consists neither in sterile or transitory affection, nor in a certain vain credulity, but proceeds from true faith, by which we are led to know the excellence of the Mother of God, and we are moved to a filial love toward our mother and to the imitation of her virtues" (nos. 66, 67).

On February 2, 1974, Pope Paul VI issued an Apostolic Exhortation in which he spoke of authentic veneration of Mary. Such veneration, he said, is truly Christian, and he pointed to its place in the liturgy. Many forms of devotion should be rescued from the neglect into which they have fallen. Specifically, the Pope called for greater use of the rosary and the Litany of the Blessed Virgin.

He also set down four features of true Marian devotions in our day:

1) Marian devotions must have a Biblical imprint. The prayers and chants used therein should draw their inspiration and wording from the Bible. Above all, they should be imbued with the great themes of the Christian message.

2) Marian devotions must be harmonized with the liturgy and not merged into it. They should somehow derive their inspiration from it. Also, because of the liturgy's preeminence they should orient the Christian people to it.

3) Marian devotions must be ecumenical in character. Every care must be taken to avoid any exaggeration which would mislead other Christian brethren about the true teaching of the Church. They must inculcate a better understanding of Mary's place in the Mystery of Christ and of the Church on the part of our separated brethren, thus smoothing the path to Christian unity.

4) Marian devotions must be in harmony with modern anthropological studies—by paying close attention to the findings of the human sciences. They must take account of the profound changes that have occurred in the psycho-sociological field in which the modern person lives and works.

The Pope urged devotion to Mary upon pastors and others engaged in pastoral work for the blessings it brings. All in all, he affirmed what has always been the mind of the Church, that, abuses aside, veneration of Mary does not detract from Christ but points to Him and redounds to His glory.

AT MARY'S WORD JESUS PERFORMED THE FIRST OF HIS SIGNS
"The wine ran out [at the marriage feast of Cana] and Jesus'
mother told him, 'They have no wine.' " Jesus told the waiters to
fill six stone water jars with water and take some to the chief
waiter, who tasted it and found it to be choice wine (Jn 2:3-11).

51. *Who was the foster father and guardian of Jesus?*

The foster father and guardian of Jesus was St. Joseph.

Jesus did not have an earthly father, such as we have. His father is God the Father in heaven. Sacred Scripture tells us very little about St. Joseph himself. It merely states that he was an upright or "just" man (Mt 1:19). In biblical language this means that he rendered to God and to fellow humans what was rightly theirs, e.g., the love and worship and obedience we owe to God.

This "justice," with which the Bible credits St. Joseph, is basic to the practice of the Christian life; to possess it is to possess, in principle, every Christian virtue. The Church celebrates on March 19 the feast of St. Joseph as Husband of the Mother of God, and on May 1 his feast as Patron of Workers, since it was by his work as a carpenter that he supported the Holy Family.

When the Bible speaks of "brothers" of Jesus, this does not mean that Mary and Joseph had other children, aside from Jesus. Though married, they lived a virginal life. In the Bible, "brothers" or "sisters" often mean no more than close relatives. Lot, for example, is called brother of Abraham, though he was only a nephew (Gn 13:8).

As late as 1552, the Protestant reformer Zwingli defended the perpetual virginity of Mary and declared that the "brothers" of Jesus were only relatives. Martin Luther himself called Mary a perpetual virgin who gave birth, while remaining a virgin, to an only child Jesus. He also preached the Immaculate Conception in the very same sense as later defined by the Church, in 1854.

52. *How we know that Jesus was the promised Messiah?*

We know that Jesus Christ was the promised Messiah because in Him everything was fulfilled that the Prophets had foretold of the Redeemer.

"Philip sought out Nathaniel and told him, 'We have found the one Moses spoke of in the law—the prophets too—Jesus, son of Joseph, from Nazareth" (Jn 1:45).

Specifically, the Prophets foretold of the Redeemer:

1) The time and place of his birth, and his birth from a virgin. *"But you, Bethlehem-Ephrathah, too small to be among the clans of Judah, from you shall come forth for me one who is to be ruler in Israel" (Mi 5:3; Mt 2:6). — "The scepter shall not depart from Judah ... until he comes to whom it belongs; and to him shall be the obedience of the peoples" (Gn 49:10). — "The virgin shall be with child, and bear a son, and shall call him Immanuel [God with us]" (Is 7:14).*

2. His divinity and miracles. *"Here is your God ... he comes to save you. Then will the eyes of the blind be opened, the ears of the deaf be cleared. Then will the lame leap like a stag, then the tongue of the dumb will sing" (Is 35:4-6).*

3. His suffering and Death. *"I am a worm, not a man; the scorn of men, despised by the people. All who see me scoff at me; they mock me with parted lips, they wag their heads. They have pierced my hands and my feet. They divide my garments among them, and for my vesture they cast lots" (Ps 22:7-8, 17, 19). — "They put gall in my food, and in my thirst they gave me vinegar to drink" (Ps 69:22).*

4) His Resurrection and Ascension. *"My body abides in confidence, because you will not abandon my soul to the nether world, nor will you suffer your faithful one to undergo corruption" (Ps 16:9-10). — "You have ascended on high. Chant praise to the Lord, who rides on the heights of the ancient heavens" (Ps 68:19, 33-34).*

5) His Glorification in heaven and His worldwide blessed Kingdom on earth. *"The Lord said to my Lord: 'Sit at my right hand till I make your enemies your footstool.' The Lord has sworn, and he will not repent: 'You are a priest forever, according to the order of Melchizedek' " (Ps 110:1, 4). — "Justice shall flower in his days, and profound peace. May he rule from sea to sea. All kings shall pay him homage, all nations shall serve him" (Ps 72:7, 8, 11).*

53. *How did Jesus Christ prove that He was God?*

Jesus Christ proved that He was God
1. by His miracles
2. and by His prophecies.

1) Jesus worked miracles, i.e., works so extraordinary that they cannot be done through natural powers but only through the almighty power of God. He changed water into wine; He fed several thousand with a few loaves of bread; He calmed the raging sea in an instant, healed by mere word sick people of every kind, drove out the devil, and raised the dead to life. "These very works which I perform testify on my behalf that the Father has sent me" (Jn 5:36).

The truth of the miracles needs no defense. They are as certain as the Gospels themselves and simply belong to the good news that Jesus brought. If we took away the miracles of Jesus, we would rob the Gospels of their unique power and do violence to their content. The miracles are signs that through Jesus God brought salvation to the world.

2) Jesus foretold things such as no human person could have known in advance, e.g., the betrayal of Judas, the flight of the Apostles, Peter's denial, the manner of His own death, the fact of His Resurrection and Ascension.

Fourth Article of Faith

"Suffered under Pontius Pilate, was crucified, died, and was buried."

54. *What did Jesus suffer for us at the end of His life?*

Jesus sweat drops of blood, was scourged, crowned with thorns, laden with the heavy Cross and crucified.

The sentence of death was passed upon Jesus by the Roman procurator Pontius Pilate. He had been appointed fifth procurator of Judea in the 26 by the Emperor Tiberius and governed until the year 36. He wanted to set Jesus free but finally handed Him over for fear of being denounced to the Emperor (Jn 19:12).

Jesus could suffer and die because He was man as well as God, and He permitted His human nature to endure every pain just as though He were only man and not at all God. "My heart is nearly broken with sorrow" (Mt 26:38). — "Come, all you who pass by the way, look and see whether there is any suffering like my suffering" (Lam 1:12).

Regarding the Death of Christ the Second Vatican Council declared in its Declaration on the Relation of the Church to Non-Christian Religions: *"True, the Jewish authorities and those who followed their lead pressed for the death of Christ; still, what happened in His passion cannot be charged against all the Jews, without distinction, then alive, nor against the Jews of today. Although the Church is the new people of God, the Jews should not be presented as rejected or accursed by God, as if this followed from the Holy Scriptures. . . .*

"Besides, as the Church has always held and holds now, Christ underwent His passion and death freely, because of the sins of human beings and out of infinite love, in order that all may reach salvation. It is, therefore, the burden of the Church's preaching to proclaim the Cross of Christ as the sign of God's all-embracing love and as the fountain from which every grace flows" (no. 4).

On October 22, 1974, Pope Paul VI instituted a special Commission for Religious Relations with the Jews and assigned it to the Secretariat for Promoting Christian Unity, then headed by Cardinal Willebrands. This was followed on December 1, 1974, by a document from the Vatican titled "Guidelines for Religious Relations with the Jews," and signed by Cardinal Willebrands. Its purpose was to promote better understanding between Christians and Jews. In particular, the document condemned anti-Semitism in all its manifestations.

The *Way of the Cross* is a devotion that commemorates the last sufferings of Jesus. The 14 stations are founded on the Gospels or suggested by them. Only the 6th station, Veronica and the veil, is based on legend. Since the beginning of the 16th century the number of stations has been set at 14. Prior to that it had varied but was never less than seven. In the Way of the Cross we follow Jesus on His journey to Calvary. The devotion, while recommended at all times, is especially appropriate during Lent.

55. *What is meant by: "Jesus died"?*

"Jesus died" means: His soul left the body, but as God He remained united both with His soul and with His body.

Jesus could not die as God, only as man. But as man He was truly dead, and not just in appearance. The Gospels state the fact very plainly. "Jesus uttered a loud cry and said, 'Father, into your hands I commend my spirit.' After he said this, he expired" (Lk 23:46; Jn 19:30).

The Death of Jesus was marked by signs and wonders. The veil of the Temple was rent in two. The earth quaked and boulders split, while tombs opened and many bodies of saints were raised. "Surely this was an innocent man; this was the Son of God" (Lk 23:47; Mt 27:54).

For the most part, these extraordinary events had been foretold by the Prophets for the "Day of the Lord" (Is 26:19; Ez 37:12; Dn 12:2; Am 8:3). The tearing of the Temple veil symbolizes an end to the Old Testament system of worship, particularly its liturgy of animal sacrifices (cf. Heb 9:12; 10:20). The dead who were raised were among the just of the Old Testament but now they belonged to Christ, whose own Resurrection was the signal for them also to emerge from their tomb. Very probably, too, they accompanied Him to heaven.

Jesus wanted to be buried to make His Death more difficult to deny and His Resurrection more glorious and deserving of belief.

56. *For whom did Jesus Christ die?*

Jesus Christ died for everyone.

God "wants all men to be saved and come to know the truth" (1 Tm 2:4). "He [Jesus Christ] is an offering for our sins, and not for our sins only, but for those of the whole world" (1 Jn 2:2).

Christ is the Redeemer of the world; He died for all. Nevertheless, to be saved every individual must receive the grace of Christ personally and cooperate with it.

Fifth Article of Faith

"He descended into hell; the third day He arose again from the dead."

57. *What is meant by: "He descended into hell"?*

"He descended into hell" means: After the death of Jesus His soul descended to the abode of the dead, i.e., to the souls of those who had died in the state of righteousness with God.

These souls could not go to heaven because heaven had been closed on account of sin and remained closed until reopened through the suffering and death of Christ. Christ descended into hell, i.e., He appeared to these righteous souls to announce to them their redemption. And at His Ascension He also brought them with Him into heaven.

Therefore, the "hell" where Christ descended is not the place or state of the damned. It is rather the place or state of the just souls of the Old Testament, Adam and Eve, Noah, Abraham, Moses, the Prophets, and all who had died in the state of grace. This descent, or appearance, is alluded to—if not directly stated—in several places of the New Testament; e.g., Mt 12:40; Mt 27:52ff; Acts 2:24-27. Another reference occurs in 1 Pt 3:19-20, but this passage is variously interpreted. It probably means that the risen Christ made known to the imprisoned souls His victory over sin and death.

With His descent into hell Christ, Who Himself had died, entered into communion with other dead who were capable of redemption, those who had not been condemned to the real hell. Lastly, it is worth noting that this teaching of our faith receives mention at Mass, in Eucharistic Prayer IV right after the Consecration, where "we recall Christ's Death, His descent among the dead. . . ."

58. What did Jesus do on the third day after His Death?

On the third day after His Death Jesus reunited His soul with His body and rose in glory from the grave.

The Resurrection of Christ is the greatest and most important event of our Catholic faith because, as St. Paul says, "if Christ has not been raised, our preaching is void of content and your faith is empty too" (1 Cor 15:14).

59. How do we know that our Lord rose from the dead?

We know that our Lord rose from the dead principally from the testimony of the Apostles, who saw the Risen Christ with their own eyes, who spoke with Him, touched Him, and gave their lives for Him.

Throughout the Christian Era there have been those who doubted or denied the Resurrection of Christ. Frequently they dismiss it as a product of the Apostles' imagination or something which the Apostles wanted so much to happen that they believed it happened. How far from the truth this is should be obvious upon reading the Gospel accounts and

THE RESURRECTION IS JESUS' GREATEST MIRACLE

On three separate occasions Jesus told his apostles that he would rise on the third day after his death (Mk 8:31; 9:31; 10:34). On the Sunday after his death he rose by his divine power, a glorious Victor, as he had promised (Mt 28:6; 1 Cor 15:4ff).

seeing how much it took to convince the Apostles of the Resurrection. Read Matthew 28, Mark 16, Luke 24, and John 20.

Much is sometimes made of the discrepancies in the Gospel accounts of the Resurrection and appearances of Jesus. But these discrepancies concern details and are easily accounted for. (To illustrate, different witnesses to an automobile accident may give slightly differing accounts, but the accident itself remains a fact.) All the Gospel accounts agree that Jesus rose and made appearances to the Apostles and others. The discrepancies, such as they are, serve rather to establish the truth of the Resurrection and appearances of Jesus, much more than if each account duplicated the others in every detail.

Though no one, so far as is known, saw Christ rise from the dead, the facts in the case are undeniable. Jesus had died. On the third day His tomb was found empty. The appearances followed and the disciples believed. For them, the Resurrection made the difference. In the case of the Apostles in particular, so absolute was their belief in the Risen Christ that every one, according to the unanimous tradition of the Church, died for it. This is eloquent testimony to the truth of what they believed, since no one embraces death for a lie or fabrication, least of all a cruel martyr's death.

60. *What does the Resurrection of Jesus prove to us?*

The Resurrection of Jesus proves to us
1. that Jesus is the Son of God,
2. and that one day we also shall rise.

1) "Destroy this temple, and in three days I will raise it up" (Jn 2:19).

2) "Just as in Adam all die, so in Christ all will come to life again" (1 Cor 12:22).

During the French Revolution attempts were made to eradicate Christianity and replace it with a human religion. A champion of the movement complained that it was not making much headway. A colleague known for his practice of the "new" morality replied: "Get yourself crucified on Friday and rise from the dead on Sunday. Then you will make headway."

Sixth Article of Faith

"He ascended into heaven, and sits at the right hand of God, the Father almighty."

61. *What happened forty days after the Resurrection of Jesus?*

On the fortieth day after the Resurrection Jesus ascended into heaven.

Christ's Ascension should not be pictured as a sort of voyage into outer space. Though a real departure, it was essentially a supernatural event that eludes human expression. The cloud that took Jesus away suggests the hidden presence of the divine Majesty. The angels assured the Apostles that Jesus would return, but the time of the return remains God's secret. For their part, the Apostles were to be witnesses of Christ "to the ends of the earth."

The number 40 leaves room for plus or minus. It is a round number as much symbolical as literal. In addition, Lk 24:50 gives the impression of an invisible ascension of Christ to the Father on Easter Sunday. But the Ascension forty days after the Resurrection (Acts 1:3) was a visible departure, the end of Christ's visible appearances to the Apostles.

62. *What is meant by: "and sits at the right hand of God, the Father almighty"?*

"And sits at the right hand of God, the Father almighty," means: Even as man, Jesus participates in the power and glory of the heavenly Father in heaven.

"Set your heart on what pertains to higher realms where Christ is seated at God's right hand" (Col 3:1). — "Your attitude must be that of Christ: Though he was God . . . he emptied himself and took the form of a slave, being born in the likeness of men. . . . Because of this, God highly exalted him and bestowed on him the name above every other name, so that at Jesus' name every knee must bend . . . and every tongue proclaim to the glory of God the Father: Jesus Christ is Lord" (Phil 2:5-11).

Seventh Article of Faith

"From thence He shall come to judge the living and the dead."

63. *Why will Jesus come again at the end of the world?*

Jesus will come again at the end of the world to judge all people and bring the Redemption to final fulfillment.

This judgment is called the General Judgment.

"This Jesus who has been taken from you will return, just as you saw him go up into the heavens" (Acts 1:11). — "See, he comes amid the clouds! Every eye shall see him, even of those who pierced him. All the peoples of the earth shall lament him bitterly" (Rv 1:7).

In the Dogmatic Constitution on the Church, Vatican II comments: "Since we know not the day nor the hour, on our Lord's advice we must be constantly vigilant. Thus, when we have finished the course of our earthly life, we may merit to enter into the marriage feast with Him and to be numbered among the blessed. Thus we may not be ordered to go into eternal fire like the wicked and slothful servant, into the exterior darkness where there will be the weeping and the gnashing of teeth.

"For before we reign with Christ in glory, all of us will be made manifest before the tribunal of Christ, so that each one may receive his or her recompense, good or bad, according to his or her life in the body. Then at the end of the world they who have done right shall rise to life; the evildoers shall rise to be damned.

"We reckon, therefore, that the sufferings of the present time are as nothing compared with the glory to be revealed in us. Strong in faith we await . . . , the appearing of the glory of the great God and Savior Christ Jesus, Who will give a new form to this lowly body of ours and remake it according to the pattern of His glorified body and Who will come to be glorified in His holy ones and adored by all who have believed" (no. 48).

In this excerpt the Council utilized the following scriptural verses: Heb 9:27; Mt 25:31-46; 25:26; 25:41; 22:13 and 25:30; 2 Cor 5:10; Jn 5:29; Mt 25:46; Rom 8:18; 2 Tm 2:11-12; Ti 2:13; Phil 3:21; 2 Thes 1:10.

64. *What do we know about the end of the world?*

We know that the end of the world is coming, but we do not know when or how it will come.

In the *Pastoral Constitution on the Church in the Modern World,* Vatican II affirms: "We do not know the time for the consummation of the earth and of humanity, nor do we know how all things will be transformed. As deformed by sin, the shape of this world will pass away; but we are taught that God is preparing a new dwelling place and a new earth where justice will abide, and whose blessedness will answer and surpass all the longings for peace which spring up in the human heart.

"Then, with death overcome, the children of God will be raised up in Christ, and what was sown in weakness and corruption will be invested with incorruptibility. Enduring with charity and its fruits, all that creation which God made on man's account will be unchained from the bondage of vanity" (no. 39).

That the world as we know it will come to an end is also indicated by scientific data. Herewith two examples: the rotation of the earth (its turning on its axis) loses a few seconds every 100 years. If this continues—and everything points that way—there will be a time when the rotation comes to an end; and when it does, all life will cease, too. Or consider this: The sun's temperatures are astronomical, from 20 to 40 million centigrade. The heat radiates from the sun and is scattered in space. Only a small fraction reaches the earth. But the sun's heat is cooling off and in time, even if only after millions upon millions of years, will be completely spent; and when it is, life on earth cannot survive.

Belief in the end of the world is also found in non-Christian religions. This could be a remnant of the original Revelation God made to mankind.

In the Old Testament it is Isaiah especially who speaks of an end to the world (13:9-10; 24:19-20; 51:6). There are numerous references in the New Testament. Christ Himself points to it, as in Mt 24:35, Mk 13:24-25, Lk 21:25. St. Paul refers to it in Rom 8:21 and 1 Cor 7:31, and the Book of Revelation mentions new heavens and a new earth (21:1ff). In his Second Epistle (3:10ff) St. Peter says that the heavens will be destroyed by fire and a new heaven and a new earth will appear.

These predictions do not mean that the world or the universe will be annihilated but that it will undergo a radical change, a transformation. Other than this, nothing is revealed in the Bible about the physical characteristics of the new heavens and the new earth. Anyone who claims to know more or presents specifics on the authority of the Bible only brings doubt and ridicule upon the Word of God.

The time of the end also has not been revealed. Neither the Old nor the New Testament gives this information. In the Book of Revelation (20:4) we read of Christ's 1,000-year reign which supposedly precedes the end. But like other numerical indications in this Book, the 1,000 years are symbolical, not literal. This, however, has not discouraged various religious sects of the past and present from predicting the time of the end. Seventh-Day Adventists once put it for the year 1844. With Jehovah's Witnesses it has been the year 1874, then 1914, and most recently 1925.

As we approach the year 2000, doubtless there will be renewed speculation about the end of the world, and doubtless Sacred Scripture will be quoted to support each one's prognostication, with no better results than in the past. What our Lord said still stands: "As for the exact day or hour, no one knows it . . . but the Father only" (Mt 24:36). The esteemed biblical scholar Joseph Lagrange (d. 1938), with these words of Christ in mind, said: "What remains the most certain is also the most useful, the certainty that this Mystery will not be revealed and so we must always be prepared."

65. What do we know about the Last Judgment?

About the Last Judgment, we know only that everyone will appear before Christ to be judged.

This is the General Judgment, which takes place at the end of time, whereas the Particular Judgment occurs immediately after death. In the General Judgment all who ever lived will appear before Christ. Our life, its good and bad, will pass in review. The General Judgment, however, does not change or modify the Particular Judgment but is a sort of public manifestation of the latter. It is called Last because it marks the Last Day, the fulfillment of human history; and General because it embraces all mankind. It is Christ's judgment; He will conduct it (Jn 5:22), because all things have been made subject to Him through His Death and Resurrection (1 Cor 15:23ff). And Satan's rule, such as it is, will then be destroyed forever.

As a public manifestation of the individual judgment at death, the General Judgment reflects the corporate nature of every human being and the corresponding duties and responsibilities. With regard to Christians in particular, it recalls our incorporation in Christ and in the body of Christ. It reminds us that as Christians we live not to ourselves but as members of Christ and members of one another in Christ and will be judged on that basis. Our Lord's description of this Judgment in Mt 25:31-46 is awesome. The Christian takes the lesson to heart.

See also Questions 119, 120.

Eighth Article of Faith

"I believe in the Holy Spirit."

66. *Who is the Holy Spirit?*

The Holy Spirit is the third Person of the Blessed Trinity, true God like the Father and the Son.

The Holy Spirit is a complete and distinct Person, not just an attribute of the Father or the Son. He is the Love between the Father and the Son, love of such infinite fullness that it constitutes a third divine Person in the one divine nature. He is also called Paraclete or Counselor, of whom Christ spoke in His Last Discourse: "I will ask the Father and he will give you another Paraclete—to be with you always: the Spirit of truth, whom the world cannot accept, since it neither sees him nor recognizes him" (Jn 14:16-17).

Of the three divine Persons, the Holy Spirit is perhaps least known and certainly least describable. This may be the reason that by and large the Holy Spirit does not seem to attract as much devotion among the faithful as the Father or the Son. Whatever the reason, the neglect is cause for regret —and pastoral initiative. One hopeful sign, if properly guided, is the contemporary Charismatic Movement with its emphasis on the role of the Spirit in the Christian life.

At the baptism of Christ the Holy Spirit appeared in the form of a dove: "After Jesus was baptized, he came directly out of the water. Suddenly the sky opened and he saw the Spirit of God descend like a dove and hover over him. With that, a voice from the heavens said, 'This is my beloved Son. My favor rests on him'" (Mt 3:16-17). The Holy Spirit appeared in the form of a dove for a number of reasons. As symbol the dove, then as now, signified peace and reconciliation, which made it a perfect representation for the Spirit. In addition, the dove stands for divine inspiration of the Scriptures. And among the ancients it figured as symbol for divinity, as the Jews were aware, and therefore it underscored the divinity of the Holy Spirit.

67. *When did the Holy Spirit descend upon the Apostles?*

The Holy Spirit descended upon the Apostles on the day of Pentecost in the form of fiery tongues.

The Jews themselves had a feast of Pentecost, also called Feast of Weeks, which was one of the three pilgrimage feasts and was celebrated 50 days after Passover. According to Jewish tradition, Moses received the Tables of the Law 50 days after the flight from Egypt. That the Holy Spirit was sent on this day, the day of the great Jewish feast of Pentecost, shows the importance which God the Father attached to the sending. Moreover, because many Jews from all over the world had come to Jerusalem for the feast, they could bear witness back home to the descent of the Spirit, a providential arrangement that was very useful for the spread of the Gospel.

The Holy Spirit had been active in just souls of the past and also in the Apostles before the feast of Pentecost, but on this day He came bringing the fullness of His grace and gifts.

The Holy Spirit

1) sanctified the Apostles;

2) enlightened them so that they understood the teaching of Jesus clearly and correctly;

3) strengthened them so that they preached it unafraid;

4) and bestowed on them the gift of speaking in foreign tongues and working miracles.

The Holy Spirit descended in the form of fiery tongues (Acts 2:3). The fiery tongues point to a divine presence, not fear-inspiring as on Mount Sinai (Ex 24:17), but conveying supernatural illumination and blessedness. The tongues themselves suggest the speaking in every language. As flames, they symbolize the divine enlightenment and burning zeal which the Holy Spirit produced in the Apostles. At the miracle of Pentecost the words of the Precursor of Jesus, John the Baptist, were fulfilled: "There is one to come who is mightier than I. . . . He will baptize you in the Holy Spirit and fire" (Lk 3:16).

In the Dogmatic Constitution on the Church, Vatican II explains: "The Lord Jesus . . . sent them [the Apostles] first to the children of Israel and then to all nations, so that as sharers in His power they might make all people His disciples, and sanctify and govern them, and thus spread His Church, and by ministering to it under the guidance of the Lord, direct it all days even to the consummation of the world.

"They were fully confirmed in this mission on the day of Pentecost in accordance with the Lord's promise: 'You will receive power when the Holy Spirit comes down on you; then you are to be my witnesses in Jerusalem, throughout Judea and in Samaria, yes, even to the ends of the earth.'

"Bishops, with their helpers, the priests and deacons, have taken up the service of the community, presiding in place of God over the flock. . . . Therefore, the Sacred Council teaches that bishops by divine institution have succeeded to the place of the Apostles, as shepherds of the Church" (nos. 19, 20).

Ninth Article of Faith

"The Holy Catholic Church, the Communion of Saints."

68. *How did God prepare the Church in the Old Testament?*

God chose Abraham and his posterity as His people.

Vatican II says in the *Dogmatic Constitution on the Church:* "God planned to assemble in the holy Church all those who would believe in Christ. Already from the beginning of the world the foreshadowing of the Church took place. She was prepared for in a remarkable way throughout the history of the people of Israel and by means of the Old Covenant. . . .

"God, however, does not make human beings holy and save them merely as individuals, without bond or link between them but by bringing them together as one people, a people which acknowledges Him in truth and serves Him in holiness. He therefore chose the race of Israel as a people unto Himself. With it He set up a covenant. Step by step He taught and prepared this people, making known in its history both Himself and the decree of His will and making it holy unto Himself. All these things, however, were done by way of preparation and as a figure of that new and perfect covenant, which was to be ratified in Christ, and of that fuller revelation which was to be given through the very Word of God made flesh" (nos. 2, 9).

"Through Christ and in Christ we are Abraham's spiritual descendants; spiritually, we are Semites," declared Pope Pius XI (d. 1939).

The word "church" stems from the Hebrew *kahal* (Greek: *kyriakon)* meaning: house of the Lord, the building and by extension the family or people of God—in the Old Testament, the People Israel.

69. *What is the Church?*

The Church is: (1) the Mystical Body of Christ; (2) the visible Kingdom of Christ on earth with Pope, bishops, priests, and laity; (3) the People of God— three aspects of one and the same Church.

Vatican II enlarges upon this answer in the *Dogmatic Constitution on the Church:* "In the human nature united to Himself the Son of God, by overcoming death through His own Death and Resurrection, redeemed human beings and remolded them into a new creation. By communicating His Spirit, Christ made His brothers and sisters, called together from all nations, mystically the components of His own Body. In that Body the life of Christ is poured into the believers who, through the Sacraments, are united in a hidden and real way to Christ. . . .

"Christ, the one Mediator, established and continually sustains here on earth His holy Church . . . as an entity with visible delineation through which He communicated truth and grace to all. But, the society structured with hierarchical organs and the Mystical Body of Christ are not to be considered as two realities, nor are the visible assembly and the spiritual community, nor the earthly Church and the Church enriched with heavenly things; rather they form one complex reality which coalesces from a divine and a human element.

"For this reason . . . it is compared to the mystery of the incarnate Word. As the assumed nature, inseparably united to Him, serves the divine Word as a living organ of salvation, so, in a similar way, does the visible social structure of the Church serve the Spirit of Christ, Who vivifies it, in the building up of the body" (nos. 7, 8).

In the *Decree on Ecumenism,* the Council declares: "It is only through Christ's Catholic Church, which is 'the all-embracing means of salvation,' that [one] can benefit fully from the means of salvation" (no. 3). In the *Pastoral Constitution on the Church in the Modern World* (no. 45) and in the *Decree on the Missionary Activity of the Church* (no. 1), the Catholic Church is called "the universal sacrament of salvation." And in the *Declaration on Religious Freedom* we read: "The Council professes its belief that God Himself has made known to mankind the way in which human beings are to serve Him, and thus be saved in Christ and come to blessedness. We believe that this one true religion subsists in the Catholic and Apostolic Church, to which the Lord Jesus committed the duty of spreading it abroad among all people" (no. 1).

70. *Do baptized non-Catholics also belong to the Catholic Church?*

In a certain sense, baptized non-Catholics also belong to the Catholic Church.

In the *Decree on Ecumenism,* Vatican II explains: "All who believe in Christ and have been truly baptized are in communion with the Catholic Church even though this communion is imperfect. The differences that exist in varying degrees between them and the Catholic Church—whether in doctrine and sometimes in discipline, or concerning the structure of the Church—do indeed create many obstacles, sometimes serious ones, to full ecclesiastical communion. The ecumenical movement is striving to overcome these obstacles.

"But even in spite of them it remains true that all who have been justified by faith in Baptism are members of Christ's body, and have a right to be called Christian, and so are correctly accepted as brothers and sisters by the children of the Catholic Church" (no. 3).

A Catholic living in the state of grievous sin (mortal sin) still belongs to the Church. But he or she is like a dead member of a body, because this sin destroys the life of grace that unites us with God.

71. *Who founded the Church?*

Jesus Himself founded the Church.

Vatican II says in the *Dogmatic Constitution on the Church:* "The mystery of the holy Church is manifest in its very foundation. The Lord Jesus set it on its course by preaching the Good News, that is, the coming of the Kingdom of God, which, for centuries, had been promised in the Scriptures: 'This is the time of fulfillment. The reign of God is at hand!' (Mk 1:15). In the word, in the works, and in the presence of Christ, this kingdom was clearly open to the view of human beings" (no. 5).

72. How did Jesus begin in founding the Church?

Jesus gathered disciples around Him, selected twelve to be His Apostles, and made Peter His Vicar (or representative) on earth.

In the *Dogmatic Constitution on the Church,* Vatican II sets forth: "The Lord Jesus, after praying to the Father, calling to Himself those whom He desired appointed twelve men who would stay with Him, and whom He would send to preach the Kingdom of God (cf. Mt 10:1-42 and Mk 3:13-19); and these Apostles He formed after the manner of a college or a stable group, over which He placed Peter chosen from among them. He sent them first to the children of Israel and then to all nations, so that as sharers in His power they might make all peoples His disciples, and sanctify and govern them. They would thus spread His Church, and by ministering to it under the guidance of the Lord, would direct it all days even to the consummation of the world" (no. 19).

73. Who is the visible head of the whole Church?

The visible head of the whole Church is the Pope, the successor to St. Peter, to whom Christ said:

"You are 'Rock' [Greek *Petros,* hence Peter], and on this rock I will build my church, and the jaws of death [literally, the gates of Sheol, hell, nether world] shall not prevail against it. I will entrust to you the keys of the kingdom of heaven. Whatever you declare bound on earth shall be bound in heaven; whatever you declare loosed on earth shall be loosed in heaven" (Mt 16:18-19).

"Feed my lambs, feed my sheep" (Jn 21:15-17).

Jesus is the invisible head of the Church. "He is head of the body, the church" (Col 1:18). But the Church is also a visible community or society. A visible society cannot endure without a visible head.

Vatican II, in its *Dogmatic Constitution on the Church,* states: "This Sacred Council, following closely in the footsteps of the First Vatican Council, with that Council teaches and declares that Jesus Christ, the eternal Shepherd, established His holy Church, having sent forth the Apostles as He Himself had been sent by the Father; and He willed that their successors, namely, the bishops, should be shepherds in His Church even to the consummation of the world.

"In order that the episcopate itself might be one and undivided, He placed Blessed Peter over the other Apostles, and instituted in him a permanent and visible source and foundation of unity of faith and communion. And all this teaching about the institution, the perpetuity, the meaning and reason for the sacred primacy of the Roman Pontiff and of his infallible magisterium, this Sacred Council again proposes to be firmly believed by all the faithful" (no. 18).

After Christ's Ascension the Apostle Peter, whose name had been Simon but was changed by Christ, did in fact exercise the office of head of the Church; e.g., at the choosing of the Apostle Matthias (Acts 1:15-26), on the day of Pentecost (Acts 2:1-41), at the Council of Jerusalem (Acts 15:1-29). He was also head of the Apostles and was recognized as such from the beginning. St. Cyril of Jerusalem (d. 386) calls him "head and prince of the Apostles and supreme teacher of the Church" *(Catech. 22, 11).*

Peter preached in Rome and also died there. Today no serious scholar denies this. Similarly, even among Protestant biblical scholars there is a growing recognition that Mt 16:18-19, where Christ makes Peter the head and foundation of the Church, is a presentation of Christ's own words and not an afterthought that originated with the Christian community in the early days of the Church.

It is remarkable, nevertheless, that a number of other passages about Peter in the New Testament date from a time after his death, which is a clear demonstration that the second generation of Christians was not less affirmative of Peter's special position in the Church than was the first generation. This affirmation concerned not only Peter's special position but that of his successors as well. In Jn 21:15-17, for example, Christ interrogates Peter on his love of the Lord and commands him to feed His sheep. Yet John's Gospel was written at least 30 or 40 years after Peter's death. Clearly, to the Christians of John's Gospel Peter's headship was not simply a personal prerogative, to cease with his death. Since Christ founded His Church on Peter and promised that it would endure till the end of time (Mt 28:20), the foundation also had to endure, namely in the successors of Peter.

Christ's promise to Peter in Mt 16:18-19 is couched in symbolical language. The "jaws of death" (literally, gates of Sheol, hell) refers to all powers of evil, spiritual and temporal, that would rise against the Church. But Christ promises that they will not succeed. The "keys of the kingdom of heaven" according to Jewish conception symbolized rulership in the house. Christ is the supreme Ruler, but He delegates authority over the house (Church) to His vicar or representative.

"Bind and loose" in a strict sense means that Peter received the power of excommunication from and admission to the ecclesial community. In the broad sense, these words declare that Peter and his successors are empowered to decide what is to be believed as true and what is to be rejected as false. They also authorize Peter and his successors to determine discipline, rules of conduct, in the Church.

What is promised in Matthew's Gospel becomes fact in John's. The "feed my sheep, my lambs" of Jn 21:15-17 is the inauguration of the Apostle Peter to primacy among the Apostles and to headship over the whole Church.

74. What is the Pope?

The Pope as bishop of Rome is the successor of St. Peter and therefore the representative of Christ on earth and the supreme shepherd of the faithful.

Formerly, the Pope was also a temporal ruler, being head of rather extensive geographical areas of Italy known as the Papal States. With the political unification of Italy in the 19th century the Papal States were taken over by the secular power and incorporated into modern Italy. In 1929 a papal state of sorts was reconstituted within Rome and called Vatican City, the smallest independent country in the world with an area of 1/6 square mile. Though minimal in size, the independent papal state of Vatican City is extremely important as symbol: it tells the world that the Papacy is not under the domination of any secular power.

From 1309 to 1377 the Popes by force of circumstances beyond their control resided in the city of Avignon in France. But the rightful seat of the Pope is and always will be Rome. Some Church Fathers, in fact, speak of the Pope as heir to the Chair of Peter. Apostolic See and Holy See are other designations for the Pope or his office.

In 535 Pope Mercurius became the first to change his name on assuming the papacy; he took the name John II. The next one to change his name does not appear until the year 955. After that, it became the common practice. Up to now 81 different names have been chosen, of which 46 occur only once (among them, Linus, Cornelius, Eusebius, Hilary, and Valentine). The most frequent name is John, which 25 Popes have taken, including the present Pope John Paul II. Since Pope Sixtus V (d. 1590) only 13 new names appear, names not chosen before, and of these Urban and Alexander have lain idle for more than 200 years. In the last 200 years the most common names have been Benedict, Clement, Gregory, Innocent, Pius, and Leo. When Cardinal Montini took the name Paul VI in 1963, he was the first Paul since 1621. Something new, or at least uncommon, occurred when his successors opted for the double names of John Paul I and John Paul II.

There have been wide differences in the length of papal reigns. The shortest was that of Stephen II in 752, which lasted only three days. Not the shortest but short by any measure was the recent Pope Paul I's one-month reign. The longest has been Pius IX's, which covered 32 years, from 1846 to 1878. Leo XIII reigned for 25 years (d. 1903), Pius XII for 19 (d. 1958), and his successor John XXIII had a relatively brief papacy but will be remembered for convening the Second Vatican Council.

Great diversity also is found in the nationality of Popes when viewed from the beginning. To the present, in addition to the 205 Italian Popes there have been 15 Greek, 15 French, seven German (the last being Hadrian VI, d. 1523), five Syrian, three African, two Spanish, and some others. In modern times, Popes have been Italian. But with the enlargement of the college of Cardinals under John XXIII and Paul VI the election of a non-Italian Pope was only a matter of time. The eventuality was realized, perhaps sooner than anyone had anticipated, in Pope John Paul II, who is not only non-Italian but the first Polish Pope. However, the nationality of a Pope is incidental. What sets him off from other bishops or cardinals is not where he was born or who were his parents but the fact that he succeeds to the office and bishopric of St. Peter as Vicar of Christ on earth.

When a Pope addresses himself in writing to the whole world or to the whole Catholic world, usually he deals with important matters of faith and morals or expounds and interprets the Catholic position as regards prevailing trends of thought in the world, the workings of the Zeitgeist. Since Benedict XIV (d. 1748), these writings have been called Encyclicals.

However, it was not until Gregory XVI (d. 1846) that encyclicals became more frequent. This Pope wrote 16, Pius IX 33, and Leo XIII 50, and Pius XXII 41, among which are the great Encyclicals on Worship (Mediator Dei), on the Mystical Body (Mystici Corporis), and Scripture Studies (Divino Afflante Spiritu). It was also Pius XII who set down the authority of Encyclicals as pertaining to the Ordinary Teaching Authority of the Church. Pope John XXIII left eight Encyclicals (among which was Pacem in Terris) and Paul VI left seven, including Humanae Vitae.

75. *What is the Roman Curia?*

The Roman Curia is all of the administrative bodies which the Pope uses to help him in governing the Church.

In the early Church there was no Curia—nor was one needed, given the infant nature of the Church. Besides, the Church was under constant persecution, which hindered its public organization. The first beginnings of the Curia go back to the 6th century. But not until the 12th century was there anything like the modern administrative bodies which, since the 16th century, have been called Congregations. In addition to various other departments, there now are nine Congregations, each of which usually is headed by a Cardinal.

Originally, Cardinals were clergy attached to any one of the principal Churches in Rome. Subsequently bishops of neighboring dioceses of Rome came to be called Cardinals, and only since the end of the 12th century have other bishops been appointed to the college of Cardinals. In 1586 Sixtus V limited the number to 70, which stood until John XXIII, the first Pope to increase it. Paul VI went further still and added Cardinals from all parts of the world. Today, as a result, Italians are a small minority of the Sacred College. In recent years there have been as many as 130 Cardinals, who serve as important counselors to the Pope and also elect his successor.

Of rather recent origin is the auxiliary body called Synod of Bishops, which was established by Pope Paul VI on September 15, 1965, at the beginning of the Fourth Session of the Second Vatican Council. The prerogative of convening the Synod belongs to the Pope, who also, usually in consultation with representative bishops, determines the topics to be discussed and presides over the proceedings. Of the approximately 200 bishops nominated to a Synod, the Pope personally chooses 15 percent; the rest are designated by Episcopal Conferences throughout the world.

In the Decree Concerning the Pastoral Office of Bishops in the Church, *Vatican II says of the Synod: "Bishops chosen from various parts of the world, in ways and manners established or to be established by the Roman Pontiff, render more effective assistance to the supreme pastor of the Church in a deliberative body which will be called by the proper name of* Synod of Bishops. *Since it shall be acting in the name of the entire Catholic episcopate, it will at the same time show that all the bishops in hierarchical communion partake of the solicitude for the universal Church" (no. 5). Several conventions of the Synod have been held, the latest, the sixth, being the one of September, 1980.*

76. What is a bishop?

A bishop is a successor of the Apostles.

Vatican II, in the *Decree Concerning the Pastoral Office of Bishops in the Church,* states: "The bishops themselves, having been appointed by the Holy Spirit, are successors of the Apostles as pastors of souls. Together with the Supreme Pontiff and under his authority they are sent to continue throughout the ages the work of Christ, the eternal Pastor. Christ gave the Apostles and their successors the command and the power to teach all nations, to sanctify human beings in the truth, and to feed them. Bishops, therefore, have been made true and authentic teachers of the faith, pontiffs, and pastors through the Holy Spirit, Who has been given to them. . . .

"A diocese is a portion of the people of God which is entrusted to a bishop to be shepherded by him with the cooperation of the presbytery. Thus by adhering to its pastor and gathered together by him through the Gospel and the Eucharist in the Holy Spirit, it constitutes a particular church in which the one, holy, catholic, and apostolic Church of Christ is truly present and operative.

"Individual bishops who have been entrusted with the care of a particular church—under the authority of the Supreme Pontiff—feed their sheep in the name of the Lord as their own, ordinary, and immediate pastors, performing for them the office of teaching, sanctifying, and governing" (nos. 2, 11).

The territorial limits within which a bishop governs constitute a diocese or bishopric. Larger dioceses generally have one or more auxiliary (assistant) bishops, who are true bishops but exercise their office under the direction of the Ordinary, i.e., the ruling bishop.

The bishop guides and governs his diocese. He proclaims the word of God, personally and through his commissioned priests and deacons. Many blessings are reserved to him. He normally administers the Sacrament of Confirmation, and only he can administer the Sacrament of Holy Orders. He blesses (or consecrates) new churches, altars, and bells. The appointment of pastors, chaplains, and other ministers of his diocese ultimately rests with him. Periodically, as at the beginning of Lent, he addresses pastoral letters to his people. It is up to him to see that purity of Catholic doctrine is maintained in his diocese.

77. *What is a General Council?*

A General Council is an assembly of all the bishops of the world, presided over by the Pope or his official representative.

Only the Pope can convene a General Council. He also presides, personally or through his representative. He determines the topics to be considered and the parliamentary procedures to be observed. He alone can suspend or adjourn the Council and declare its proceedings terminated. Only after he has confirmed and proclaimed the results of the Council do they become binding upon the Church. If the Pope dies during the Council, it is automatically adjourned until the new Pope reassembles it, which he is not obliged to do.

Besides bishops, heads of religious orders (abbots-primate, ministers-general, etc.) are invited to a General Council. Priests, theologians, and lay people may be present as periti, *experts in their field to advise their bishops but they do not have the right to vote. Women and non-Catholics may be granted admission as observers.*

Not counting the Council of Jerusalem, which brought together the Apostles for the last time, there have been 21 General Councils. The first was the Council of Nicaea in Asia Minor, in the year 325. Four General Councils were held in Constantinople, five in the Lateran in Rome, two in Lyons, France. The 16th General Council (1414-1418) met in the city of Constance; this Council ended the 40-year upheaval that had produced rival Popes.

The 19th General Council met in Trent in northern Italy; it spanned the years 1545-1563, not in continuous session but in three intermittent intervals. The 20th General Council was the First Vatican, 1869-1870. Because of the capture of the Papal States by Italian troops the Council was suspended and never reconvened. The Second Vatican Council convened in four sessions between the years 1962 and 1965. About 2,500 bishops took part. It will no doubt prove to have been one of the most important General Councils in the history of the Church.

78. *What is a priest?*

A priest is one who has received the Sacrament of Holy Orders and through this Sacrament has become an anointed minister of the Church.

The terms "secular" and "regular" describe the two general kinds of clergy. Secular priests live in and belong to a diocese and exercise their priestly functions under the jurisdiction of a bishop. Because the live in they world they are called secular. Regular priests belong to a religious order, e.g., Capuchins, Benedictines, etc., and normally live in a monastery or religious house. They are called regular (from *regula,* rule) because they follow a certain Rule, like the Rule of St. Benedict, St. Francis, St. Ignatius, and others.

Most seculars, and some regulars, are active in the parishes of their diocese. The head of the parish is the pastor. In larger parishes there are assistant or associate pastors (sometimes co-pastors). Primarily the pastor and the associate pastors are charged by the bishop with the spiritual care of people of the parish. In the name and by authority of the bishop they instruct the people in Catholic doctrine, adminster the holy Sacraments, conduct divine services, and in general seek to promote observance of the Commandments of God and the Church both in private and in public life.

Vatican II, in its Decree on the Ministry and Life of Priests, says: "In the measure in which they participate in the office of the Apostles, God gives priests a special grace to be ministers of Christ among the people. They perform the sacred duty of preaching the Gospel, so that the offering of the people can be made acceptable and sanctified by the Holy Spirit. . . . Since no one can be saved who does not first believe, priests, as co-workers with their bishops, have the primary duty of proclaiming the Gospel of God to all. . . .

"Exercising the office of Christ, the Shepherd and Head, and according to their share of His authority, priests, in the name of the bishop, gather the family of God together as a brotherhood enlivened by one spirit. Through Christ they lead them in the Holy Spirit to God the Father. For the exercise of this ministry, as for the other priestly duties, spiritual power is conferred upon them for the building up of the Church. In building up of the Church, priests must treat all with exceptional kindness in imitation of the Lord. They should act toward people, not as seeking to please them, but in accord with the demands of Christian doctrine and life. They should teach them and admonish them as beloved children, according to the words of the Apostle: 'Stay with this task whether convenient or inconvenient—correcting, reproving, appealing—constantly teaching and never losing patience (2 Tm 4:2)' " (nos. 2, 4, 6).

Nothing is more desirable in a parish than the family spirit, for the parish is a family of God and under the leadership *of its priests does the work of God. If the priest serves his people, the faithful have also to serve and work with and for their priests.* The aforesaid Decree on the Ministry of Priests says this: *"The Christian faithful, for their part, should realize their obligations to their priests, and with filial love they should follow them as their pastors and fathers. In like manner, sharing their cares, they should help their priests by prayer and work insofar as possible so that their priests might more readily overcome difficulties and be able to fulfill their duties more fruitfully"* (no. 9).

The faithful are also called the laity. Vatican II, in its Dogmatic Constitution on the Church, explains: *"The term laity is here understood to mean all the faithful except those in holy orders and those in the state of religious life specially approved by the Church. These faithful are by Baptism made one body with Christ and are constituted among the People of God; they are in their own way made sharers in the priestly, prophetical, and kingly functions of Christ; and they carry out for their own part the mission of the whole Christian people in the Church and in the world. . . .*

"The laity . . . are called upon, as living members, to expend all their energy for the growth of the Church and its continuous sanctification. . . . Through their Baptism and Confirmation all are commissioned to this apostolate by the Lord Himself. . . . The laity are called in a special way to make the Church present and operative in those places and circumstances where only through them can it become the salt of the earth" (nos. 31, 33).

Short and to the point is the Decree on the Apostolate of the Laity: *"On all Christians is laid the preeminent responsibility of working to make the divine message of salvation known and accepted by all throughout the world"* (no. 3).

79. *What is a deacon?*

A deacon is one who has received the Sacrament of Holy Orders not for the priesthood but for a ministry of service to God's people through the liturgy, word, and charity.

JESUS URGED OFFERING SACRIFICE AFTER RECONCILIATION
"If you bring your gift to the altar and there recall that your brother has anything against you, leave your gift at the altar, go first to be reconciled with your brother, and then come and offer your gift" (Mt 5:23f).

Deacon in Greek means assistant or server. The first deacons were instituted by the Apostles to attend to the material needs of the people (Acts 6:1-6). By the end of the first century, the order formed a distinct hierarchical rank in the third place after bishops and priests. Deacons assisted at the Eucharist and Baptism, led the people in prayer, chanted the Gospel, and received the people's offerings.

During the Middle Ages, the diaconate became merely the final stage in the preparation for the priesthood. Only those were ordained deacons who intended to become priests. And their must important function was to participate in liturgical ceremonies.

The Second Vatican Council increased the number of the deacon's functions: "It is the duty of the deacon . . . to administer Baptism solemnly, to be custodian and dispenser of the Eucharist, to assist at and bless marriages in the name of the Church, to bring Viaticum to the dying, to read the Sacred Scripture to the faithful, to instruct and exhort the people, to preside at the worship and prayer of the faithful, to administer Sacramentals, and to officiate at funeral and burial services. [Deacons are] dedicated to duties of charity and administration" *(Const. on the Church,* no. 29).

The Permanent Diaconate. The Council also decreed that the diaconate be restored as a permanent and separate rank in the Latin Church and that married men be ordained to this rank. On June 27, 1967, Pope Paul VI restored the permanent diaconate, making it possible for men to become deacons permanently, without going on to the priesthood.

This order may be received by unmarried men, 25 or older, who cannot then marry, and by married men, 35 or older, with the consent of their wives. A 2 or 3 year period of preparation and formation is required and deacons then carry out their ministry under the direction of the bishop and with the priests with whom they are associated.

80.   *What are the marks of the true Church?*

The true Church has these four marks: It is one, holy, catholic, and apostolic.

These four marks became part of the Nicene Creed as early as the year 381, when the First Council of Constantinople added the words: "I believe in one, holy, catholic, and apostolic Church."

Vatican II speaks about these marks in various places.

1) Unity (oneness): "The mystery of the unity of the Church . . . finds its highest exemplar and source in the unity of the Persons of the Trinity: the Father and the Son in the Holy Spirit, one God" (Decree on Ecumenism, no. 2).

2) Holiness: "The Church is believed to be indefectibly holy" (Dogmatic Constitution on the Church, no. 39).

3) Catholicity (universality): "This characteristic of universality which adorns the people of God is a gift from the Lord Himself. By reason of it, the Catholic Church strives constantly . . . to bring all humanity . . . back to its source in Christ, with Him as its head and united in His Spirit" (Dogmatic Constitution on the Church, no. 13).

4) Apostolicity: "The Bishops themselves, having been appointed by the Holy Spirit, are successors of the Apostles as pastors of souls" (Decree Concerning the Pastoral Office of Bishops in the Church, no. 2).

81. *Which is the only Church that has these four marks?*

The only Church that has these four marks is the Roman Catholic Church.

The *Dogmatic Constitution on the Church* says:"This [the Catholic Church] is the one Church of Christ which in the Creed is professed as one, holy, catholic, and apostolic" (no. 8). — In the *Declaration on Religious Freedom,* Vatican II says: "We believe that this one true religion subsists in the Catholic and Apostolic Church, to which the Lord Jesus committed the duty of spreading it abroad among all people" (no. 1).

82. *Is the Roman Catholic Church one?*

The Roman Catholic Church is one, because it has (1) the same teaching everywhere, (2) the same sacraments, and (3) the same Head.

Doubtless, disagreements can arise in the Church. Even in the beginning there were certain practical matters which, at least until resolved, divided the Christian community (Acts 11:2-3 and 21:20ff). But the essential content of the faith has weathered all storms. After the Council of Trent theological debate centered on the efficacy of divine grace, but no one questioned the fact that the human will remains free even under the attraction of grace.

Today, as in the past, when theologians are at variance with the dogmas of the Church, they are in error and cannot justify their deviations on the ground of ecumenism or adaptation to the times. Attempts to make the teachings of faith more acceptable to the contemporary mind must not adulterate or falsify the Catholic faith.

On September 22, 1967, the Bishops of Germany issued a statement in which they warned that "new developments in theology must be compatible with the old, i.e., the established truths of faith." They pointed out that anything that tends to undermine the centrality of Christ in the Christian life and faith ceases to be true and serves neither God nor the best interests of the world itself. "Contemporary questioning of the faith," they continued, "may make it necessary to take a fresh look at the truths of faith, and in the process new emphases may suggest themselves. But this is not the same as casting doubt on the faith but serves to gain better understanding of divine Revelation and the teachings of the Church. We are convinced, and experience bears us out, that there is never any reason to deny the Catholic faith for the sake of some other truth or to deny some other truth for the sake of the Catholic faith."

Truth, that is, is one and does not contradict itself. the words of the German Bishops have far wider application than to their flock; they apply to the Church and to theologians everywhere.

Though convinced of being the Church founded by Jesus Christ, the Catholic Church nevertheless welcomes the ecumenical movement because its aim is the restoration of Christian unity. In the Decree on Ecumenism, *Vatican II says: "Today, in many parts of the world, under the inspiring grace of the Holy Spirit, many efforts are being made in prayer, word, and action to attain that fullness of unity which Jesus Christ desires. The Sacred Council exhorts all the Catholic faithful to recognize the signs of the times and to take an active and intelligent part in the work of ecumenism.*

"The term 'ecumenical movement' indicates the initiatives and activities planned and undertaken, according to the various needs of the Church and as opportunities offer, to promote Christian unity. These are: first, every effort to avoid expressions, judgments, and actions which do not represent the conditions of our separated brothers and sisters with truth and fairness . . . then, 'dialogue' between competent experts from different Churches and Communities. . . .

"There can be no ecumenism worthy of the name without a change of heart. . . . All the faithful should remember that the more effort they make to live holier lives according to the Gospel, the better will they further Christian unity and put it into practice. For the closer their union with the Father, the Word, and the Spirit, the more deeply and easily will they be able to grow in mutual familial love. This change of heart and holiness of life, along with public and private prayer for the unity of Christians, should be regarded as the soul of the whole ecumenical movement, and merits the name, 'spiritual ecumenism' " (nos. 4, 7, 8).

83. *Is the Roman Catholic Church holy?*

The Roman Catholic Church is holy because (1) its Founder is holy, (2) its teaching is holy, (3) its Sac-

raments are holy and produce holiness, and (4) among its members are always holy people.

In the *Constitution on the Church,* Vatican II comments: "The Church . . . is believed to be indefectibly holy. Indeed Christ, the Son of God, Who with the Father and the Spirit is praised as 'uniquely holy,' loved the Church as His bride, delivering Himself up for her. He did this that He might sanctify her. . . . The followers of Christ are called by God, not because of their works but according to His own purpose and grace. They are justified in the Lord Jesus, because in the baptism of faith they truly become children of God and sharers in the divine nature. In this way they are really made holy. Then too, by God's gift, they must hold on to and complete in their lives this holiness they have received" (nos. 39, 40).

Of course, there are also sinners in the Catholic Church, because some Catholics do not live according to their faith and the Commandments of God and the Church. Our Lord tells of this failure in the parable of the good seed and the weeds (Mt 13:24-30). Vatican II, in the Pastoral Constitution on the Church in the Modern World, *confesses: "The Church . . . is very well aware that among her members, both clerical and lay, some have been unfaithful to the Spirit of God during the course of many centuries; in the present age, too, it does not escape the Church how great a distance lies between the message she offers and the human failings of those to whom the Gospel is entrusted. Whatever be the judgment of history on these defects, we ought to be conscious of them, and struggle against them energetically, lest they inflict harm on the spread of the Gospel" (no. 43).*

84. *Is the Roman Church catholic, i.e., all-embracing and universal?*

The Roman Church is catholic, i.e., all-embracing and universal, because it was founded for all peoples and all times and as a matter of fact has spread over all the world.

Tertullian, one of the first Christian Apologists, wrote toward the end of the second century *(Apology, 37)*: "We are but of yesterday, yet we have filled every place among you—cities, islands, fortresses, towns, marketplaces, camps, tribes, town councils, the palace, the senate, the forum; we have left you nothing but the temples of your gods." The picture may be overdrawn, but the reality was there just the same.

Vatican II, in the *Dogmatic Constitution on the Church,* says: "All human beings are called to belong to the new people of God. Wherefore this people, while remaining one and only one, is to be spread throughout the whole world and must exist in all ages, so that the decree of God's will may be fulfilled" (no. 13).

85. *Is the Roman Catholic Church apostolic?*

The Roman Catholic Church is apostolic because
1. **it preaches the same doctrine as the Apostles;**
2. **it confers the same Sacraments as the Apostles,**
3. **and its Pope and bishops are the legitimate successors of the Apostles.**

St. Irenaeus, who was bishop of Lyons, France, in the last quarter of the second century, provides the first historical list of Popes from St. Peter to his day. It appears in a work of his with the title *Against Heresies* (3, 3, 1-3). This list is an invaluable document, accepted as authentic by Catholic and non-Catholic scholars alike.

In the Dogmatic Constitution on the Church, *Vatican II says: "For the nurturing and constant growth of the People of God, Christ the Lord instituted in His Church a variety of ministries, which work for the good of the whole body. . . . The divine mission entrusted by Christ to the Apostles will last until the end of the world, since the Gospel they are to teach is for all time the source of all life for the Church. And for this reason the Apostles, appointed as rulers in this society, took care to appoint successors. . . . And just as the office granted individually to Peter, the first among the Apostles, is permanent and is to be transmitted to his successors, so also the Apostles' office of nurturing the Church is permanent, and is to be exercised without interruption by the sacred order of bishops" (nos. 18, 20).*

86. What threefold office did Christ assign to His Church?

Christ assigned to His Church the threefold office
1. to teach what He taught,
2. to confer His means of grace (the Sacraments),
3. and to govern the faithful.

"As the Father has sent me, so I send you" (Jn 20:21). "Go, therefore, and make disciples of all the nations. Baptize them in the name of the Father, and of the Son, and of the Holy Spirit. Teach them to carry out everything I have commanded you" (Mt 28:19-20). — This threefold mission of the Church is called the teaching office, the priestly office, and the pastoral office.

Vatican II, in the Dogmatic Constitution on the Church, says: "Episcopal consecration, together with the office of sanctifying, also confers the office of teaching and of governing, which, however, of its very nature, can be exercised only in hierarchical communion with the head and the members of the college. For from the tradition . . . it is clear that, by means of the imposition of hands and the words of consecration, the grace of the Holy Spirit is so conferred, and the sacred character so impressed, that bishops in an eminent and visible way sustain the roles of Christ Himself as Teacher, Shepherd, and High Priest, and that they act in His person" (no. 21).

87. *From what is the Church preserved by the Holy Spirit?*

The Church is preserved by the Holy Spirit from all error in her teaching on faith and morals.

Christ promised the gift of infallibility to the Church primarily through Peter and his successors. See Luke 22:31-32 and John 21:15-17. These passages of Luke and John indicate that the supremacy of St. Peter was to be exercised above all, but not only, in the realm of faith. In being made supreme custodian of the faith Peter also was made head of the future Church and head of his fellow Apostles.

The necessity of the grace of infallibility for Peter's role as supreme head and shepherd is self-evident. Without inerrancy in matters of faith and morals Peter could never have been Rock and foundation of the Church, nor could he have strengthened his brothers in their faith. Moreover, infallibility was joined to the office, not the person, of Peter. Peter would die, but the Church would go on, and with it the rock and foundation that only the grace of infallibility ensures. See also Question 73.

88. *Through whom does the Church make her infallible pronouncements?*

The Church makes her infallible pronouncements either through the Pope and Bishops together, or through the Pope alone.

In the history of the Church there is ample evidence for both ways. St. Cyprian, in the year 252, wrote to Pope Cornelius affirming that in a question of faith the Pope is not susceptible to error—or is infallible. By their writings and actions Popes have demonstrated over and over their belief in the infallibility of their office, Popes like Gelasius I (d. 496), Gregory the Great (d. 604), and others. In 1854 Pius IX exercised infallibility in defining the dogma of the Immaculate

Conception of Mary, and in 1950 Pius XII did the same in defining the bodily assumption of Mary into heaven. Neither convened a Council for the purpose. As for the Councils, convened and confirmed by the Pope they have always been considered infallible in matter of faith and morals. See also Question 77.

89. When is the Pope infallible in his pronouncements?

The Pope is infallible in his pronouncements when in his capacity as supreme shepherd and teacher of the Church he declares, i.e., defines, that a given doctrine concerning faith or morals must be held by all the faithful.

The doctrine of papal infallibility, always a universal belief in the Church, was defined at the First Vatican Council on July 18, 1870, in the course of its Fourth Public Session. The doctrine is set forth in the Council's *Dogmatic Constitution Pastor Aeternus:* "As circumstances dictated, the Roman Pontiffs have at times called together ecumenical councils or sought the views of the Church throughout the world; at other times they have made use of regional councils, or other helps supplied by divine Providence. After taking such measures, they have with God's help defined as doctrines that must be held those which they had recognized . . . to be in conformity with the Sacred Scriptures and with the apostolic tradition. . . .

"Therefore, adhering faithfully to the tradition received from the beginning of the Christian faith . . . , with the approval of the sacred Council we teach and define that it is a divinely revealed dogma: that the Roman Pontiff, when he speaks *ex cathedra,* that is, when acting in the office of shepherd and teacher of all Christians, he defines, by virtue of his supreme apostolic authority, doctrine concerning faith or morals to be held by the whole Church, he possesses through the divine assistance promised to him in the person of St. Peter that infallibility with which the divine Redeemer willed His Church to be endowed in defining doctrine concerning faith or morals."

Perhaps what this definition of papal infallibility does not say is as important as what it says. It does not say that every time the Pope speaks on a subject he is infallible, or that he can manufacture new doctrines at will, doctrines no one in the Church ever heard of, and enjoin them on the faithful. The Pope is not infallible as a private person: e.g., if a Pope resigned and went into retirement, which is possible but not likely, his infallibility would cease with his papacy.

The Pope is not infallible as learned or as priest and bishop, nor in his moral life, nor in his political philosophy and diplomatic dealings with secular powers. He is not even infallible in the way he governs the Church: the counselors he chooses, the Cardinals he creates, the bishops he appoints. He is infallible solely in his capacity as supreme Shepherd and Teacher of the Church and when in this capacity he proclaims that a given doctrine of faith or morals must be held by all members of the Church.

90. *What does the Second Vatican Council teach about infallibility?*

The Second Vatican Council teaches about infallibility what the Church has always believed, but the Council gives more prominence than heretofore to the collegial, though not individual, infallibility of the bishops of the world.

The *Dogmatic Constitution on the Church* says: "Although the individual bishops do not enjoy the prerogative of infallibility, they nevertheless proclaim Christ's doctrine infallibly. This is so, even when they are dispersed around the world, provided that they maintain the bond of communion among themselves and with the successor of Peter, authentically teach matters of faith and morals, and are in agreement on one position as definitively to be held. This authority is even more clearly verified when, gathered together in an ecumenical council, they are teachers and judges of faith and morals for the universal Church. Their definitions must then be adhered to with the submission of faith.

"This infallibility . . . extends as far as extends the deposit of Revelation, which must be religiously guarded and faithfully expounded. This is the infallibility which the Roman Pontiff, the head of the college of bishops, enjoys in virtue of his office, when, as the supreme shepherd and teacher of all the faithful . . . by a definitive act he proclaims a doctrine of faith or morals" (no. 25).

91. Why is the Roman Catholic Church called the Church of salvation?

The Roman Catholic Church is called the Church of salvation because she alone received from Christ, the sole Redeemer, the mission and means to bring people to eternal salvation.

The axiom *extra ecclesiam nulla salus,* "outside the Church, no salvation," was coined by St. Cyprian (d. 258). Perhaps no assertion about the Church has been misunderstood as much as this. In 1949 Rome issued an official clarification which stated that the axiom is not to be taken in the strictly literal sense. Clement XI (d. 1721) and Pius IX (d. 1878) had spoken to the same effect.

But just as in the Old Testament there was only one ark of deliverance from bodily death, so in the New Testament there is only one ark of salvation, namely the Catholic Church. Christ said: "If he ignores . . . the church, then treat him as you would a Gentile or a tax collector [i.e., public sinner]" (Mt 18:17). It is possible, however, to be outside the Church through no fault of one's own. If such persons try to follow God's will as they know it, they can be presumed to be in God's grace and to belong to the Church inwardly, though not outwardly. They belong, as it were, to the soul of the Church and therefore can be saved. But they are deprived of many means or channels of grace found only in the true

Church, e.g., the Holy Sacrifice of the Mass, the Real Presence in the Eucharist, sacramental absolution of sins.

Touching this question, Vatican II says in the Dogmatic Constitution on the Church: *"Basing itself upon Sacred Scripture and Tradition, [the Council] teaches that the Church, now sojourning on earth as an exile, is necessary for salvation. Christ, present to us in His Body, which is the Church, is the one Mediator and the unique way of salvation. In explicit terms He Himself affirmed the necessity of faith and Baptism and thereby affirmed also the necessity of the Church, for through Baptism as through a door people enter the Church. Whosoever, therefore, knowing that the Catholic Church was made necessary by Christ, would refuse to enter it or to remain in it, could not be saved" (no. 14).*

As for all Catholics being saved, the Council said: *"Those are not saved . . . who, though part of the body of the Church, do not persevere in charity. They remain indeed in the bosom of the Church, but, as it were, only in a 'bodily' manner and not 'in their heart.' All the Church's children should remember that their exalted status is to be attributed not to their own merits but to the special grace of Christ. If they fail moreover to respond to that grace in thought, word, and deed, not only will they not be saved but they will be the more severely judged"* (ibid.).

92. *What can they expect who never learn of God or the Church?*

Christ died for all and wants all to be saved. Those mentioned in the question can be saved if they do God's will as made known to them through the natural moral law.

This answer accords with what Pius IX wrote in 1863 to the Bishops of Italy. It also reflects the teaching of Vatican II in the *Dogmatic Constitution on the Church:* "Those also can attain to salvation who through no fault of their own do not know the Gospel of Christ or His Church, yet sincerely seek

God and moved by grace strive by their deeds to do His will as it is known to them through the dictates of conscience. Nor does Divine Providence deny the helps necessary for salvation to those who, without blame on their part, have not yet arrived at an explicit knowledge of God and with His grace strive to live a good live" (no. 16).

93. *What are missionaries?*

Missionaries are priests, Religious, and lay people sent by the Church to preach the Gospel to those who do not yet know Christ.

In the *Decree on the Missionary Activity of the Church* we read: "They are assigned with a special vocation who, being endowed with a suitable natural temperament, and being fit as regards talent and other qualities, have been trained to undertake mission work . . . be they priests, Religious, or lay people. Sent by legitimate authority, they go out in faith and obedience to those who are far from Christ. They are set apart for the work for which they have been taken up, as ministers of the Gospel, 'that the offering up of the Gentiles may become acceptable, being sanctified by the Holy Spirit' (Rom 15:16). . . .

"Missionaries must be ready to stay at their vocation for an entire lifetime, and to renounce themselves and all those whom they thus far considered as their own, and instead to 'make themselves all things to all people' (1 Cor 9:22). . . . They must have the spirit of initiative in the beginning, as well as that of constancy in carrying through what they have begun; they must be persevering in difficulties, patient and strong of heart in bearing with solitude, fatigue, and fruitless labor. . . . They will with a noble spirit adapt themselves to the people's foreign way of doing things and to changing circumstances. . . . Anyone who is going to encounter another people should have a great esteem for their patrimony and their language and their customs" (nos. 23-26).

94. *Why must the Church engage in missionary work?*

The Church must engage in missionary work because she was commanded by Christ to do so.

Christ gave this command to the Apostles in the following words: "Full authority has been given to me both in heaven and on earth; go, therefore, and make disciples of all the nations. Baptize them in the name of the Father, and of the Son, and of the Holy Spirit. Teach them to carry out everything I have commanded you. And know that I am with you always, until the end of the world" (Mt 28:18-20).

As defined in the Decree on the Missionary Activity of the Church, *"missions is the term usually given to those particular undertakings by which the heralds of the Gospel, sent out by the Church and going forth into the whole world, carry out the task of preaching the Gospel and planting the Church among peoples or groups who do not yet believe in Christ. These undertakings are brought to completion by missionary activity and are mostly exercised in certain territories recognized by the Holy See. The proper purpose of this misssionary activity is evangelization, and the planting of the Church among those peoples and groups where it has not yet taken root.*

"This missionary activity derives its reason from the will of God, Who wishes all human beings to be saved and to come to the knowledge of the truth. . . . Therefore, all must be converted to Him, made known by the Church's preaching, and all must be incorporated into Him by Baptism, and into the Church which is His Body. . . . Finally, by means of this missionary activity, God is fully glorified, provided that people fully and consciously accept His work of salvation, which He has accomplished in Christ" (nos. 6, 7).

95. *How can we help the missionaries?*

We can help the missionaries by prayer, works of penance, and material support, usually in the form of monetary contributions.

JESUS WENT ABOUT HELPING PEOPLE AND DOING GOOD
"When the men of that place recognized [Jesus] they . . .
brought him all the afflicted with the plea that he let them do no
more than touch the tassel of his cloak. As many as touched it
were fully restored to health" (Mt 14:35f).

The *Decree on the Missionary Activity of the Church* eluci-
dates: "Since the whole Church is missionary, and the work
of evangelization is a basic duty of the People of God, this sacred Synod invites all to a deep interior renewal so that, with
a vivid awareness of their own responsibility for the spreading of the Gospel, they may do their share in missionary
work among the nations. . . .

"Yet, let all realize that their first and most important obligation for the spread of the faith is this: to lead a profoundly
Christian life. For their fervor in the service of God and their
charity toward others will cause a new spiritual wind to blow
for the whole Church, which will then appear as a sign lifted
up among the nations.

"In those lands which are already Christian, lay people cooperate in the work of evangelization by nurturing in themselves and in others a knowledge and love of the missions; by
stimulating vocations in their own family, in Catholic associations, and in the schools; by offering subsidies of every
kind, that they may offer to others that gift of faith which
they have received gratis" (nos. 35, 36, 41).

96. What is the Society for the Propagation of the Faith?

**The Society for the Propagation of the Faith is a
Pontifical Society which supports the missionary
activity of the Church throughout the world. It
serves both foreign and home missions.**

The work of foreign missions is widely recognized and ap-
plauded even outside the Church. Home missions—missions
in the home country, as in the United States—are not always
as well known. Their work is among particular groups or in
particular places where Christ may already be known but
where the knowledge or practice of the Catholic faith barely
survives for lack of priests or catechists and other personnel
and resources. There are numerous areas in the United
States without a priest or an established parish. Among the

ethnic groups reached by the home missions are the Native Americans, the black people, the Hispanic people, more recently the Vietnamese refugees, and still others as need arises.

97. *Who belong to the Communion of Saints?*

To the Communion of Saints belong:
1. people on earth who believe in Christ,
2. the souls in purgatory
3. and the Saints in heaven.

Belief in the Communion of Saints goes back to the very beginnings of the Church. The "Saints" in question are not only canonized ones. The Bible generally uses the word for all who are united with God through sanctifying grace and belong to the people of God. This is the sense of the expression "Communion of Saints."

In the Dogmatic Constitution on the Church, *Vatican II says: "Until the Lord shall come in His majesty . . . some of His disciples are exiles on earth, some having died are purified, and others are in glory beholding 'clearly God Himself triune and one, as He is'; but all in various ways and degrees are in communion in the same charity of God and neighbor. . . . For all who are in Christ, having His Spirit, form one Church and cleave together in Him. . . . This Sacred Council accepts with great devotion this venerable faith of our ancestors regarding this vital fellowship with our brothers and sisters who are in heavenly glory or who having died are still being purified" (nos. 49, 51).*

98. *How can we help the souls in purgatory?*

We can help the souls in purgatory by prayer, by good works and indulgences, and particularly by the Holy Sacrifice of the Mass.

As she lay dying, St. Monica (d. 387) said to her son St. Augustine: "Bury me anywhere. All I ask is that you remember me at the altar of the Lord." — The Second Vatican Council says in the *Dogmatic Constitution on the Church:* "Fully conscious of this communion of the whole Mystical Body of Jesus Christ, the pilgrim Church from the very first ages of the Christian religion has cultivated with great peity the memory of the dead, and 'because it is a holy and wholesome thought to pray for the dead that they may be loosed from their sins' (2 Mc 12:45-46), also offers suffrages for them" (no. 50).

99. Why do we venerate the Saints?

We venerate the Saints because they are friends of God and because God Himself honors them.

Many people have a wrong idea about Saints. In order to live a holy life it is not necessary to do anything spectacular or to work miracles. Saints may indeed perform the miraculous, but that is rather a sign of their holiness, not the cause of it. To live in a saintly manner means to live for God in whatever vocation or circumstances of life He has placed us.

Saints are like a mirror in which we can read the goodness and the holiness of God Himself. The honor we pay them redounds to His honor and glory, since it was by His gifts of grace that they were able to become the Saints they are.

100. What does the Church teach about veneration of the Saints?

The Church teaches that it is good and useful to venerate the Saints and to invoke their help.

Veneration of the Saints has been approved and recommended by the Councils of the Church, e.g., by Trent in its Session of December 3, 1563, and most recently by the Second Vatican. Since honor to the Saints is honor to God, Catholics are encouraged to make devotion to the Saints a part of their life, especially devotion to their Patron Saints and the Patron of their parish and their country.

God Himself honors and glorifies Saints. Christ said: *"If anyone serves me, him the Father will honor" (Jn 12:26).* Veneration of the Saints also creates incentives to follow the example of their holy life. *"Can't you do what they did?"* asks St. Augustine, saying in effect that Saints are not a breed apart but weak human beings like the rest of us, who become strong and holy through the help of God's grace.

It is both proper and helpful to ask the Saints in heaven to intercede for us. We ask people on earth to pray for us. All the more reason to ask the Saints in heaven for their prayer and intercession. And if on earth the fervent petition of a holy person is powerful (Jas 5:16), much more powerful is the prayer of a Saint in heaven.

In the Dogmatic Constitution on the Church *of Vatican II we are taught: "Nor is it by the title of example only that we cherish the memory of those in heaven, but still more in order that the union of the whole Church may be strengthened in the Spirit by the practice of fraternal charity. For just as Christian communion among wayfarers brings us closer to Christ, so our companionship with the Saints joins us to Christ, from Whom as from its Fountain and Head issues every grace and the very life of the people of God.*

"It is supremely fitting, therefore, that we love those friends and coheirs of Jesus Christ, who are also our brothers and sisters and extraordinary benefactors, that we render due thanks to God for them and suppliantly invoke them and have recourse to their prayers, their power and help in obtaining benefits from God through His Son, Jesus Christ, Who is our Redeemer and Savior. For every genuine testimony of love shown by us to those in heaven by its very nature tends toward and terminates in Christ as the 'crown of all Saints,' and through Him, in God Who is wonderful in His Saints and is magnified in them" (no. 50).

101. *Do we give Saints the same honor that we give to God?*

We do not give Saints the same honor that we give to God. We honor God with worship of Him as supreme Lord. We honor the Saints with veneration of them as His faithful servants.

By asking the prayers of the Saints we do not detract from God's honor. The Saints can accomplish nothing on their own, nor do we ask them to. As the Blessed of heaven they appear before God bearing our petitions. Too often, however, our prayer is poor and listless, and excessively self-centered. This prayer the Saints receive and invest with their superabundant merits and their perfect love of God. What was a prayer of inordinate petition becomes a prayer adjusted to the great plans of God, one more pleasing and acceptable to His will.

Vatican II, in the Dogmatic Constitution on the Church, says: "By reason of the fact that those in heaven are more closely united with Christ, they establish the whole Church more firmly in holiness, lend nobility to the worship which the Church offers to God here on earth and in many ways contribute to its greater edification. For after they have been received into their heavenly home and are present to the Lord, through Him and with Him and in Him they do not cease to intercede with the Father for us. They show forth the merits which they won on earth through the one Mediator between God and human beings, Christ Jesus. There they served God in all things and filled up in their flesh those things which were lacking of the sufferings of Christ for His Body which is the Church. Thus by their familial interest our weakness is greatly strengthened" (no. 49).

102. *Why does the Church honor relics of the Saints?*

The Church honors relics of the Saints,
1. **because the bodies of the Saints were temples of the Holy Spirit and will rise in glory;**
2. **because God has often honored relics by working miracles through them.**

The word "relics" derives from the Latin *relinquere*, "to leave behind." Hence, it refers to what is left of the Saints (their body or parts thereof, their clothing, artifacts, instruments of torture and martyrdom, and the like). Instances of veneration of relics occur in the Bible itself:

"When the [dead] man came in contact with the bones of Elisha, he came back to life" (2 Kgs 13:21).—Even St. Peter's shadow was sought for healing of the sick (Acts 5:15).—In the case of St. Paul, "handkerchiefs or cloths which had touched his skin were applied to the sick [and] their diseases were cured and evil spirits departed from them" (Acts 19:12).

Vatican II, in its *Constitution on the Sacred Liturgy,* lauds veneration of the Saints and their relics (no. 111).

103. *Why do we honor images of Christ and the Saints?*

We honor images of Christ and the Saints
1. **because in the images we honor Christ and the Saints themselves;**
2. **because the images inspire us to love and imitate Christ and the Saints.**

The veneration we pay to images is directed to the person represented. It is the person, not the image, that we ask for help or seek to imitate in our life. Human beings have honored their heroes, in pictures, in statues, and in festivals. What greater heroes to a Catholic than the Saints, let alone our Lord Himself?

In 1970 there still were over 780 million people in the world who could neither read nor write. Christ also must be brought to them. Images (pictures, statues, crucifixes, whatever) are proven means of making Christ and the Saints better known to them. But even people who arc litcratc arc not above such things. Images inspire good thoughts, keep us attentive in prayer, remind us of God's goal for us and how to get there. In the *Constitution on the Sacred Liturgy,* the Second Vatican Council says: "The practice of placing sacred images in churches so that they may be venerated by the faithful is to be maintained" (no. 125).

104. *Isn't veneration of images contrary to the Bible?*

Veneration of images is not contrary to the Bible, because the Bible only forbids the making and worshiping of idols (representations of false gods).

Veneration of images is not worship of images. We only worship God, not any image, of Him or His Saints. The Old Testament prescription against idols can be read in Ex 20:4-5 and Dt 4:15-19. The New Testament has nothing for or against veneration of images. But though not in the letter, it is certainly in the spirit of the New Testament to venerate images of our Lord, and of His Blessed Mother, His Apostles, His Martyrs and Saints.

Protestant Churches, which for the most part used to be opposed to sacred images, have in recent decades shown a more favorable attitude. There seems to be a growing recognition that sacred images are in fact a scriptural sermon, not in word but in form or color or both. Consider the religious imagery of a stained glass window, or the homiletic effect of a statue of Christ or a painting of the Blessed Mother. Never mind that the painting or statue is not worthy of the masters, a Raphael, a Michelangelo. Good religious art is preferable to bad, of course, but the underlying principle is the same, namely, what the Bible preaches through the spoken or printed word it can also preach through the depicted word.

105. *What is done at the beatification or canonization of a Saint?*

At the beatification or canonization of a Saint the Pope proclaims that the person lived a holy life on earth and is now with God in glory.

The number of Saints is countless. In the Book of Revelation, or Apocalypse, St. John says: "I saw before me a huge crowd which no one could count from every nation and race, people and tongue" (7:9). One hagiographer lists some 12,800 Saints and Blessed by name and date. Large as this number may seem, it is undoubtedly a mere handful compared to the total number of people (Saints) in heaven.

Before a beatification or canonization can take place, the life of the person concerned must be thoroughly investigated. This is a long and rigorous process which may go on for decades, even centuries. Proof must be established, on the basis of numerous witnesses, that the person lived the Christian life and virtues in a heroic manner and that through his/her intercession miracles have occurred. These miracles also are thoroughly probed before being declared authentic. The records and depositions relating to a canonization usually comprise many volumes.

Tenth Article of Faith

"I believe in . . . the forgiveness of sins."

106. *What do we profess in the words: "forgiveness of sins"?*

In the words "forgiveness of sins," we profess that Jesus Christ gave His Church power and authority to forgive sins and punishment due to sin.

All persons who truly repent of their sins will receive God's pardon. But they must have the intention to receive, at opportunity, the Sacraments which Christ instituted for the forgiveness of sins. For unbaptized adults this means at least an implicit desire for the holy Sacrament of Baptism. For baptized persons who commit sins after Baptism it means the Sacrament of Penance or Reconciliation (confession). Contrition, as well as the Sacraments of Baptism and Penance, is treated in Part II of this Catechism.

Eleventh and Twelfth Articles of Faith

"I believe in ... the resurrection of the body and life everlasting."

107. What takes place in human death?

In human death the soul departs from the body.

The body is buried in the cemetery, in a blessed grave. — Primitive man buried his dead. The practice of cremation does not appear in Europe until the third millennium before Christ, only to disappear again, or nearly so, in the immediate centuries before Christ. We know from the Bible that the Israelites respected the dead and always gave them burial, as seen in the case of the elder Tobit (Tb 1:17ff; 2:4). Christians did the same, from the start, always burying their dead.

Cremation in modern times derives from the French Revolution. Continental Freemasonry also promoted it, among other reasons to counter the Christian belief in immortality. Because of the irreligious campaign associated with it, the Church forbade the practice. But times have changed and by and large cremation has ceased to be a vehicle of anti-Catholicism. The Church, accordingly, has relaxed its former discipline and since June, 1964, gives Catholics the option of cremation.

108. *What do we know about our death?*

About our death we only know that it is coming; we do not know when or where or how?

Consequently, we should be ready at all times, as our Lord admonishes: "Keep your eyes open, for you know not the day or the hour" (Mt 25:13).

In the Pastoral Constitution on the Church in the Modern World, *Vatican II says: "Although the mystery of death utterly beggars the imagination, the Church has been taught by divine Revelation and firmly teaches that human beings have been created by God for a blissful purpose beyond the reach of earthly misery. In addition, that bodily death from which the human race would have been immune had it not sinned will be vanquished according to the Christian faith, when human beings who were ruined by their own doing are restored to wholeness by an almighty and merciful Savior.*

"For God has called human beings and still calls them so that with their entire being they might be joined to Him in an endless sharing of a divine life beyond all corruption. Christ won this victory when He rose to life, for by His death He freed human beings from death. Hence for all thoughtful persons, a solidly established faith provides the answer to their anxiety about what the future holds for them" (no. 18).

109. *What happens with the soul after death?*

After death the soul appears before the judgment seat of God.

This truth is clearly taught in the Bible. The Old Testament says in the Book of Sirach (11:26): "It is easy with the Lord on the day of death to repay man according to his deeds." — In the New Testament St. Paul writes: "Every one of us will have to give an account of himself before God" (Rom 14:12). And in Heb 9:27: "It is appointed that men die once, and after death be judged." The primitive Greek text of this quotation from Hebrews makes it clear that "once" means "once only," that death is unrepeatable.

This rules out the idea of reincarnation, an un-Christian belief according to which the soul after death enters another body, even of a brute animal, as often as necessary until it is completely cleansed.

Also excluded is the notion that after death a person can still decide for or against Christ. If this were true, no one would decide against Christ because the soul separated from the body knows only one desire, to be united with Christ. Death has final consequences for everyone, because it determines one's fate forever. St. Cyprian (d. 258) wrote: "Once we are departed from this world. there is no room for repentance, no profit from remorse. Eternal life is won or lost here on earth."

Vatican II in the Dogmatic Constitution on the Church, says: *"Before we reign with Christ in glory, all of us will be made manifest 'before the tribunal of Christ, so that each one may receive his recompense, good or bad, according to his life in the body' " (2 Cor 5:10) (no. 48).*

110. *Which souls go straight to heaven?*

Those souls go straight to heaven who die in the state of sanctifying grace and are free of all sin and all punishment due to sin.

"Nothing profane [unclean] shall enter it [heaven]" (Rv 21:27). — Vatican II, in its Dogmatic Constitution on the Church *(no. 49), expresses the Catholic teaching that those in heaven, in glory, behold God Himself triune and one, as He is. — Concerning heaven, Pope Paul VI said in his general audience of May 22, 1974: "We now live in time, but one day we shall live forever in the Kingdom of heaven. This does not mean the blue sky above but the new state of existence produced in mysterious and wonderful manner according to God's creative plan and by His power. It is a Kingdom in which we share even now in virtue of certain supernatural*

conditions and gifts like faith, grace, and divine love. We are partly of earth and partly of heaven. We must know how to live simultaneously on earth and in heaven."

111. What makes the happiness of the blessed in heaven?

1. The blessed in heaven see God and live in indescribable joy;
2. they are free of all evil.

1) "Now we see indistinctly, as in a mirror; then we shall see face to face" (1 Cor 13:12). — "Eye has not seen, ear has not heard, nor has it so much as dawned on man what God has prepared for those who love him" (1 Cor 2:9).

There are degrees of reward and therefore of happiness in heaven. "Each will receive his wages in proportion to his toil" (1 Cor 3:8). "He who sows bountifully will reap bountifully" (2 Cor 9:6). This is part of the mystery of heaven, that there are degrees of happiness yet each degree is perfect happiness for the soul and eventually for the body.

2. "[God] shall wipe every tear from their eyes, and there shall be no more death or mourning, crying out or pain" (Rv 21:4).

N.B. *The blessed in heaven are not only the canonized Saints but all who have died and gone to heaven.*

112. Which souls go to purgatory?

Those souls go to purgatory who die in the grace of God but are not free of all venial sin and all punishment due to sin.

The German word for purgatory is *Fegfeuer,* literally "cleansing fire." It suggests that the pain of the soul in purgatory may be compared to the pain the body suffers from fire. The word "purgatory" transcribes the Latin *purgatorium,* a place of purging or purification.

From the beginning, Christians believed that after this life sin may still be atoned for and temporal punishment of sin satisfied. This is evident from their practice of praying for the dead and offering the sacrifice of the Eucharist (Holy Mass) for them. Many a grave of Christian antiquity bears an inscription requesting prayer for the person buried there. This would be pointless if the only possibility was heaven or hell, because those in heaven do not need our prayer and those in hell cannot benefit from it, hell being eternal. Already in Tertullian's time (ca. 200) Christians celebrated anniversary Masses for the dead. St. Cyprian (d. 258) also mentions this practice, and Church Fathers after him all encourage Masses for the dead.

What the Old Testament says in 2 Mc 12:46 presupposes after-death purification, as do the words of our Lord in Mt 12:32, because here also the possibility of satisfaction for sin in the hereafter is at least raised. A similar conclusion may be drawn from 1 Cor 3:11-15, even though the passage does not speak directly of a place of purification.

The Church does not presume to know more about purgatory than what can be gathered from God's revelation. Her official teaching, which does not cater to idle curiosity, is sparing and clear-cut: (1) There is a purgatory, a place or state of purification. (2) Purgatory itself ceases with the Last Judgment, hence is not eternal. (3) We can help the souls in purgatory through our prayers, good works, and pious practices generally.

Protestantism on the whole frowns on the idea of purgatory. The attitude stems from its particular view of justification. Yet, as a Protestant theologian of the 19th century wrote: "Most people die too good for hell and certainly too bad for heaven. In this matter, it must be frankly admitted, the Protestantism of the Reformation is left groping in the dark."

113. *Why do we call the souls in purgatory the "poor" souls?*

We call them the "poor" souls because they
1. are suffering souls,
2. are still separated from God in heaven
3. and can do nothing of themselves to shorten their purgatory.

Nevertheless, they can also be called happy souls. For one thing, they are in the state of sanctifying grace and so are worthy children of God. In addition, they are no longer subject to sin, which méans they are assured of heaven, a certainty that tempers the pain of purgatory. The pain is real but not without solace, the solace of heaven glimpsed and guaranteed, though delayed. Purgatory, therefore, is not next door to hell but next door to heaven.

114. *Is there a hell?*

That there is a hell we know from Sacred Scripture, especially from the words of Jesus Himself.

In the Old Testament the Prophet Isaiah spoke of a place where the worm shall not die nor the fire be· extinguished (66:24). Even if, as is commonly held, chapter 66 of Isaiah (as well as some others) is a later addition from about the year 520 B.C., it does show that as far back as then people spoke along the lines of an everlasting hell. The Book of Daniel, which in its present form dates from about the year 170 B.C., says: "Many of those who sleep in the dust of the earth shall awake; some shall live forever, others shall be an everlasting horror and disgrace" (12:2).

Altogether, one can point to more than 70 places in the Bible that relate to hell. Christ Himself refers to it 25 times. A few examples:

Mt 5:29f: "If your right eye is your trouble, gouge it out and throw it away! Better to lose part of your body than to have it all cast into Gehenna [hell]."

Mt 10:28: "Do not fear those who deprive the body of life but cannot destroy the soul. Rather, fear him who can destroy both body and soul in Gehenna."

In Christ's description of the Last Judgment the doctrine of an everlasting hell is clearly stated: "Out of my sight, you condemned, into that everlasting fire prepared for the devil and his angels" (Mt 25:41). In His parables also, Christ makes frequent reference to hell: e.g., parable of the weeds and the wheat (Mt 13:24f), the merciless servant (Mt 18:23), the wedding feast (Mt 22:2ff), the rich man and Lazarus (Lk 16:19ff).

Consequently, the Church always has taught that there is a hell, a place or state of eternal damnation, of eternal banishment from God, where the lost suffer everlasting torment according to the enormity of their guilt. The essential pain of hell is the pain of loss, the loss of God forever. This pain is the more excruciating because in the hereafter the longing for God is relentless yet eternaly unfulfilled in the damned. There are other torments or punishments of hell; about their precise nature the Church never has made an official pronouncement, for the very good reason that nothing about that has been revealed.

To deny the Bible its teaching on hell is to reject an essential part of its message and make God a liar. Protestants in general also subscribe to belief in hell. One of their number, a Swiss university theologian, citing Mt 25:41 (quoted above) wrote in 1947: "So speaks not just anyone but the Lord Himself. So does He speak to every one of us, and here there is no glossing and explaining away, whether we like to hear what He says or not."

Certainly, the doctrine of an eternal hell is a deep mystery of faith, so great and deep that only God can fathom it. An eternal hell is the ultimate outcome, a demand as it were, of His infinite holiness, expressing His utter hatred of sin. But only God comprehends this.

115.   *Which souls go to hell?*

Those souls go to hell which pass from this life in the state of unrepented mortal sin.

Vatican II, in the *Dogmatic Constitution on the Church,* says: "They are not saved who, though part of the body of the Church, do not persevere in charity [sanctifying grace]. They remain indeed in the bosom of the Church, but, as it were, only in a 'bodily' manner and not in their heart" (no. 14).

However, we are never in a position to say that a given person died in the state of mortal sin, i.e., was without a trace of divine love at the moment of death by reason of complete and final turning from God. It is noteworthy that the Church has beatified and canonized many persons, in other words has said they are in heaven. But the Church has never pointed to anyone and said this person is in hell. We can say, however, that *if* a person dies in the state of mortal sin, hence in the state of absolute rejection of God, hell is simply the continuation of mortal sin in eternity, with all the consequences this implies.

The objection is sometimes raised that God is so good and merciful that an eternal hell is incompatible with his goodness. The objection is understandable, yet rests on a misconception. God does not damn anyone to hell. Sinners damn themselves. God takes free will seriously, so seriously that He compels no one to be saved but leaves every person the possibility of saying no. God, in turn, also must be taken seriously when He warns of the possibility of being rejected by Him for all eternity. God does not trick us into hell. Nor does anyone go there blindfolded but always with eyes open, as it were. Nevertheless, as we have said, human reason cannot fathom the mystery of hell. What we can do is to call upon God's mercy while yet there is time. Those who do will obtain the mercy that saves them from hell.

116.   What happens to the human body at the end of the world?

At the end of the world the human body is raised and united forever with the soul.

INSPIRED WORDS

"Heaven and earth shall pass away: but My words shall not pass away" (Luke 21:33).

The doctrine of plenary verbal inspiration, wrongly considered antiquated by many modern neo-evangelicals, is actually essential to the Christian faith. The Bible is not just the Word of God in a vague, general sort of way. Instead, every word is eternal and inerrant, because every word was divinely "inspired" — that is, "breathed in" — by the Holy Spirit. "All Scripture (that is, 'every writing,' every word written down or inscribed) is given by inspiration of God (not man!)" (II Timothy 3:16).

We acknowledge, of course, that problems of transmission and translation exist, but these are relatively trivial in the entire context. We also acknowledge that the *process* of inspiration may have varied, but the *end result* is as if the entire Bible had been dictated and transcribed word by word.

This is the way Jesus Christ — the Creator, the Living Word, the Author of Scripture — viewed the Scriptures. "The Scripture cannot be broken," He said (John 10:35). "Till heaven and earth pass, one jot or one tittle shall in no wise pass from the law, till all be fulfilled" (Matthew 5:18). "Then He said unto them, O fools, and slow of heart to believe all that the prophets have spoken: ... And beginning at Moses and all the prophets, He expounded unto them in all the Scriptures the things concerning Himself" (Luke 24:25,27).

The Bible, therefore, every Word of it, is divinely inspired, verbally without error, infallibly true, and of absolute authority in every area of our lives. The Words of Christ, who taught these truths, are forever "settled in heaven" (Psalm 119:89) and "shall not pass away."

It is mortally dangerous, therefore, "unto every man that heareth the Words of the prophecy of this Book" to "add unto these things (as the cultists do)," or to "take away from the Words of the Book of this prophecy (as the liberals do)" (Revelation 22:18,19). Would it not be much better to say with the psalmist, "Thy testimonies also are my delight and my counsellors" (Psalm 119:24)? HMM

THE LORD IS THY KEEPER

"The LORD is thy Keeper: the LORD is thy shade upon thy right hand. ... The LORD shall preserve thy going out and thy coming in from this time forth, and even for evermore" (Psalm 121:5,8).

One of the most precious doctrines in all of Scripture is that of the secure position of the believer in Christ Jesus. Nothing in creation is "able to separate us from the love of God, which is in Christ Jesus, our Lord" (Romans 8:39).

The Apostle Peter tells us that we who are born again are "kept by the power of God through faith unto salvation" (I Peter 1:5). Nothing we can do can merit salvation; similarly, nothing we do can keep it. This is God's work, not ours, and extends to all realms of our lives. "And the peace of God, which passeth all understanding, shall keep your hearts and minds through Christ Jesus" (Philippians 4:7). "I pray God your whole spirit and soul and body be preserved (usually translated "kept") blameless unto the coming of our Lord Jesus Christ" (I Thessalonians 5:23). "But the Lord is faithful, who shall stablish you, and keep you from evil" (II Thessalonians 3:3).

This keeping aspect of God's work for us should not be a surprise, for Christ prayed for just this. With His betrayal, trial, crucifixion, and death imminent, He prayed for all who would eventually believe on Him (John 17:20). "Holy Father, keep through Thine own name those whom Thou hast given Me. ... While I was with them in the world, I kept them in Thy name: those that Thou gavest Me I have kept, and none of them is lost. ... I pray not that thou shouldest take them out of the world, but that Thou shouldest keep them from the evil (one)" (John 17:11,12,15). Since God, the Son, prayed "according to His (i.e. the Father's) will" (I John 5:14), we know the prayer is answered, for God, the Father, would surely hear the intercessory prayer of His own beloved Son.

"Now unto Him that is able to keep you from falling, and to present you faultless before the presence of His glory with exceeding joy, To the only wise God, our Saviour, be glory and majesty, dominion and power, both now and ever. Amen." (Jude 24,25). JDM

The end of the world is also called the Last Day.

"I know that my Vindicator lives, and that he will at last stand forth upon the dust; whom I myself shall see. My own eyes, not another's, shall behold him, and from my flesh I shall see God" (Jb 19:25-26).

"An hour is coming in which all those in their tombs shall hear his [the Son of God's] voice and come forth. Those who have done right shall rise to live; the evildoers shall rise to be damned" (Jn 5:28-29).

Cardinal Faulhaber of Germany (d. 1952) once remarked: "Just as in the beginning there was the wonder of creation, so at the end of the world there will be the wonder of the resurrection of the dead."

117. *Why will the body be raised up?*

The body will be raised up to share in the reward or punishment of the soul, just as it shared in our good or evil deeds on earth.

When we fold our hands or kneel in prayer, the body participates in the prayer. When we give a needy person an alms, our hands take part in the giving. For a pilgrimage, the body must help us. Nor can we speak evil without the tongue, or damage the neighbor's property without enlisting the help of the body. Even our thoughts, in this life, cannot do without an organ of the body, the brain. (Not that the brain does the thinking, but it furnishes the materials for the mind to work on.) Rightly, therefore, does the body as well as the soul receive reward or punishment after death.

118. *Will all bodies be the same after the resurrection?*

Not all bodies will be the same after the resurrection. The bodies of the just will be glorious and beautiful; the bodies of the wicked will be unsightly and abhorrent.

The doctrine of bodily resurrection has often met with skepticism, from the early days of the Church onward. St. Paul's Athenian audience in the Areopagus listened with rapt attention—until he mentioned the raising of the dead (Acts 17:32). His Corinthian Christians had difficulties of their own, which the Apostle tried to answer as far as they can be answered this side of heaven (1 Cor 15:35ff). How are the dead to be raised up, they asked? In reply St. Paul turned to an illustration, the seed and the plant. The plant differs from the seed from which it sprang, yet the seed lives on in the plant. So will our earthly body (seed) be transformed and become a glorified body (plant). How this comes about is a mystery of God's creative power, which provides the kind of body suited to the new life after the resurrection.

The body that died was mortal; the body that is raised is immortal. The glorified body is both new and the same: new because it is glorified, the same because it is still the body we had, our body. And though the resurrected, immortal body is said to be "spiritual," it is not spiritual like an angel, in substance. In heaven, after the resurrection, human beings remain human beings, composites of soul and body, spirit and flesh, though flesh of which we have no experience save by analogy with the resurrected body of Christ. Of the resurrected, glorified body can be said what St. Paul said in another context: "Eye has not seen, ear has not heard, nor has it so much as dawned on man what God has prepared for those who love him" (1 Cor 2:9).

119.   *What is the General Judgment?*

The General Judgment is a judgment of the whole human race combined, which Jesus Christ will hold at the end of the world.

This judgment is also called the Last Judgment, and it is public. Thoughts, words, and deeds of everyone will be revealed for all to see. In this life we can deceive and dissemble—many a smiling face masks an evil heart. Weeds are not always distinguishable from the wheat. But when God comes in judgment, nothing can be hidden and we will appear in our true self. The author of the Book of Revelation offers this description:

"I saw the dead, the great and the lowly, standing before the throne. Lastly, among the scrolls, the book of the living was opened. The dead were judged according to their conduct as recorded on the scrolls. . . . Each person was judged according to his conduct" (Rv 20:12-13).

120. Why will there be a General Judgment?

There will be a General Judgment
1. **so that everyone will see that God is just and wise;**
2. **so that the good will receive deserved honor and the wicked deserved shame.**

"Then shall the just one with great assurance confront his oppressors who set at nought his labors. Seeing this, they shall be shaken with dreadful fear, and amazed at the unlooked-for salvation. They shall say among themselves, rueful and groaning through anguish of spirit: 'This is he whom once we held as a laughingstock, and as a type for mockery, fools that we were! His life we accounted madness, and his death dishonored. See how he is accounted among the sons of God; how his lot is with the saints!' " (Wis 5:1-5).

Our Lord describes this Judgment in Mt 25:31-46.

To the saved the Judge will say: "Come. You have my Father's blessing! Inherit the kingdom prepared for you from the creation of the world" (Mt 25:34).

To the reprobate He will say: "Out of my sight, you condemned, into that everlasting fire prepared for the devil and his angels!" (Mt 25:41).

121. *What happens on the Last Day to the world we see?*

On the Last Day the world we see will be transformed and made new.

Vatican II, *in its* Pastoral Constitution on the Church in the Modern World, *says: "We do not know the time for the consummation of the earth and of humanity, nor do we know how all things will be transformed. As deformed by sin, the shape of this world will pass away; but we are taught that God is preparing a new dwelling place and a new earth where justice will abide, and whose blessedness will answer and surpass all the longings for peace which spring up in the human heart" (no. 39).*

See Question 64.

Amen

The Creed ends with Amen, an expression adopted from the Old Testament. It was used, and still is, to express assent to the will or word of God. A good example is found in Dt 27:15ff, where the people say Amen to the maledictions attached to various transgressions of God's law. The usual English translation is "so be it."

In the New Testament Jesus often introduces the the word in the sense of "truly," "I assure you," etc., to emphasize what He is going to say (Mt 5:18: Amen = I assure you . . .). When the people at Mass or any divine service add their Amen to a prayer or chant of the priest they as much as say that the prayer or chant expresses their thoughts, their prayer, their praise of God; e.g., the Amen after the Great Doxology ("through Him, with Him. . .") that concludes the Eucharistic Prayer (see also 1 Cor 14:16, or Rv 5:14). The

Amen conveys the assent of the heart to the outward action. It underlines our presence and our participation, not unlike the underlining of something written to reinforce what is asserted.

Because it packs so much meaning, our Amen should always be delivered with becoming reverence and attention both in private and public worship, but especially in public, as a community. It is easy to fall into mechanical repetition of the word, but not if we keep in mind what we are saying when we say Amen.

JESUS EMPOWERED US TO LIVE IN HIM THROUGH GRACE
"Live on in me as I do in you. . . . I am the vine, you are the branches. He who lives in me will produce abundantly, for apart from me you can do nothing" (Jn 15:4f).

PART TWO: THE HOLY SACRAMENTS

Grace

122. *What is grace?*

Grace is an inward, supernatural help or gift which God bestows on us for the good of the soul.

Natural, outward gifts of the body are health, food, clothing, housing, etc.

Natural, inward gifts of the soul are intellect, will, memory, mental abilities, etc.

But grace is not a natural gift, not part of our given nature, It is something additional, over and above what constitutes human nature and surpassing it in power and goodness. For this reason it is called supernatural. Grace can come only from God. We cannot acquire it by ourselves, or by our own efforts.

A tree that grows wild can only produce wild fruit. But with the right kind of grafting it produces good fruit. Similarly, by ourselves we cannot produce good fruit. Only with the help of God's grace does that become possible.

123. *What are the principal kinds of grace?*

There are two principal kinds of grace:
1. Helping grace.
2. Sanctifying grace.

Helping grace is also called actual or transient grace: actual because it is given to perform a supernatural act or

145

acts, transient because it works on the soul in a passing manner.

Sanctifying grace, on the other hand, remains in the soul and adorns and prepares the soul to be constantly pleasing in God's sight.

124. *What does helping grace do?*

Helping grace inclines us to good deeds and helps us to perform them.

125. *How does helping grace work in us?*

1. Helping grace enlightens our mind;
2. it moves and strengthens our will.

1) "It is not that we are entitled of ourselves to take credit for anything. Our sole credit is from God" (2 Cor 3:5).

2) "It is God who, in his good will toward you, begets in you any measure of desire or achievement" (Phil 2:13).

126. *Does God give everyone the necessary grace?*

God gives everyone sufficient grace to be saved.

"God wants all men to be saved and come to know the truth" (1 Tm 2:4).

But not everyone receives the same measure of grace. A person who cooperates with God's grace will receive more than someone who neglects God and has no interest in prayer or good works, and seldom if ever goes to church.

"Oh, that today you would hear his voice: Harden not your hearts . . ." (Ps 95:8). — "We beg you not to receive the grace of God in vain" (2 Cor 6:1).

Both criminals crucified with Jesus received the grace of repentance. One responded to it and was saved. The other, as far as we know, did not respond to it.

Without grace we can nothing to please God. The monk Pelagius (d. ca. 418) denied the necessity of grace and said that it was possible to keep God's commandments without the help of His grace. St. Augustine assailed this teaching. Pelagianism, as it came to be called, was condemned by several Particular Councils of the Church and also by the General Council of Ephesus in 431.

In the Pastoral Constitution on the Church in the Modern World, *Vatican II says: "Since human freedom has been damaged by sin, only by the aid of God's grace can human beings bring their relationship with God into full flower" (no. 17).*

127. What do we become through sanctifying grace?

Through sanctifying grace we become holy and right with God; we become his children and heirs of heaven.

Sanctifying grace is first received in the Sacrament of Baptism. It removes original sin and its eternal punishment and sanctifies the soul. Since the baptized person is made just (holy) before God, the sanctifying grace of Baptism is also called the grace of justification.

Sanctifying grace is the garment without which no one is admitted to the wedding feast of heaven (Mt 22:1ff).

Sanctifying grace is the divine (supernatural) life in the souls of the just. We became partakers of God's life in the Sacrament of our rebirth, holy Baptism. Because we were born of God, we may call Him Father; and because we received Baptism and divine life through the Church, we may call the Church our mother. Christ, the "only-begotten Son of God," is our brother. As God's children, we are promised the divine inheritance, hence are heirs of heaven.

128. How do we lose sanctifying grace?

We lose sanctifying grace through any grave (mortal) sin.

The contrary opinion has always been rejected by the Church, and in 1547 the Council of Trent took occasion to declare that not only the sin of unbelief but every mortal sin results in the loss of sanctifying grace. Cited in support can be St. Paul's catalog of sins in 1 Cor 6:9f, where the Apostle writes: "Can you not realize that the unholy will not fall heir to the kingdom of God? Do not deceive yourselves: no fornicators, idolaters, or adulterers, no sexual perverts, thieves, misers, or drunkards, no slanderers or robbers will inherit God's kingdom."

Sanctifying grace can be regained through perfect contrition and the resolve to go to confession when opportunity offers.

129. *What must we do to preserve and increase sanctifying grace?*

To preserve and increase sanctifying grace we must be devoted to good works in our daily life.

Good works are not the works which St. Paul criticizes in the Epistles to the Romans and Galatians. These were outward ceremonial works of the Mosaic Law through which the Jewish people sought justification. The good works of the Christian are works of a living faith. St. James writes: "My brothers, what good is it to profess faith without practicing it? Such faith has no power to save, has it? . . . Faith that does nothing in practice is thoroughly lifeless. . . . Be assured, then, that faith without works is as dead as a body without breath" (2:14ff). Similarly, St. Peter: "Be solicitous to make your call and election permanent, brothers; surely those who do so [through good works] will never be lost" (2 Pt 1:10).

Good works to which we should apply ourselves include: (1) works of piety and penance, (2) works of love of neighbor, (3) conscientious work in our occupation, and (4) suffering borne for love of God. Sacred Scripture lays particular stress on prayer, fasting, and almsgiving. "It is better to give alms than to store up gold" (Tb 12:8).

Especially important is frequent reception of Holy Communion, because Christ in the Eucharist is the food that nourishes the divine life in our soul.

A person who is not zealous for good works becomes lukewarm and easily falls into grave sin. Without good works it is simply not possible to be saved: "Every tree that is not fruitful will be cut down and thrown into the fire" (Mt 3:10).

130. *When are our works good?*

Our works are good,
1. when they conform to God's will
2. and when we do them with a good intention.

Our intention is good when we do good for love of God and not for human praise or reward. "Be on guard against performing religious acts for people to see. Otherwise expect no recompense from your heavenly Father" (Mt 6:1).

Every morning and often through the day form a good intention in words like: "Dear Lord, all for You and for Your glory."

Good works done in the state of grace are meritorious because they share in the infinite merits of Jesus Christ, Whose living members we are through sanctifying grace. "No more than a branch can bear fruit of itself apart from the vine, can you bear fruit apart from me" (Jn 15:4).

131. *What is a Sacrament?*

A Sacrament is an outward sign instituted by Jesus Christ to give inward grace.

A sign indicates something other than itself, as smoke indicates fire. The sacramental sign is a sense-perceptible thing, like water or oil or spoken words, which points to and brings the grace of the Sacrament. Our Lord commanded the use of these outward signs partly to teach us the humility of submitting to material means for receiving spiritual grace.

The inward grace is produced by God through the sacramental sign. God can bestow grace apart from the Sacraments. But the Son of God did give us the Sacraments and made them the ordinary channels of His sanctifying grace. Hence we ignore them at our peril.

Institution by Christ is absolutely necessary, because signs or actions instituted by the Church (i.e., sacramentals) cannot produce grace in the way that a sign instituted by Christ does. Whether He instituted a given Sacrament before or after His Resurrection is irrelevant. The Church Fathers without exception attribute the origin of the Sacraments to Christ Himself, never to the Church. The Apostles also viewed themselves as administrators of the Sacraments and not as their authors (1 Cor 4:1).

Vatican II, in the Dogmatic Constitution on the Church, *says: "In that Body [the Church] the life of Christ is poured into the believers who, through the Sacraments, are united in a hidden and real way to Christ Who suffered and was glorified" (no. 7).*

And in the Constitution on the Sacred Liturgy *it adds: "The purpose of the Sacraments is to sanctify human beings, to build up the Body of Christ, and, finally to give worship to God; because they are signs they also instruct. They not only presuppose faith, but by words and objects they also nourish, strengthen, and express it; that is why they are called 'Sacraments of faith.' They do indeed impart grace, but, in addition, the very act of celebrating them most effectively disposes the faithful to receive this grace in a fruitful manner, to worship God duly, and to practice charity. It is therefore of the highest importance that the faithful ... frequent with great eagerness those Sacraments which were instituted to nourish the Christian life" (no. 59).*

132. *How many Sacraments did Christ institute?*

Jesus Christ instituted seven Sacraments:

1. **Baptism,**
2. **Confirmation,**
3. **Holy Eucharist (Sacrament of the Altar),**
4. **Penance (Reconciliation),**
5. **Anointing of the Sick,**
6. **Holy Orders,**
7. **Matrimony.**

In Baptism we receive supernatural life. Confirmation strengthens us for the practice and profession of our faith. The Holy Eucharist provides nourishment for the supernatural life. In the Sacrament of Penance supernatural life is restored or increased. The Anointing of the Sick helps the sick in body and soul. The last two Sacraments pertain to the two most important states of life: Holy Orders confers upon the priest strength and grace for his responsible office. Matrimony sanctifies man and wife in lifelong union and provides blessings for family life.

Baptism establishes the supernatural life of sanctifying grace in the soul; Penance reestablishes it when lost. Consequently, they are called Sacraments of the dead (because the soul without sanctifying grace is supernaturally dead). The other Sacraments presuppose and increase sanctifying grace, for which reason they are Sacraments of the living (because the soul with sanctifying grace is supernaturally alive). Each Sacrament also imparts its own special graces. In addition, three Sacraments—Baptism, Confirmation, Holy Orders—imprint an indelible mark (technically: character) upon the soul and therefore can be received once only.

The Church teaches that there are seven Sacraments. Even heretical groups which separated from Rome as early as the 5th century profess seven. Among such groups are Syrians, Armenians, Nestorians, and Monophysites. In the first centuries of the Church there is no evidence of contention as regards the number of Sacraments. This implies a tradition of unanimity that goes back to the Apostolic Age.

Added to this may be the witness of the Eastern Orthodox Church, which broke with Rome in 1054. This Church also holds to seven Sacraments. When efforts were made to enlist it in the Protestant cause, a Synod meeting in Constantinople in 1672 reaffirmed its belief in seven Sacraments, giving as reason that this is what the Gospels teach.

On a pastoral level, the Second Vatican Council in its Decree on the Catholic Churches of the Eastern Rite *declared that "Eastern Christians who are in fact separated in good faith from the Catholic Church, if they ask of their own accord . . . may be admitted to the Sacraments of Penance, the Eucharist, and the Anointing of the Sick. Further, Catholics may ask for these same Sacraments from those non-Catholic ministers [of the Eastern Church] " (no. 27).*

Baptism

133. *What is Baptism?*

Baptism is the Sacrament in which we are made members of the Church, empowered to participate in Christian worship, and born to eternal life by means of water and the Holy Spirit.

Among Old Testament prefigurations of Baptism are the Flood, the passage of the Israelites through the Red Sea, and Naaman the Syrian's washing in the Jordan. —The word "baptism" derives from the Greek *baptizein,* which means to submerge or immerse. Baptism by immersion was common in the early Church but became less and less practical and in time was discontinued in favor of Baptism by pouring water over the head, as we now have it.

Vatican II, in the Constitution on the Church, *says: "Incorporated in the Church through Baptism, the faithful are destined by the baptismal character for the worship of the Christian religion; reborn as children of God, they must confess before people the faith which they have received from God through the Church" (no. 11).*

In the Decree on Ecumenism, *it adds: "Whenever the Sacrament of Baptism is duly administered . . . and received with the right disposition, a person is truly incorporated into the crucified and glorified Christ, and reborn to a sharing of the divine life. . . . But of itself Baptism is only a beginning, an inauguration wholly directed toward the fullness of life in Christ. Baptism, therefore, envisages a complete profession of faith, complete incorporation in salvation such as Christ wills it to be, and finally complete ingrafting in Eucharistic communion."*

134. How is Baptism administered?

The person baptizing pours water over the head of the person being baptized and at the same time says: "I baptize you in the name of the Father, and of the Son, and of the Holy Spirit."

This formula must always be used in Baptism, which in the normal course of events should be administered by a bishop, priest, or deacon. But any persons, even non-Christians, can validly baptize, though ordinarily they should not administer the Sacrament except in emergency, when an infant or for that matter an adult seeking Baptism is in danger of dying unbaptized. It is essential, however, that the person baptizing in emergency use the correct formula and have the serious intention to baptize according to the mind of the Church.

If blessed baptismal water is not available in emergency Baptism, ordinary water may be used, from a well or kitchen faucet, from melted ice or snow, from a lake or stream or any other source. Christ chose water for this Sacrament precisely because it is easily and everywhere available and symbolizes better than anything the effects of Baptism—it washes, purifies, and makes clean, spiritually. The water must touch the body of the person baptized, hence not only the hair.

Baptism is a Sacrament of initiation into the Christian community, which has a stake in the supernatural rebirth of the child and therefore in its timely Baptism: "Now and then it is said that Baptism should be put off so that in time children can decide for themselves if they want to be Christian and what Church to belong to. This contention rests on a false notion of human freedom, and parents who act in this way abandon their responsibility. Not only do they have a perverted understanding of human freedom, but they forget that the grace of Christ's redemptive work is not an indifferent offer which can be accepted or rejected as one pleases, and without consequences. . . .

"Freedom does not mean that persons can start from scratch and decide everything in their life. Baptism is not the only thing about which the child is not consulted. It was not consulted about its birth, survival, sex, nationality, I. Q., and much more. These are given realities in anyone's life and must be faced. Christ's Redemption also is given reality; it is irrevocable and confronts all human beings, and those who knowingly reject its grace make themselves culpable" (Bishop Hengsbach).

The New Testament suggests that infant Baptism was practiced as early as the Apostles. At any rate we read of whole families being baptized, and families include children. See Acts 11:14; 16:15-33; 18:8; 1 Cor 1:16.

Recently (November 1980) the Vatican, in face of theological debate concerning it, issued a strong reaffirmation of the practice of infant Baptism.

135. Why is Baptism the most necessary Sacrament?

Baptism is the most necessary Sacrament because without Baptism no one can be saved.

"Go into the whole world and proclaim the good news to all creation. The man who believes in it and accepts baptism will be saved; the man who refuses to believe in it will be condemned" (Mk 16:15-16). To Nicodemus Christ said: "No one can enter into God's kingdom without being begotten of water and Spirit" (Jn 3:5). Jews who heard Peter's Pentecostal sermon and wanted to become Christians asked what they were to do: "You must reform and be baptized, each one of you" (Acts 2:38).

Vatican II, in the Decree on the Missionary Activity of the Church, says: "Therefore, all must be converted to Him [Christ] . . . and all must be incorporated into Him by Baptism and into the Church which is His body" (no. 7).

The necessity of Baptism (by water) applies to all who know about it. People who never have heard of Baptism can be saved if they live according to their conscience, i.e., according to the natural moral law implanted in the heart by God.

In Romans 2:14-16 we read: "When Gentiles who do not have the law keep it as by instinct, these men although without the law serve as a law for themselves. They show that the demands of the law are written in their hearts. Their conscience bears witness together with that law, and their thoughts will accuse or defend them on the day when, in accordance with the gospel I preach, God will pass judgment on the secrets of men through Christ Jesus."

Concerning the fate of infants who die unbaptized, nothing has been revealed. Theologians have taught that they go to "limbo," where they will be blessed with natural happiness but not with the supernatural happiness of the vision of God in heaven. Many contemporary theologians believe that God makes it possible for these infants to be saved, just how we do not know. But we do know that God wants everyone to be saved and that infants are incapable of personal sin. Hence, the opinion is put forward that unbaptized infants will by God's grace be admitted to heaven. What, then, of limbo?

The Church has taken no official stand on the nature or even the reality of limbo but does teach that Baptism in some form (see below) is necessary for salvation. Inevitably some infants will die unbaptized; grieving mothers can take comfort in the thought that children were the object of Christ's special love on earth, and this love is at least as great now, when He has triumphed over death and sits in glory at the Father's right hand. Inexcusable, nevertheless, are parents who delay unconscionably in getting their children baptized. The beatific vision, the vision of God in *heaven, is a gift far too precious to be exposed even to the slightest question.*

BAPTISM OF BLOOD. *From the beginning the Christian community held that Baptism of blood, i.e., martyrdom for Christ, makes up for the lack of water Baptism. They could point to our Lord's words: "Whoever loses his life for my sake will save it" (Lk 9:24). The Holy Innocents and catechumens martyred for Christ received this Baptism. Tertullian (d. ca. 220), in his work on Baptism (chap. 16), speaking of martyrdom says: "This is the Baptism that takes the place of the actual Baptism that was not received."*

BAPTISM OF DESIRE. *This baptism is received by persons who truly want to be baptized but are prevented—by an untimely death, for example. If there was a sincere desire for Baptism together with sorrow for sins committed, the desire is accounted by God as actual Baptism by water. The desire exists most clearly when it is explicit or conscious, but it may also be implicit and unconscious, as in persons who through no fault of their own do not know Christ or the Church yet strive by God's grace to do His will as they know it.*

Such persons can be presumed to have Baptism of desire, meaning they would be prepared to receive Baptism if they knew of it and Christ's command to be baptized. Some contemporary theologians would extend Baptism of desire to infants, God in some way enabling them to have this desire before death. St. Ambrose mentions Baptism of desire in his funeral sermon for the Emperor Valentinian II (d. 392), who was murdered before he could receive water Baptism.

136. *What are the effects of Baptism?*

1. **Baptism imprints the soul with the indelible mark of the Christian;**
2. **it takes away original sin, all personal sin, and all temporal and eternal punishment due to sin —assuming repentance;**
3. **it confers sanctifying grace.**

"You have been washed, consecrated, justified in the name of our Lord Jesus Christ and in the Spirit of our God" (1 Cor 6:11).

Baptism is a Sacrament of incorporation in Christ. It makes us members of the Body of Christ, members of the Catholic Church. Christ is the head, we are the members. He is the vine, we are the branches.

Though Baptism remits all sin and all punishment due to sin (assuming repentance), other consequences of original sin remain: death, temptation to evil, and the sufferings and tribulations of life. These consequences survive, not as punishment but as means of gaining merit.

The indelible mark (character) imprinted on the soul through Baptism is like a seal that identifies the Christian as belonging to Christ. St. John speaks of the seal impressed "on the foreheads of the servants of our God" (Rv 7:3; cf. 9:4; 14:1). The baptismal seal is not visible, but the Christian's conduct is, and it should testify to the invisible seal that claims us permanently for Christ.

137. Why does the Church require godparents?

Godparents, together with the parents, should make the baptismal promises for the child and be helpful to the parents in the care and upbringing of the child.

The practice of having godparents arose very early in the Church and subsequently was made a requirement of Church law. The Roman Catechism issued after the Council of Trent complained that too many godparents seemed to have no awareness of the sacredness of their responsibilities. That was 400 years ago. One is tempted to say that not much has changed, unfortunately. In the new Rite of Baptism mandated by the Second Vatican Council the responsibilities of godparents are reaffirmed and accentuated. Among other things, godparents should be practicing Catholics; otherwise they cannot be a Catholic example to the child.

"The godparent should (1) be mature enough to undertake this responsibility; (2) have received the Sacraments of initiation (Baptism, Confirmation, and the Eucharist); (3) be a member of the Catholic Church, canonically free to carry out this office. A baptized and believing Christian from a separated church or community may act as a godparent or Christian witness along with a Catholic godparent, at the request of the parents and in accord with the norms for various ecumenical cases" (Rite of Baptism for Children, *General Introduction, no. 10*).

Christian parents should give their children names of Saints, who can be an example and inspiration to the children. These names in practice should not be so corrupted and mutilated that no one knows what the real name is. Davey for David is one thing, but "Mutt" for Matthew! Some parents, wanting to be "modern," give their children names of superstars and celebrities that tickle the popular imagination but have absolutely no relationship to the Christian life. Such children are to be pitied because all through life they will have a name that not only has no Christian meaning but quite often has no meaning at all. It is a good idea for parents, when in doubt, to ask their pastor if a name they have in mind is a Saint's name.

138.   *What is the Rite of Christian Initiation of Adults?*

The Rite of Christian Initiation of Adults is the process by which adults are prepared for Baptism and reception into the Church in several stages.

The various stages of this Rite are:

1) *Pre-catechumenate:* a period of iniquiry, instruction, and evangelization. The community (including both the clergy and the laity) introduces its beliefs and life to a seeking person.

2) *Catechumenate:* a period (of several years) of formal instruction and progressive formation and familiarity with the Christian life.

3) *Election:* period of prebaptism and enlightenment, from the beginning of Lent to reception of the Sacraments of Initiation—Baptism, Confirmation, Holy Eucharist. Special rites are celebrated within the Sunday Liturgy, offering the candidates the support of the community's prayers and subjecting them to the scrutinies, introducing them to the Creed and the Lord's Prayer, and eliciting the choice of a name and final statement of intention.

4) *Post-baptismal Catechesis:* a period that draws the newly-baptized into full participation in the community through observance of the Easter Season and association with the faithful.

The candidates have sponsors who know and help them, bear witness to the community concerning their morals, faith, and intention, show the candidates the place of the Gospel in their own lives and in society, and watch over the progress of the new baptismal life.

By introducing the Rite on January 6, 1972, the Church implemented the express desire of Vatican II: "The catechumenate for adults, comprising several distinct steps, is to be restored and to be put into use. . . . By this means the period of the catechumenate, which is intended as a time of suitable instruction, may be sanctified by sacred rites to be celebrated at successive intervals" *(Constitution on the Sacred Liturgy,* no. 64).

Confirmation

---

139. *What is Confirmation?*

Confirmation is the Sacrament in which the Christian is strengthened for the mature practice and profession of the faith.

To profess one's faith means to bear witness to it in our life, so that people will see that we are Catholic. Some obvious ways of doing this are: going to Mass regularly, especially on Sundays and holydays; attending religious instruction classes; receiving the Sacraments; defending the faith against attacks, and in general living as our Catholic faith requires.

The word "confirmation" is a Latin derivative meaning to make firm or steadfast (in the faith). In the Dogmatic Constitution on the Church, *Vatican II says: "They [the faithful] are more perfectly bound to the Church by the Sacrament of Confirmation, and the Holy Spirit endows them with special strength so that they are more strictly obliged to spread and defend the faith, both by word and by deed, as true witnesses of Christ" (no. 11).*

140. *What are the sacramental effects of Confirmation?*

1. **Confirmation produces the indelible mark (character) that identifies the servant and soldier of Christ;**
2. **it gives us the fullness of the Holy Spirit, to help us remain true to the faith and to profess and defend it against enemies of the soul;**
3. **it increases sanctifying grace;**
4. **and it imparts a more intimate linking with the Holy Eucharist.**

On the day of the feast of Pentecost, the Holy Spirit came down in an extraordinary way on the Apostles as they were gathered together with Mary, the Mother of Jesus, and the group of disciples. They were so "filled with" the Holy Spirit (Acts 2:4) that by divine inspiration they began to proclaim "the mighty works of God." Peter regarded the Spirit Who had thus come down upon the Apostles as the gift of the Messianic age (see Acts 2:17f). Those who believed the Apostles' preaching were then baptized and they too received "the gift of the Holy Spirit" (Acts 2:38).

From that time on the Apostles, in fulfillment of Christ's wish, imparted the gift of the Spirit to the newly baptized by the laying on of hands to complete the grace of Baptism. Hence it is that the Epistle to the Hebrews lists among the first elements of Christian instruction the teaching about Baptism and the laying on of hands (6:2). This laying on of hands is recognized by Catholic Tradition as the beginning of the Sacrament of Confirmation, which in a certain way perpetuates the grace of Pentecost in the Church. (See Paul VI: Apos. Constitution on the Sacrament of Confirmation).

141. *How is Confirmation conferred?*

Confirmation is conferred through the anointing with chrism on the forehead, which is done by the laying on of hand, and through the words: "Be sealed with the Gift of the Holy Spirit."

The whole rite has a twofold meaning. The laying on of hands on the candidates by the Bishop is the Biblical gesture by which the giving of the Holy Spirit is invoked. The anointing with chrism and the accompanying words express clearly the effects of the giving of the Spirit. Signed with the perfumed oil, the baptized persons receive the indelible character, the seal of the Lord, together with the gift of the Spirit which conforms them more closely to Christ and gives them the grace of spreading the Lord's presence.

Formerly, in the early centuries of the Church, Confirmation was administered with Baptism or soon after; this is still the practice of Eastern Rite Catholics, who confirm infants after their Baptism. In time, in the Western Church, Confirmation came to be administered some years after Baptism. Normally, the bishop confirms. If need be, however, any priest can be authorized by the bishop to confirm.

The Holy Eucharist

142. *What is the Holy Eucharist?*

The Holy Eucharist is the Sacrament in which Christ Himself is truly though not visibly present as God and Man, with His glorified Body and Blood, under the appearances of bread and wine, to offer Himself on the altar as our Sacrifice and to give Himself as our sacrificial food.

"The Eucharist is a memorial of the Lord's passion, death, and resurrection. This holy sacrifice is both a commemoration of a past event and a celebration of it here and now. Through, with, and in the Church, Christ's sacrifice on the cross and the victory of His resurrection become present in every celebration.

"The eucharistic celebration is a holy meal which recalls the Last Supper, reminds us of our unity with one another in Christ, and anticipates the banquet of God's kingdom. In the Eucharist, Christ the Lord nourishes Christians, not only with His word but especially with His body and blood, effecting a transformation which impels them toward greater love of God and neighbor" *(National Catechetical Directory,* no. 120).

By thus increasing charity within the visible community, the Eucharist "makes the Church." It builds up the Church as the authentic community of the People of God, as the assembly of the faithful characterized by unity.

Jesus is truly present, not only in remembrance, or merely by His power and grace. Other names for the Holy Eucharist are: Body of Christ, Sacrifice of the Mass, Holy Communion, Table of the Lord, Bread of Life, Bread of Angels, Viaticum, Blessed Sacrament, Sacrament of the Altar.

143. *In what words did Jesus promise the Holy Eucharist?*

Jesus promised the Holy Eucharist in the words: "The bread I will give is my flesh, for the life of the world. At this the Jews quarreled among themselves, saying, 'How can he give us his flesh to eat?' Thereupon Jesus said to them: 'Let me solemnly assure you, if you do not eat the flesh of the Son of Man and drink his blood, you have no life in you. He who feeds on my flesh and drinks my blood has life eternal, and I will raise him up on the last day. For my flesh is real food and my blood is real drink' " (Jn 6:51-55).

Read the entire discourse of Jesus on the Bread of Life in John 6:25-58.

144.   *When did Jesus institute the Holy Eucharist?*

Jesus instituted the Holy Eucharist on the night before He suffered and died.

The institution of the Holy Eucharist is commemorated on Holy Thursday. The greatest Memorial of our Lord's Eucharist after Holy Thursday is Easter Sunday, the day after Christ's Resurrection from the dead. The Solemnity of Corpus Christi also celebrates this institution.

145.   *How did Jesus institute the Holy Eucharist?*

Jesus took bread, blessed it, broke it, gave it to his disciples and said: "Take this, all of you, and eat it; this is my body which will be given up for you."

In the same way Jesus took the cup, blessed it, gave it to his disciples and said: "Take this, all of

you, and drink from it; this is the cup of my blood, the blood of the new and everlasting covenant. It will be shed for you and for all men so that sins may be forgiven. Do this in memory of me."
(Mt 26:26-28; Mk 14:22-24; Lk 22:19-20; 1 Cor 11:23-26)

There are minor variations in the wording of the institution as recorded by the Synoptics (Mt, Mk, Lk). Their concern was not to match each other word for word but to give the substance of what Jesus said and did on the occasion, and in this they are in perfect agreement. When Jesus says (Mt, Mk) that His blood will be poured out "for the many" or "in behalf of many," He is using an Aramaicism which means the whole of humanity, or all.

146. *What happened when Jesus spoke the words: "This is My body, this is My blood"?*

When Jesus spoke the words: "This is My body, this is My blood," He changed the bread into His sacred Body and the wine into His precious Blood.

147. *What power did Jesus confer upon the Apostles with the words: "Do this in memory of Me"?*

With the words: "Do this in memory of Me," Jesus conferred upon the Apostles the power also to change bread into His sacred Body and wine into His precious Blood.

148. *To whom was the power to change bread and wine handed on?*

The power to change bread and wine was handed on to bishops and priests.

149. *When do bishops and priests exercise this power?*

Bishops and priests exercise the power to change bread and wine at the Consecration of Holy Mass.

However, when bishops and priests consecrate, they do not act in their own name but in the name and with the power of Christ. Because the Consecration takes place on the altar, the Holy Eucharist is also called the "Sacrament of the Altar."

150. *How do we know that Jesus is truly present in the Holy Eucharist?*

That Jesus is truly present in the Holy Eucharist we know

1. from the words by which Jesus promised and instituted this Sacrament;

2. from the teaching of the Apostle Paul and the Church.

For the promise and institution of the Holy Eucharist, see Questions 143 and 145.

According to the clear words of Jesus, the Holy Eucharist is the same Body and the same Blood with which Jesus as Man was born, suffered, died, and rose from the dead.

"Since Christ Himself said: 'This is My Body,' who may doubt it? Since He plainly said: 'This is My Blood,' who may question or think it is not so? Once He changed water into wine. Can He not change wine into blood?" (St. Cyril of Jerusalem, d. 386).

In his discourse on the Bread of Life Jesus contrasts His Bread with the manna that the Israelites ate in the wilderness. They ate yet died. His Bread gives eternal life. It should also be noted that at the time of Christ the figurative meaning of "eating someone's flesh" was "to hate someone with deadly hatred." Consequently, when Jesus said "he who eats

My Flesh," He could only mean it literally, because the other sense (to hate with deadly hatred) is here out of the question. (Compare our English phrase "to eat someone out," i.e., to castigate, etc.)

Christ spoke the words of institution in His native Aramaic, which has no linking verb ("to be"). Hence His actual words were: "This, My Flesh," and "This, My Blood of the Covenant." Instead of the sacrificial flesh of the Jewish Passover lying there on the table where Jesus was reclining with the Twelve, He offers Himself as the new Paschal Sacrifice.

151. What does the Apostle Paul teach about the Holy Eucharist?

The Apostle Paul teaches: "Is not the cup of blessing we bless a sharing in the blood of Christ? And is not the bread we break a sharing in the body of Christ?" (1 Cor 10:16).

152. What does the Church teach about the Holy Eucharist?

The Church teaches what she has always taught, from the time of the Apostles to the present day: that in the Holy Eucharist Jesus Christ is truly present, actually, uniquely, God and Man, whole and entire.

"We are taught that this consecrated food is the Flesh and Blood of the incarnate Son of God" (St. Justin, d. 166). — "What seems bread is not bread, though it taste so, but is the Body of Christ; what seems wine is not wine, though it seem so to the taste, but is the Blood of Christ" (St. Cyril of Jerusalem, d. 386). — "Christ was holding Himself in His own hands as He held out His sacred Body and said: 'This is My Body' " (St. Augustine, d. 430).

All Eastern Churches who separated from the Catholic Church maintain belief in the Real Presence of Christ in the Holy Eucharist.

153. *What did the Protestant Reformers teach about the Holy Eucharist?*

The Protestant Reformers taught that the words of Christ are not to be taken literally.

Ulrich Zwingli (d. 1551) said that the words "this is My Body, this is My Blood" mean: this bread is a sign of My Body, this wine is a sign of My Blood. Hence, the bread and wine are only symbols for Christ's Body and Blood.

Martin Luther (d. 1546) taught that in the celebration of the Eucharist bread and wine are not changed but at the moment of Communion the faith of the communicant somehow brings the Body of Christ into the bread and the Blood of Christ into wine. Therefore, when believing communicants receive the bread they also receive the Body of Christ, and when receiving the wine also receive the Blood of Christ.

John Calvin (d. 1564) taught that what is received in the Eucharist is not Christ's Body and Blood but Christ's Spirit and power.

The contemporary ecumenical process is marked by interfaith discussion on the Eucharist (and other doctrinal points) between the Catholic Church and separated Christian bodies. Such attempts to identify and build on common ground warrant our prayerful support.

154. *Under what appearances is Jesus Christ present in the Holy Eucharist?*

Jesus Christ is present in the Holy Eucharist under the appearances of bread and wine, which are the outward signs of this Sacrament.

Jesus chose bread and wine as the outward signs of this Sacrament because bread and wine best symbolize the inward grace of the Sacrament.

155. *What is meant by the "appearances of bread and wine"?*

By the "appearances of bread and wine" is meant what the senses perceive: form, color, taste, and smell of bread and wine.

Jesus Christ veils Himself from our senses,

1) so that we may approach this holy Sacrament with childlike trust;

2) so that through firm faith in His presence we may gain much merit: "Blest are they who have not seen and have believed" (Jn 20:29).

156. *Is only the Body of Christ present under the form of bread, and only the Blood of Christ under the form of wine?*

No, both the Body and the Blood are present under each form, i.e., both are present under the appearances of bread, and both are present under the appearances of wine.

The Jesus Who is present in the Holy Eucharist is not dead but living. Therefore He is present whole and entire in each of the outward signs (appearances of bread and wine), present in each with flesh and blood, with body and soul, and as God and Man.

As the human soul is totally present in every part of the human body, so Jesus is totally present in the least particle of the consecrated host and in the least drop of the consecrated chalice.

Only the bread (the host), not the unseen Christ it contains, can be broken or divided.

157. *Why, then, did Jesus institute the Holy Eucharist under two outward signs, the form of bread and the form of wine?*

Jesus instituted the Holy Eucharist under the two outward signs so that the Mass would more clearly present the Sacrifice on the Cross, where the Blood was separated from the Body, and at the same time would graphically express the meal-aspect of the rite, which recalls the Last Supper.

158. *What is a sacrifice?*

A sacrifice is a visible gift offered to God for the purpose of worshiping Him and honoring Him as highest Lord.

The word "sacrifice" is a Latin derivative meaning "to make sacred," hence to dedicate or offer to God. When a soldier dies for his country, we say that he made the supreme sacrifice. When the father of a family works hard and denies himself many things for the sake of his children, we say that he sacrifices himself for them. If the soldier or the father makes this sacrifice also for love of God, he fulfills the meaning of sacrifice as something given to God for His honor and glory. In this sense, people of the Old Testament offered sacrifices to God: e.g., Cain and Abel, Noah, Abraham, Melchizedek, the Prophets, the priests of the temple in Jerusalem, and others. The Gospels tell of the poor widow who made an offering of her last pennies to the temple treasury, a real sacrifice for her (Mk 12: 42; Lk 21:2).

In the Dogmatic Constitution on the Church, *Vatican II* says of the laity: "*All their works, prayers, and apostolic endeavors, their ordinary married and family life, their daily occupations, their physical and mental relaxation, if carried out in the Spirit, and even the hardships of life, if patiently borne—all those become 'spiritual sacrifices acceptable to God through Jesus Christ' (1 Pt 2:5). Together with the offer-*

ing of the Lord's Body, they are most fittingly offered in the celebration of the Eucharist. Thus, like those everywhere who adore in holy activity, the laity consecrate the world itself to God" (no. 34).

159. What is the Sacrifice of the New Covenant?

The Sacrifice of the New Covenant is the Sacrifice of Jesus Christ on the Cross, which becomes present in an unbloody manner in the Sacrifice of the Mass (the Eucharist).

See Questions 142, 144, 145ff.

In the *Dogmatic Constitution on the Church,* Vatican II says: "As often as the Sacrifice of the Cross in which Christ our Passover was sacrificed (1 Cor 5:7) is celebrated on the altar, the work of our Redemption is carried on, and, in the Sacrament of the Eucharistic Bread, the unity of all believers who form one body in Christ (1 Cor 10:17) is both expressed and brought about. All human beings are called to this union with Christ, Who is the light of the world, from Whom we go forth, through Whom we live, and toward Whom our whole life strains" (no. 3).

In the *Constitution on the Sacred Liturgy* we read: "At the Last Supper, on the night when He was betrayed, our Savior instituted the Eucharistic Sacrifice of His Body and Blood. He did this in order to perpetuate the Sacrifice of the Cross throughout the centuries until He should come again, and so to entrust to His beloved spouse, the Church, a memorial of His Death and Resurrection: a Sacrament of love, a sign of unity, a bond of charity, a Paschal banquet in which Christ is eaten, the mind is filled with grace, and a pledge of future glory is given to us" (no. 37).

160. What is the Holy Sacrifice of the Mass?

The Holy Sacrifice of the Mass is the perpetual unbloody sacrifice of the New Covenant in which the Sacrifice of the Cross is made sacramentally yet truly present.

Simply stated, the Mass is the same sacrifice as the Sacrifice of the Cross.

The word "Mass" derives from the Latin "missa," which stems from the Latin verb "mittere," to send out or away, and more immediately from the Latin noun "missio," a mission or sending. The first meaning of "missa," then, is sending away or dismissal, like the dismissal or dissolution of an official assembly which, among the Romans, was done with a certain solemnity. Similarly, at the end of Mass we have in Latin "Ite, missa est": "Go, it is dismissal" (in the new Liturgy: "The Mass is ended"). It was not long before this term of dismissal was used as a name for the entire celebration of the Eucharist. St. Ambrose seems to have been the first to use it in this sense, in 385, and we find it in general use as early as the 5th century.

The "Ite, missa est" also admits of the interpretation: "Go, it is mission time," time for us to go into the world and into our daily life, and fulfill our mission as Christians, other Christs.

More and more the name "Mass" is being replaced by "Eucharistic Sacrifice" or simply "Eucharist." These designations have merit, but so does "Mass," which ought not be allowed or even compelled to suffer oblivion. It has been much too regnant and time-honored a name for a fate of that kind.

The connection between the Last Supper, the Sacrifice of the Cross, and the Sacrifice of the Mass:

In any discussion of this kind we must remember that we are dealing with a profound mystery of faith and can never explain it to our satisfaction. There comes a point beyond which our finite understanding cannot go and faith in Christ's words must take over.

In the Epistle to the Hebrews we read that Christ offered His Sacrifice, Himself, "once for all" (7:27). There is, accordingly, only one, numerically one, sacrifice of the New Covenant. Consequently, the Mass is not a new sacrifice, different from the Sacrifice of the Cross. Nor does it "repeat" or "multiply" it. The Mass *is* the Sacrifice of the Cross made liturgically yet truly present in all its essential reality under the sacramental signs of bread and wine, signs Christ Himself instituted. In itself, and viewed from God's standpoint, the Sacrifice of Christ is timeless, i.e., without the accidents of time, place, etc. On the Cross it bore the dimension of time, and through the Mass it continues to enter the dimension of time. It is made present in time, inserted as it were in our history and in the particular moment of history that Mass is celebrated. Hence, there is no question of "repeating" Christ's Sacrifice in the Mass, or of adding to or subtracting anything from it.

Moreover, we should not view Christ's Sacrifice on the Cross in isolation from the rest of His redemptive work. In Hebrews 10:5-7, we read that Christ offered Himself to His Father from the moment of His entrance into the world. This oblation of Himself to the Father He never dismissed from His mind but throughout His life He spoke of doing the Father's will (Mt 3:13; Lk 2:21f; Jn 4:35, etc.). Thus, the offering on the Cross is the outward culmination of His lifelong inward offering of Himself to the Father. Moreover, this offering of Himself continues after His Resurrection and Ascension (cf. 1 Jn 2:1-2; Heb 7:35; 8:1; 9:24).

At the Last Supper Christ offered liturgically the Sacrifice He would offer bloodily on the Cross. Hence the Last Supper can also be called the liturgical enactment of the Sacrifice on the Cross. That the Last Supper involved a true sacrifice follows, among other things, from the words Christ used on the occasion, saying: "This is my body to be given for you" (Lk 22:19). In the Old Testament economy of sacrifice a body that is "given" is a sacrifice. And as the Sinai covenant was ratified with the blood of sacrifice (Ex 24:8), so the New Covenant is established and sealed with the blood of Christ in the cup.

Particularly relevant to this discussion is the oldest manual of Christian belief and practice, the *Didache* (so-called *Teaching of the Twelve Apostles)*, which stems from about the year 100. There we read (14:1-3): "On the Lord's

Day come together, break the bread, and celebrate the Eucharist. First, however, confess your sins so that your sacrifice may be pure. . . . For so did the Lord say: 'In every place and at all times a pure sacrifice shall be offered to Me. For I am a great King, says the Lord, and my name is great among the Gentiles.' "

The reference to the prophecy of Malachi (1:11) is unmistakable: "From the rising of the sun, even to its setting, my name is great among the nations. And everywhere they bring sacrifice to my name, and a pure offering." The inference is obvious: St. Irenaeus, who died as bishop of Lyons ca. 200, also writes in his work *Against Heresies* (IV, 17, 5) that in the Mass the prophecy of Malachi is fulfilled.

Irenaeus thus testifies to the belief of the early Church that what Malachi had foretold comes to pass in the Sacrifice of the Mass. The prophecy itself compels this conclusion, because the technical language of the primitive text points not only to an unbloody sacrifice but to one that is continual and offered everywhere. These features obviously do not apply to the historical Sacrifice on the Cross; they can only refer to its being made present in the Sacrifice of the Mass, as the early Christians already believed.

The Council of Trent addressed itself directly to the question of the Mass as sacrifice. In its session of September 17, 1562, it declared that the Mass is not only a meal or remembrance of a past sacrifice but a true sacrifice with propitiatory and supplicatory value. It was offered by Christ and at His command by the Apostles. And it is offered by their successors, the bishops, who have the power to ordain priests and commission them to celebrate Mass.

But the Mass is not a self-standing reality, as though it could exist without the Sacrifice of the Cross. Nor, as we have said, does it "repeat" or even "renew" that sacrifice. The Mass is the Sacrifice of the Cross made sacramentally yet truly present in time. It perpetuates the reality of this Sacrifice in human history, making it truly and really present through time whenever and wherever Mass is celebrated.

JESUS CELEBRATED THE FIRST MASS AT THE LAST SUPPER
"Jesus took the cup, blessed it, gave it to his disciples and said:
'Take this, all of you, and drink from it; this is the cup of my
blood. . . . Do this in memory of me" (Mt 26:26ff; Mk 14:22ff;
Lk 22:19f; 1 Cor 11:23ff).

Making Christ's Sacrifice present at the altar adds nothing to it. As the Sacrifice of One Who is both God and Man, it has infinite value and its power to redeem is similarly unlimited. But the Mass makes it possible for us to enter more directly into Christ's Sacrifice and make it more perfectly our own, as our Lord commanded at the Last Supper. We for our part can bring something to it, our own total surrender to God, the oblation of our own will to the Father's will, so that joined with Christ in His Sacrifice He may "present us to God holy, free of reproach and blame" (Col 1:22).

Finally, we should be ever mindful of what was said at the beginning, that the Sacrifice of the Mass is a profound mystery of our faith. It is laudable to try to learn more about it, but in this life at any rate it will always elude comprehension. The worshiper "in spirit and in truth" accepts it in faith—faith and the humility of faith.

161. Since what time has the Catholic Church offered the Sacrifice of the Mass?

The Catholic Church has offered the Sacrifice of the Mass since the time of the Apostles.

With the words "Do this as a remembrance of me" (Lk 22:19) Christ gave the Apostles and their successors the power and the command to celebrate Holy Mass.

Writing around the year 57, Paul admonishes the Corinthians to assemble "to eat ... the Lord's Supper.... Every time you eat this bread and drink this cup you proclaim the death of the Lord until he comes" (1 Cor 12:20). — "Daily, Christ's precious Body and Blood is offered on the table filled with mystery" (St. Hippolytus, ca. 230). — "We offer in the Church the holy, life-giving and unbloody sacrifice" (St. Cyril of Alexandria, d. 444).

162. To whom is the Holy Sacrifice of the Mass offered?

The Holy Sacrifice of the Mass is offered to God the Father.

At Mass we also remember the Saints, to ask them for their intercession or to thank God for the graces He gave them and through them to us.

163. Who celebrates the Mass?

1. **The principal celebrant of the Mass is Christ Himself.**
2. **The second celebrant is the general body of the faithful and the community here and now assembled.**
3. **The third celebrant is the bearer of the official priesthood who stands at the altar.**

"Christ is always present in His Church, especially in her liturgical celebrations. He is present . . . in the person of His minister. . . . The Liturgy is considered as an excercise of the priestly office of Jesus Christ; . . . in the Liturgy the whole public worship is performed by the Mystical Body of Jesus Christ, that is, by the Head and His members" (Vatican II: *Constitution on the Sacred Liturgy,* no. 7).

164. Who benefits from the spiritual fruits of the Mass?

All members of the Church, living and dead, benefit from the spiritual fruits of the Mass.

Persons who devoutly participate at Mass or have Mass celebrated for themselves benefit in a special way. It is a pious practice to ask that Mass be offered for some spiritual or temporal need, for a deceased loved one, for the Poor Souls, or simply in thanksgiving to God.

It is customary for a person who wants a Mass offered for his or her intention to give the priest an alms, i.e., a Mass stipend. The stipend is not a payment for the graces of the Mass, which would be the sin of simony. It is a contribution to the support of the priest. It expresses a desire to share more personally in the fruits of the Mass by adding to it "a form of sacrifice which contributes in a particular way to the needs of the Church and especially to the sustenance of its ministers" (Paul VI, *Apostolic Letter on Mass Stipends,* June 13, 1974). No Mass, however, can be offered exclusively for a private intention. Every Mass of its very nature is offered to glorify God, to bring salvation to all the world, and the infinite fruits of Christ to all the faithful.

The Mass stipend grew out of the Preparation of the Gifts ("Offertory") of the Mass. The faithful brought bread and wine and other gifts to be blessed and offered at the altar. These offerings, or some of them, were used after Mass for the agape, the meal shared after Mass by the faithful in attendance. When the custom of the agape meal ceased, the priests used the offerings for the poor and their own support. In time, from the 8th century on, instead of gifts in kind the faithful brought a monetary alms. Thus the principle of the Mass stipend was established.

Nevertheless, as far as the fruits of the Mass are concerned, the rich person who can afford many stipends is not necessarily better off than the poor person, to whom even one stipend may be a considerable sum. First, no priest denies a request for a Mass just because no stipend is tendered. But most importantly, the outward gift, the stipend alone, is not what determines whether a person's share in the fruits of the Mass is large or small. The inner attitude of the soul, the offering of ourselves to God, and the surrender to His will, counts more with Him than the outward gift of the stipend. What our Lord said of the widow's mite applies here (Mk 12:41-44), a clear case where less was more.

165.   *Do the people have a part in the Mass?*

In the Mass (as in all liturgical celebrations) each person has an office to perform; the people take part by means of acclamations, responses, psalmody, antiphons, and songs, as well as by actions,

gestures, bodily attitudes, and a reverent silence at the proper time.

In order that the faithful of a community who come together may fully represent the Church, their Assembly must have a quality essential to the Church, *a hierarchical* structure of persons differing in rank and function.

The distribution of liturgical roles is of the highest importance as a sign; this sign clearly manifests that the Assembly is not a haphazard gathering of people, but a manifestation of the Church. It is the combined action of those exercising different roles which comprises the Liturgy.

The Assembly is composed of (1) the presiding priest and his ministers at the altar (for example, servers and deacon), (2) other liturgical ministers, such as readers, commentator, leader of song, extraordinary ministers of Communion, and ushers, and (3) the people in the pews. Each of these has a role to carry out in the celebration.

166.   *What are the "people's parts" of the Mass?*

The "people's parts" are those parts of the Mass that pertain to the people as their right and duty flowing from the general priesthood bestowed on them by Baptism.

The Second Vatican Council stated in the *Constitution on the Sacred Liturgy:* "The revision of liturgical books must carefully attend to the provision of rubrics also for the people's parts" (no. 31).

The Eucharistic celebration is an action of the community assembled together to render worship to God. This requires both *external* and *internal* participation on the part of all present. One type of participation alone is not sufficient.

We must enlist not only our minds and our hearts in the service of God's worship but our bodies as well: our tongues and lips, our hands and feet, our arms and legs, etc. The whole person who is called upon to praise and glorify the Creator.

This does not mean that we must be preoccupied with external responses to every word or action of the celebrant and ministers. It does mean, however, that we must make an effort to respond whenever we can, without making our response a mere formality which has no interior attitude behind it. By dwelling on the content of our parts, we can participate at Mass *fully, actively, and consciously* as desired by the Church.

For the people's parts run throughout the entire celebration and they are so varied as to dissipate boredom and encourage true worship in us. They include simple responses such as "Amen," "Thanks be to God," and "Glory to you, Lord," as well as second halves of dialogues, such as "We lift them up to the Lord" and "It is right to give him thanks and praise," in addition to chants and prayers.

Among the latter are the Penitential Rite, the Profession of the Faith, the General Intercessions (Prayer of the Faithful), and the Lord's Prayer. Then there are the parts which in themselves constitute a rite or action: the Gloria, the Responsorial Psalm, the Sanctus, and the Memorial Acclamation at the Consecration, as well as the Song after Communion. Finally, some of the parts accompany a rite such as the songs at the entrance, offertory, breaking of the bread, and Communion. (See General Instruction to the Roman Missal, nos. 14-17.)

In an address delivered on March 17, 1965, Pope Paul VI said: "Previously, our presence [at Mass] was sufficient; now we demand attention and action . . . ; now we must listen and pray. The congregation will be alive and active—participation means that the activity flows from the soul, whether it be through paying attention, responding, singing, or gesturing."

167. *How can we best celebrate the Mass?*

We can best celebrate the Mass by a full, conscious, and active participation that is both external and internal as well as sacramental (through Communion).

We must be united in faith and love and avoid any appearance of singularity or division. It is as a *group* that the Word of God is addressed to us and that we are invited to pray, to sing, to perform actions and take certain positions. It is therefore as a group that we should respond.

Lest this common participation degenerate into mere outward conformity for the sake of good order, it should be motivated by a deep religious sense of our office to be a sign of the Mystery of the Church.

168.   What benefit do we derive from the Mass?

Through the Mass we encounter Christ in His saving Mysteries and are filled with grace.

"Recalling thus the Mysteries of Redemption, the Church opens to the faithful the riches of her Lord's powers and merits, so that these are in some way made present for all time, and the faithful are enabled to lay hold upon them and become filled with saving grace" (Vatican II: *Constitution on the Sacred Liturgy,* no. 102).

The greater is our love for God and Christ and the greater is the love we infuse into our participation, so much the greater will be our fruits. Since Christ is acting in the Liturgy, the deeper our desire to be one with Him and His members, the more abundantly will He enrich our souls with His graces.

169.   What else does the Mass do for us?

The Mass instructs us in the Faith, for the Church teaches as she sanctifies.

"Although the Sacred Liturgy is above all things the worship of the Divine Majesty, it likewise contains much instruction for the faithful. For in the Liturgy God speaks to His people and Christ is still proclaiming His Gospel. And the people reply to God both by song and by prayer" *(Constitution on the Sacred Liturgy,* no. 33).

"The ordinary and privileged teaching of the Church is given in the Liturgy" (Pius XI).

Together with Sacred History, the Liturgy is one of the two sources of Catechesis (teaching of the Faith). The unfolding of the liturgical year instructs and forms Christians by bringing them into contact with the person of the Savior through the actualization of successive events in the life of Christ —from His eagerly awaited birth at Christmas to His glorious life as Mystical Head poured out at Pentecost through the action of the Holy Spirit and always acting in His Church.

170. What is the altar?

The altar is the table of sacrifice on which the Sacrifice of the Mass is offered.

At the Last Supper Christ used a table. The early Christians also used ordinary tables. Even today the part of the altar on which the sacrifice is offered is called *mensa*, table. Altars in general still resemble, some more some less, a table. We could also say they are like a closed coffin, because they may contain relics of saints. The altar represents Christ, the "corner stone" of the Church. Five crosses are engraved on the top, recalling the five wounds of Christ.

In the Constitution on the Sacred Liturgy, *Vatican II directs that norms governing the "construction of sacred buildings, the shape and construction of altars," be revised. This revision was embodied in the "General Instruction of the Roman Missal," revised by decree of the Second Vatican Council and published by authority of Pope Paul VI: "The main altar should be freestanding so that the ministers can easily walk around it and Mass can be celebrated facing the people. It should be placed in a central position which draws the attention of the whole congregation" (no. 262).*

171. What is the Roman Missal?

The Roman Missal is the book that contains the texts and rites for the celebration of Mass. It is

divided into two parts, which are now published in separate volumes: The *Sacramentary* contains the Prayers (including the Order of Mass) and is used at the altar; the *Lectionary* contains the Biblical Readings and is used at the ambo.

In the primitive Church, the Prayers and Readings for the Eucharist were decided upon by each bishop for his own church in accord with local tradition. As time went on, Prayers began to be gathered together for various occasions and eventually gave rise to collections of Prayers, called *Sacramentaries.* Bible Readings also began to be fixed for certain occasions and gave rise to *Gospel Books* and *Lectionaries.*

Around the 10th century, both Prayers and readings began to be collected into one book, which came to be known as a *Missal* or *Mass Book.* The most famous such book was the *Roman Missal,* that is, the one in accord with the Roman Church, which became widespread through its use by the mendicant Friars and the traveling officials of the Roman Curia. In 1570, in line with the directives of the Council of Trent, Pius V published a revised edition of the *Roman Missal* which became the one used throughout the world.

In 1963, the Second Vatican Council, in its *Constitution on the Sacred Liturgy* (no. 25), decreed that this Missal be revised and made intelligible to people of our day. The reform was carried out in two parts in the official Latin edition. In 1970, the new *Lectionary* was issued in three volumes and the new *Sacramentary* was published in one volume. In the United States, this new Roman Missal went into effect in two phases. In 1970 the new Readings were issued in the new *Lectionary for Mass* and in 1974 the new Prayers were issued in the new *Sacramentary.*

172. *What is the "People's Missal"?*

The "People's Missal" is a small-size version of the large Roman Missal, intended to aid the par-

ticipation of the people at Mass. As such, this Missal is a Catechism, Prayer Book, Bible, and Book of Worship all rolled into one.

Over the years many methods have been used to render the Mystery of the Eucharist more comprehensible to the people as it unfolds in the Liturgical Year. There were the "Mystagogical Explanations" of the Fathers of the Church, the early "Commentaries on the Mass," and the "Mass Explanations" of the Carolingian days.

The Middle Ages saw the rise of "Theological Treatments" and "Allegorical Interpretations" that were in keeping with the mentality of that time. Finally, the beginnings of the popular Missal took place after the Council of Trent when the official Mass texts were collected into one source—the *Roman Missal* of Pius V. These forerunners of the "People's Missals" were originally made up of extracts from the Altar Missal with explanations, since the Canon could not be printed in the vernacular.

In the late 19th and early 20th century, the pioneers of the Liturgical Movement created the "People's Missal" so that the faithful could *closely follow* the words and actions of the priest during the Latin Mass. It was the Missal which encouraged and brought about the participation of the Assembly even in Latin Masses.

As a result, there arose a genuine spirituality of the Liturgical Year which was helped by the researches of the Liturgical Movement and the Biblical Renewal. The Missal became a wonderful instrument of Eucharistic spirituality for the people.

If we are to profit spiritually from the ineffable riches which God has placed at our fingertips in the Liturgy we must *know, love,* and *live* it. The best way to do so is by participating *fully, consciously,* and *actively* in that Liturgy.

We must become so involved in the Eucharist *(know it)* that we will make it part of us *(love it)* and bring its effects into our everyday activities *(live it).*

The Missal aids participation by presenting the people with the opportunity to meditate on the liturgical texts before the Eucharist and to go over them afterward. It can be a springboard for attaining a complete knowledge of and genuine love for the Liturgy, inasmuch as it provides at least a minimum knowledge of what is taking place in the Liturgy.

The watchword of those who used Missals in their heyday was: "Follow the Mass with a Missal." With this in mind, some Catholics are beginning to fashion a new watchword: "You don't need a Missal to follow the Mass anymore. But you need a Missal to make the Mass follow you home and in your daily life."

The Missal gives us a *knowledge of the Mystery of Faith.* It is a textbook of the teachings of the Church. But it is not something dead. It is a living instrument of Christian knowledge.

The Missal is a *prayerbook* of our own. It teaches us to pray with the "mind of the Church." This eliminates the dangers of self-centered prayers.

The Missal is an excellent *introduction to the Bible.* It provides us with the Church's commentary on the Word of God and shows us the Bible *in action* in the Liturgy.

Finally, the Missal provides a wonderful *introduction to the Eucharist* and its place in the Sacramental Order. It gives a Liturgical Culture that no other book can impart.

Hence, the Missal is more than simply a must book for those who have a greater role in Liturgies, such as members of the Liturgy Committee, lectors, extraordinary ministers, and choristers. It is this and much more.

The Missal is the one book that is indispensable for us—because it contains all others. It is our *Catechism,* our *Prayer Book,* our *Bible,* and our *Book of Worship* all rolled into one.

173.   Why are candles lighted at Mass?

Candles are lighted at Mass to symbolize Christ as Light of the World and to adorn the celebration.

Christ said: "I am the light of the world. No follower of mine shall ever walk in darkness; no, he shall possess the light of life" (Jn 8:12).

Originally candles were used for purely practical reasons, i.e., to provide light when Mass was celebrated at night. Soon, however, they were also used at daytime Masses. St. Jerome (d. 420) calls the use of candles an old custom, an expression of joy. St. Isidore of Seville (d. 636) gives the reason mentioned in the answer above. He refers to Jn. 1:9 and says that candles symbolize the light of which the Gospel speaks. Already in his day candles burned all during Mass but the candlesticks (candelabra), instead of being on the altar, were placed where the altar boys stood (presumably to tend them). Only since the 12th century have the candles been set on the altar, next to the crucifix. Today in many churches we see a preference for the older custom of not having them on the altar, as well as a tendency to have as few as possible. Yet there is no question that a goodly number of burning candles on or about the altar, especially on feast days, do add luster to the celebration.

Candles spend themselves to give light and warmth. In this they symbolize not only Christ but also the selfless care of Christians for their fellow humans.

174. *In what language is Holy Mass celebrated?*

Formerly, in the Roman Rite, Holy Mass was celebrated in Latin. Today it may be celebrated in the vernacular—that is, the language of the people gathered together for the Eucharist.

In the worship of the primitive Church, the language used was Aramaic, spoken in and around Jerusalem. This quickly gave way to Greek as the Church spread westward. In the 4th century (under Pope Damasus ca. 385), Latin became the official language of the Liturgy of the West.

In the Churches of the Eastern Rite, many different languages were adopted for liturgical use. The practice was to use the vernacular or a language closely related to the native tongue of the people.

In the West, Latin remained as the sole liturgical language until the promulgation of the *Constitution on the Sacred Liturgy* by the Second Vatican Council on December 4, 1963. This stipulated that the people have a right and a duty to participate in the liturgy fully, consciously, and actively. And in order to attain this goal more readily the liturgy was to be revised and the vernacular could be used so that the prayers and ceremonies of divine worship would be more informative and meaningful for all (nos. 11, 14, and 36). Since that time, the vernacular has been introduced into the liturgy of all countries, in accord with the new Liturgical Books approved by the Holy See.

At the same time, Latin remains the official liturgical language of the Western Church *(ibid.,* no. 36) A Latin Mass can be celebrated within the new revised rites as found in the Appendix to the *Sacramentary.* However, the stipulation is that the people who attend it be given the materials for participating in the Mass: "Steps should be taken so that the faithful may also be able to say or sing together in Latin those parts of the Ordinary of the Mass which pertain to them" *(Ibid.,* no. 54).

175. *Which are the liturgical colors for Mass?*

The liturgical colors are: white, red, green, violet, and black. Gold may be used for the first three.

White (the color of joy and innocence) is used for feasts of the Lord other than that of His Passion, as well as feasts of the Mother of God, the Angels, and the Saints who were not martyrs. (It may also be used in funeral Masses.)

Red (the color of love and blood) is used on Passion Sunday and Good Friday, Pentecost, celebrations of the Passion, birthday feasts of the Apostles and Evangelists, and feasts of Saints who were martyrs.

Green (the color of hope) is used on Sundays and Week-days of Ordinary Time (after Epiphany and Pentecost).

Violet (the color of penance) is used in Advent and Lent. It may also be used in Masses for the dead.

Black (the color of mourning) may be used in Masses for the dead. But other colors may also be used in keeping with the greater emphasis on the resurrection.

176. Why does the priest wear special garments for Mass?

The priest wears vestments for Mass:
1. **to indicate that he does not act and pray in his own name but in the name and power of Jesus Christ;**
2. **to stress the sacred character of the celebration.**

Christ and the Apostles did not wear special garments at the Last Supper. Since the 4th century, however, the Church has prescribed vestments for Mass, and this prescription remains in effect.

"Clothes make the man." This applies in a sense to the liturgy, to the vestments worn at Mass. "They give visible form to the human desire to find value, importance, and meaning in life. They are a symbol of the redeemed person, who had 'put on' Christ (Rom 13:14)" (Bishop Hengsbach).

In the Old Testament God gave precise instructions regarding vesture for divine worship (Lv 8:1ff). Then, and still more now, sacred vestments directed attention to the invisible realities in which we believe. In our day particularly, it is important that even by his vestments the priest at the altar show that he is not "doing his own thing" and does not speak and act in his own name—that by himself he can do nothing, and only by the power of Christ does he fulfill his service.

177. *What are the divisions of the Mass?*

The divisions of the Mass are:
1. **Introductory Rites,**
2. **Liturgy of the Word,**
3. **Liturgy of the Eucharist,**
4. **Concluding Rite.**

Eucharist means thanksgiving. We give thanks to the Father in heaven by offering the sacrifice of His Son, Christ our Lord and Redeemer.

178. *What does the "Introductory Rites" include?*

The "Introductory Rites" includes: Entrance Song (or Antiphon), Greeting, Penitential Rite or Rite of Blessing and Sprinkling Holy Water, Kyrie (Lord, Have Mercy), Gloria (Glory to God), and Opening Prayer. The purpose of this is to prepare us as a community to meet Christ as He comes in Word and Sacrament. We gather as a worshiping community to celebrate our unity with Him and with one another.

These parts of the Introductory Rites are succinctly described in the General Instruction of the Roman Missal (nos. 24-32):

Entrance Song: After the people have assembled, the Entrance Song begins, and the priest and ministers come in. The purpose of this Song is to open the celebration, deepen the unity of the people, introduce them to the mystery of the Season or feast, and accompany the procession. If there is no singing, the Antiphon in the Missal is recited either by the people or by some of them or by a reader. Otherwise it is said by the priest after the greeting.

Greeting of the People: As a sign of veneration and greeting, the priest and ordained ministers kiss the altar. Then the priest and congregation make the Sign of the Cross.

THE MASS IS THE MEMORIAL OF CHRIST'S DEATH

"Two insurgents were crucified along with him. . . . People going by kept insulting him. . . . Near the cross of Jesus stood his mother. . . . Jesus cried out in a loud voice, and then gave up his spirit" (Mt 27:38f; Jn 19:25; Mt 27:50).

Through a greeting the priest expresses the presence of the Lord to the assembled community. This greeting and the people's response manifest the Mystery of the Church that is gathered here.

Penitential Rite: After greeting the people, the priest or other suitable minister may very briefly introduce the Mass of the day. Then the priest invites the congregation to take part in the Penitential Rite, which is a general confession made by the entire assembly and is concluded by the priest's absolution.

Kyrie (Lord, Have Mercy): The Kyrie is now begun, unless it has already been included as part of the Penitential Rite. This acclamation, which praises the Lord and implores His mercy, is ordinarily made by all, that is, with parts for the people and for the choir or cantor.

Gloria (Glory to God): This is an ancient hymn in which the Church, assembled in the Spirit, praises and prays to the Father and the Lamb. If it is not sung, it is recited by all together or in alternation.

Opening Prayer: Next the priest invites the people to pray, and together they spend some moments in silence so that they may realize that they are in God's presence and may make their petitions. The priest then says the Prayer which expresses the theme of the celebration and by the words of the priest a petition is addressed to God the Father through the mediation of Christ in the Holy Spirit.

179.   *What does the Liturgy of the Word include?*

The Liturgy of the Word includes:

1. **Readings from the Old and New Testaments as well as a Responsorial Psalm—God's Word listened to;**
2. **Homily—God's Word explained;**
3. **Profession of Faith—God's Word accepted and held fast;**
4. **General Intercession—God's Word appealed to.**

Readings from Scripture and the Chants between the Readings form the main part of the Liturgy of the Word. The Homily, Profession of Faith, and General Intercessions or Prayer of the Faithful develop and complete it. In the Readings, explained by the Homily, God speaks to His people of redemption and salvation and nourishes their spirit; Christ is present among the faithful through His Word. Through the Responsorial Psalm and Alleluia Verse the people make God's Word their own and express their adherence to it through the Profession of Faith. Finally, moved by this Word, they pray in the General Intercessions (Prayer of the Faithful) for the world's salvation.

180. *What does the Liturgy of the Eucharist include?*

The Liturgy of the Eucharist includes:
1. **Preparation of the Gifts: Presentation.**
2. **Eucharistic Prayer: Enactment and Offering of the Sacrifice.**
3. **Communion Rite: Partaking of the Sacrificial Meal.**

The General Instruction of the Roman Missal nicely summarizes the main parts of the Liturgy of the Eucharist and their themes (no. 48):

At the Last Supper Christ instituted the Paschal Sacrifice and Meal. In this meal the Sacrifice of the Cross is continually made present in the Church when the priest, representing Christ, carries out what the Lord did and handed over to His disciples to do in His memory.

Christ took bread and the cup, gave thanks, broke, and gave to His disciples, saying: "Take and eat, this is My Body. Take and drink, this is the cup of My Blood. Do this in memory of Me." The Church has arranged the celebration of the Eucharistic Liturgy to correspond to these words and actions of Christ:

1) In the Preparation of the Gifts, bread, wine, and water are brought to the altar, the same elements which Christ used.

2) The Eucharistic Prayer is the hymn of thanksgiving to God for the whole work of salvation; the offerings become the Body and Blood of Christ.

3) The breaking of the one Bread is a sign of the unity of the faithful, and in Communion they receive the Body and Blood of Christ as the Apostles did from His hands.

181. What takes place at the Preparation of the Gifts?

At the Preparation of the Gifts, the priest prepares the altar and the gifts, prays over the bread and wine, and helps the Assembly get ready for the tremendous Sacrifice which will shortly take place in an unbloody manner.

The General Instruction of the Roman Missal describes this rite in the following way (nos. 49-53):

First, the altar, the Lord's table, is prepared as the center of the Eucharistic Liturgy. The corporal, purificator, chalice, and Missal are placed on it.

The offerings are then brought forward, by the faithful if possible. These are placed on the altar with the accompanying prayers, which speak of God's creative action but also of the constitutive action of human beings. The rite of carrying up the gifts continues the ancient custom when the people brought bread and wine for the Liturgy from their homes. This is also the time to bring forward or to collect money of gifts for the poor and the Church.

The procession with the gifts is accompanied by the *Offertory Song*. The gifts on the altar may be incensed, symbolizing the Church's offering and prayer going up to God.

The priest *washes his hands* as an expression of his desire for inward purification. Then the Preparation of the Gifts concludes with the *invitation to pray* with the priest and the *Prayer over the Gifts* in which the priest asks in the name of the Assembly that the gifts may please God.

"A little water is added to the wine. This was customary in our Lord's time, not only among the Jews, but also among the Greeks and the Romans, and it was done for a practical reason: the wine of the ancients was very heavy and very heady, and one could drink it only after greatly diluting it with water. But very soon, this utilitarian action took on a symbolic meaning and value. It is already known in the 2nd century, in the 3rd century St. Cyprian will explain it as an important teaching, and it will remain traditional. Water, the Book of Revelation tells us, represents the peoples (Rv 17:15). Hence, this mingling has been looked upon as signifying the union in Christ of the Divine nature and the human nature.... We ask that, as Christ became man, we ourselves might be divinized" (A. M. Roguet, The New Mass, pp. 104f).

182. What takes place during the Eucharistic Prayer?

The Eucharistic Prayer is the center and high point of the Mass which makes Christ present for us in His Passion, Death, and Resurrection. During it, the whole congregation joins Christ in acknowledging the works of God and in offering the Sacrifice.

The General Instruction of the Roman Missal (no. 55) sets forth the chief elements of the Eucharistic Prayer:

1) *Thanksgiving* (expressed especially in the Preface): in the name of the entire people of God, the priest praises the Father and gives Him thanks for the work of salvation or for some special aspect of it in keeping with the day, feast, or Season.

2) *Acclamation:* united with the angels, the congregation sings or recites the Sanctus. This acclamation forms part of the Eucharistic Prayer, and all the people join with the priest in singing or reciting it.

3) *Epiclesis:* in special invocations the Church calls on the Holy Spirit and asks that the gifts offered by human beings may be consecrated, that is, become the Body and Blood of

Christ and that the Victim may become a source of salvation for those who are to share in Communion.

4) *Narrative of the Institution and Consecration:* in the words and actions of Christ, the Sacrifice He instituted at the Last Supper is celebrated, when under the appearances of bread and wine He offered His Body and Blood, gave them to His Apostles to eat and drink, and commanded them to carry on this Mystery.

5) *Anamnesis:* in fulfillment of the command received from Christ through the Apostles, the Church keeps His memorial by recalling especially His Passion, Death, Resurrection, and Ascension.

6) *Offering:* in this memorial, the Church—and in particular the Church here and now assembled—offers the Victim to the Father in the Holy Spirit. The Church's intention is that the faithful not only offer the spotless Victim but also learn to offer themselves and daily to be drawn into ever more perfect union, through Christ the Mediator, with the Father and with each other, so that at last God may be all in all.

7) *Intercessions:* the intercessions make it clear that the Eucharist is celebrated in communion with the whole Church of heaven and earth, and that the offering is made for the Church and all its members, living and dead, who are called to share in the salvation and redemption acquired by the Body and Blood of Christ.

8) *Final Doxology:* the praise of God is expressed in the Doxology which is confirmed and concluded by the acclamation of the people.

All should listen to the Eucharistic Prayer in silent reverence and share in it by making the acclamations.

183.   *What takes place at the Consecration?*

At the Consecration the priest changes the bread into the sacred Body of Jesus, and the wine into His sacred Blood.

After the Consecration of the bread the priests holds the Host aloft, and after the Consecration of the wine he does the same with the Chalice, so that we may adore Christ under the appearances of bread and wine. Gazing at the Host and Chalice, we may offer silent prayer like:

Jesus, I live for You, I die for You, Yours I am in life and death.

Jesus, take pity on me, have mercy on me, forgive me all my sins.

Dear Lord, change also my heart, so that I may be a good Catholic. With Your help, may all my thoughts, words, and deeds be pleasing to You.

Or, we may simply gaze believingly on the consecrated species (bread and wine) and adore in silence.

184. What is the Memorial Acclamation?

It is the acclamation at the heart of the Mass by which the people recognize that in the Eucharist the Mystery of Faith is realized, concretely recalled, and offered to our communion.

At this high point of the Eucharistic Liturgy we are called to unite ourselves to the whole economy of salvation, the entire plan of God's love, for the salvation of the world: "Let us recall the Mystery of Salvation."

We do so by responding with one of the four formulas of the Memorial Acclamation: "(1) Christ has died, / Christ is risen, / Christ will come again. / (2) Dying you destroyed our death, / rising you restored our life. / Lord Jesus, come in glory. / (3) When we eat this bread and drink this cup, / we proclaim your death, Lord Jesus, / until you come in glory. / (4) Lord, by your cross and resurrection / you have set us free. / You are the Savior of the world."

It is noteworthy to mention that instead of being addressed to the Father—as is the whole Eucharistic Prayer uttered by the priest—our acclamation is addressed to Jesus in keeping with the spontaneous movement of popular devotion. (Unfortunately, the English translation of the first acclamation above does not retain this important feature of the Latin acclamations—it speaks of Christ but not to Him.)

185. What is the Great Amen?

The Great Amen is the response of the people at the end of the Eucharistic Prayer that gives their assent and affirmation to all that has been done.

This Amen says that we have joined in praising the Father for all His wonderful works and have offered ourselves with Jesus; now we are ready to receive Jesus in Communion.

The Great Amen is a time-honored way in which the Christian Assemblies have given their okay over the years. St. Justin describes this same Acclamation in Roman Liturgies around the year 150. He notes that the people render their assent to the president's prayer by saying "Amen," which is the Hebrew word for "So be it!" "Let it be!"

186. What is the Communion Rite?

The Communion Rite is the conclusion of the Mass. It is the part when God gives a gift to us after we have presented our gift to Him. In both cases the gift is the same—Jesus Christ, the Son of God and Savior of the world. It includes the Lord's Prayer, Sign of Peace, Breaking of the Bread, Lamb of God, Communion of priest and people, and Prayer after Communion.

The General Instruction of the Roman Missal (no. 56) gives a good summary of the parts just mentioned. The following is based on it.

Lord's Prayer: This is a petition both for daily food, which for Christians means also the Eucharistic Bread, and for forgiveness from sin, so that what is holy will be given to the holy.

Sign of Peace: Before they share in the same Bread, the people express their love for one another and beg for peace and unity in the Church and with all mankind.

Breaking of the Bread: This gesture of Christ at the Last Supper gave the entire Eucharistic action its name in apostolic times. In addition to its practical aspect, it signifies that in Communion we who are many are made one Body in the one Bread of life which is Christ.

Lamb of God: This is sung or recited during the Breaking of Bread.

Communion of Priest and People: The priest prepares himself to receive the Body and Blood of Christ by praying quietly. The faithful also do this by praying in silence. The actual rite of administering Communion is itself filled with meaning. The people are *invited* to receive Communion in words from Sacred Scripture: "This is the Lamb of God / who takes away the sins of the world" / (Jn 1:36). "Happy are those who are called to his supper" (Rv 19:9). We accept the invitation also in words from the Scriptures: "Lord, I am not worthy to receive you, / but only say the word and I shall be healed" (Mt 8:9).

Communion Procession: Communion is administered via a procession accompanied by song. This expresses the real unity, spiritual joy, and brotherly love of the people assembled to offer and communicate. At this point, Holy Communion far surpasses a private act of devotion. It is the action of the community whose members are praying for closer unity with Christ and through Him with all the other members of the Assembly and all Christians of the world.

Formula of Administration: The formula of administration and the response of the communicants are very clear and filled with meaning. "The body of Christ: *Amen.*" In St. Cyprian's words: "Remember tnat it is not idly that you say *Amen.* You are professing that you receive the Body of Christ. . . . You answer *Amen,* that is, It is true! Thus, *keep in your heart what you profess with your lips!*"

Silence after Communion: There is also place for private devotion here. After the procession, there is a time of silence and song, if desired. This time may be given to private devotion—but in a communal setting. The Mass and Communion are never our private preserve. They are always communal.

Prayer after Communion: The rite comes to an end with the Prayer after Communion which asks for the fruits of Communion for the whole Church. Our *Amen* evinces our desire to be united with others in our daily lives.

187. What is the Concluding Rite?

The Concluding Rite is the rite that brings the Eucharist to a close with a Blessing and Dismissal, and sends us forth to love and serve the Lord.

After brief announcements, if there are any, the priest *greets* the congregation, gives them his *blessing,* and *dismisses* them with the mission to love and serve the Lord. The *Recessional Procession* then takes place. We join in singing while the ministers and other designated officers of the Mass process out. It is our farewell to them for being helpful in re-enacting and re-presenting the wondrous Mystery of the Mass.

The Mass should bear fruit in our lives. Partaking in the Eucharist means a renewed commitment to God and human beings. We have prayed: "[God], we offer you in thanksgiving this holy and living sacrifice. Look with favor on your Church's offering, and see the Victim [Christ] whose death has reconciled us to yourself.... May he make us an everlasting gift to you" (Eucharistic Prayer III). We hope to make this commitment real during the week "strengthened by the Bread of heaven.

188. What do we receive in Holy Communion?

In Holy Communion we receive the Risen and Glorified Body and Blood of our Lord Jesus Christ as food for eternal life.

Communion means "union with."

189. *By what words did Jesus Christ command us to receive Holy Communion?*

Jesus Christ commanded us to receive Holy Communion by the words: "Let me solemnly assure you, if you do not eat the flesh of the Son of Man and drink his blood, you have no life in you" (Jn 6:53).

Christ did not say how often we should receive Communion. But the Church, which governs in the name of Christ, commands us to receive Communion at least once a year, between the beginning of Lent and the end of the Easter Season. (In the United States the time for the "Easter Duty" is from the first Sunday of Lent to Trinity Sunday inclusive.) In addition, we have a duty to receive in danger of death. This is the minimum. If we love Christ, we will want to receive frequently, daily if possible, as the Church encourages us to do.

For worthy reception of Holy Communion, one must be a baptized Catholic in the state of grace and believe what the Church teaches about this Sacrament. One must also have the right intention, which in the words of Pope Pius X means that "we approach the table of the Lord not simply out of habit, vanity or other human motive, but to please God, to increase our love and union with Him, and as a divine remedy for our weaknesses and faults" (e.g., common sins of the tongue, against charity and the like). — Children also should be encouraged to receive frequent or daily Communion and be taught the right intention.

190. *Why does Holy Communion under one form suffice?*

Holy Communion under one form suffices because even under one form Christ is totally present and received.

Our Lord speaks of receiving Holy Communion under one kind as well as under both but asserts the same grace and efficacy for each kind: "If anyone eats this bread he shall live forever" (Jn 6:51, 58). — Similarly St. Paul: "Whoever eats the bread or drinks the cup of the Lord unworthily sins against the body and blood of the Lord" (1 Cor 11:27). — Even in the early days of the Church many Christians, such as the sick, the imprisoned, and hermits, received Communion under one form, the bread. — Christ's words, "All of you must drink from it," were for the Apostles and their successors whenever they offered the Eucharistic sacrifice.

191. *What are the benefits of the restored option to receive Communion under both kinds?*

The restored option to receive Communion under both kinds is in closer accord with the words of Jesus, rests on strong theological bases, and makes the meaning of Communion clearer and more understandable.

We can enumerate the benefits of receiving Communion under both kinds—that is, under the Sacred Species of Bread and Wine—in part as follows: (1) It stresses the *meal aspect* of the Eucharist and makes it more understandable. (2) It makes the connection between the Eucharistic Meal and the Heavenly Banquet in the Father's Kingdom easier to grasp (see Mt 26:27-29). (3) It shows more clearly how the New and Eternal Covenant is ratified in the Blood of the Lord and strongly reminds us of both Old and New Testament images which speak of *an agreement sealed in blood* between God and human beings. (4) It recalls the *roots* of the Mass *in the Jewish Passover Meal,* a ritual ceremony in which the drinking of wine took place at designated intervals and was accompanied by brief prayers or explanations (see 1 Cor 10:16). (5) It brings out the special, festive, joyful *banquet notion* of the Mass. We celebrate in the context of a sacred meal our Lord's Resurrection from sin and death as well as our own. Bread is a staple food and wine adds a sign of specialness and festivity.

In 1977, the U.S. Bishops' Committee on the Liturgy issued a booklet entitled *The Body of Christ* which nicely summarized the history of this practice:

"The meaning of Holy Communion is more clearly signified when the faithful receive under both kinds, when the members of a congregation not only eat the Lord's Body, but actually drink His Blood under the appearance of wine. It was because of this fuller sign value that the Church from the outset until the 13th century in the West (continuing on to the present in the East) consistently and commonly distributed Communion under both kinds to the laity. This was throughout those years and remains today the fullest expression and most perfect fulfillment of what our Lord said, did and directed: "Let me solemnly assure you, if you do not eat the flesh of the Son of Man and drink His blood, you have no life in you" (Jn 6:53).

"At the same time, the Church always gave Communion under the one kind when circumstances so dictated, and recognized this as a valid, complete, true sacrament. This, Christians received under the sign of Bread alone when communicating at home or when the Eucharist was offered to the sick, to prisoners, or to monks living in isolation. Similarly, Communion under the appearance of wine alone for infants and the gravely ill formed a standard and accepted custom throughout this period.

"Practical difficulties and poor attitudes linked to produce a change in the 13th and 14th centuries. There was, naturally, no denial, but in fact a greater affirmation of the truth that each kind, bread or wine, contained the whole Christ, present Body and Blood, Soul and Divinity, in all the fullness and power of His Life, Sufferings and Resurrection. But the faithful, for complicated historical reasons, approached the Sacraments much less frequently and, unfortunately, failed to realize that the sacrifice and sacrificial meal are one in the Mass. These doctrinal and devotional attitudes, combined with contagion in times of rampant diseases, the possibility of irreverence or spilling, the hesitation of some communicants to drink from the common cup, the large numbers at Easter and other special feasts, and the scarcity of wine in northern countries, led to a gradual abandonment of Communion under both kinds.

"A reaction set in during the 14th century and many reformers urged a return to the early Christian tradition. However, in doing so some maintained that Communion under the sign of bread alone was invalid, a deprivation, an incomplete and erroneous fulfillment of the Lord's teaching in John's gospel. Roman Catholics reacted in the face of those attacks and discouraged or forbade reintroduction of the practice under such doctrinal conditions.

"The Second Vatican Council decreed the restoration of this practice on occasions when it would be pastorally effective and spiritually beneficial (Constitution on the Sacred Liturgy, no. 55). . . .

"The revised Roman Missal specifies fourteen cases when Communion may be distributed under both kinds. . . . The National Conference of Catholic Bishops in the United States . . . added [five] instances. . . .

"In effect Communion under both kinds would then be allowed according to the new legislation on almost any occasion in which a small group gathers for Mass and even in some circumstances when a large congregation celebrates the Eucharist" (pp. 26-29).

192. *What are the benefits of the restored option to receive Communion in the hand?*

The restored option to receive Communion in the hand is in closer accord with the words of Jesus, rests on theological bases, and makes the meaning of Communion clearer and more understandable.

We can enumerate the benefits of receiving Communion in the hand in part as follows: (1) It teaches that *our entire body,* including hand as well as tongue, *shares equally in* the *goodness of God's creation* and in the holiness achieved through Christ's entrance into the world as the Word made flesh (see Gn 1:31; Jn 1:14-16). (2) It reminds us that through the Sacraments of Christian Initiation (Baptism, Confirmation, and Eucharist) we have become temples of the living God (see 2 Cor 6:16), a chosen race, a royal priesthood, a holy nation (see 1 Pt 2:9). We are cleansed and consecrated, rendered sharers in Christ's priesthood, and made a new creation. (3) It forms a positive, human, understandable response to Jesus' invitation to "take and eat." We actually reach out, receive the Lord's Body into our hands, and then communicate ourselves. (4) It appears to be a *more mature* and *adult gesture*. In our culture, normally only infants and the infirm receive food into their mouths from another's hand. (5) It is a more relaxed and hygienic method of distributing Communion. (6) It links together the *presentation of the gifts* and the *reception of the Lord*. The same hands that brought forward and offered the bread and wine earlier in the Mass now receive back these transformed gifts.

The Bishops' Committee booklet on the Body of Christ states:

"For the past thousand years the customary manner of distributing or receiving Communion in the Western Church has been for the minister of the Eucharist to place the consecrated particle directly on the tongue of the communicant. Around the time of Vatican Council II, however, the various liturgical restorations which preceded and followed the Constitution on the Liturgy created the desire in scattered sections of the Church for a return to the practice of the early Christian centuries in which the Eucharistic Bread was placed in the hands of the faithful who then placed it in their own mouths.

"The procedure spread gradually, sometimes without prior approval of the Holy See and occasionally without appropriate preparation of the people. Aware of this, Pope Paul VI surveyed each bishop of the entire Latin Church as to the appropriateness of introducing the option of Communion in the hand. In view of the response, the Holy Father judged that a conference of bishops, by a two-thirds majority, could

petition the Holy See for permission. At its Spring, 1977 session, 190 of the 274 members of the United States hierarchy endorsed this option for the individual communicant, thus attaining the necessary two-thirds majority. Confirmation of this decision by the Holy See was obtained on June 17, 1977" (p. 10).

193.   What are the effects of Holy Communion?

1. **Holy Communion brings us in closest union with Christ and increases sanctifying grace;**
2. **it reduces our inclination to evil and gives strength and desire to lead a good life;**
3. **it remits venial sin and guards against mortal sin;**
4. **it is a pledge of future resurrection and blessedness.**

"The man who feeds on my flesh and drinks my blood remains in me, and I in him. Just as the Father who has life sent me, and I have life because of the Father, so the man who feeds on me will have life because of me" (Jn 6:56-57).

"He who feeds on my flesh and drinks my blood has life eternal, and I will raise him up on the last day" (Jn 6:54).

194.   Who does not gain these benefits of Holy Communion?

A person who receives Communion unworthily, i.e., in mortal sin, does not gain its benefits.

195.   What does the apostle Paul say about unworthy Communion?

The apostle Paul says: "Whoever eats the bread or drinks the cup of the Lord unworthily sins against the body and blood of the Lord. He ... eats and drinks a judgment on himself" (1 Cor 11:27, 29).

Unworthy Communion is a sacrilege an act of extreme disrespect and ingratitude toward our Lord.

196. What must we do to receive Communion worthily?

To receive Communion worthily we must prepare ourselves in body and soul.

"A man should examine himself first; only then should he eat of the bread and drink of the cup" (1 Cor 11:28).

197. How do we prepare the soul?

1. **If we are in mortal sin, we must first make a good sacramental Confession;**
2. **we should also be sorry for our venial sins and strive to overcome them;**
3. **we should participate fully, consciously, and actively in the Mass.**

In general, preparation of the soul is remote or proximate. Remote: by the kind of Catholic life we live overall. Proximate: participation in the Mass, including the acts of prayer and devotion immediately before receiving Holy Communion; these include the prayers of preparation in the Mass itself as well as more personal silent preparation as time permits and the Spirit moves.

Sacramental Confession of mortal sin before Holy Communion is the rule. We may ordinarily not receive Communion simply after making an act of perfect contrition. There may be times when a person in mortal sin cannot easily forgo Holy Communion. In these exceptional circumstances, if sacramental Confession is not immediately possible, it suffices to make an act of perfect contrition with the resolve to confess sacramentally at the next practical opportunity, or at least within a reasonable time. This resolve is critical, because without it no contrition can be perfect.

JESUS REWARDED HUMILITY IN THOSE RECEIVING HIM

"The centurion said [to Jesus], 'I am not worthy to have you under my roof. Just give an order and my boy will get better. . . .' Jesus said, 'Go home. It shall be done because you trusted' " (Mt 8:8, 13).

198. *How do we prepare the body?*

1. **We must abstain from food and liquids (water excepted) one hour before receiving Holy Communion.**
2. **We should also be dressed in a way that shows respect for the Sacrament.**

This bodily preparation not only has a penitential purpose but also honors the sacredness of the Holy Eucharist. Water and necessary medicine do not break the Eucharistic fast.

Fasting for some time before Holy Communion has existed since about the 4th century. Through the Middle Ages the accepted rule was not to eat or drink from midnight on. The Roman Catechism issued by Pope Pius V (d. 1572) after the Council of Trent retained this regulation. It was also kept in force in the 1918 Code of Canon Law.

Change came with World War II, when circumstances of war often made it necessary to put off Mass until late afternoon or an evening hour. The Pope, in consequence, allowed various modifications of the midnight rule. With the continued growth of evening Masses after the war, restoration of the rule was not practical. Accordingly, in 1953 and again in 1957 Pope Pius XII made further modifications, the effect of which was to reduce the fast to three hours for solid foods and one hour for liquids. Yet even this was a hardship for many workers, since it did not leave them sufficient time to eat supper and still be fasting before evening Mass. Hence, it was a welcome move when in November, 1964, Pope Paul VI set the fast at one hour before Communion, both for solid foods and liquids. (Water, as we have said, and medicines never break the Eucharistic fast.)

As for proper dress, common sense should prevail. The Church does not presume to dictate fashion, so long as modesty is preserved. But what might be appropriate for the beach or ballroom is hardly right for church. Just the same, the spirit is more important than the letter, and many times "come as you are" is the way to come, if the alternative is not to come at all.

199. *How should we approach the Table of the Lord?*

We should approach the Table of the Lord with great reverence, hands folded and eyes guarded.

Some people may think this is overdoing it. But to approach with arms swinging and eyes roaming certainly is no improvement, no great mark of respect for the Blessed Sacrament. We ought to bear in mind Whom we go to meet and receive in the Eucharist. Cluny monks of the past offer an example in point. The wheat for the host was sown and harvested to the accompaniment of psalm singing. The choicest kernels were sifted out and brought to the mill, the monks praying the while. And when the flour was ready, they first prayed a part of their choir office and only then set to work on the baking, but in the prayerful silence of their rule. If these monks invested this process, from the planting to the baking, with such great respect, it was because of their reverence for what the product, the host, was to become: the Body of Christ. Some of this reverence could serve us still.

200. *What should we do after Holy Communion?*

After receiving Holy Communion we should give fervent thanks to God.

These are precious moments, right after Holy Communion. Speak to Jesus with the simplicity of a child. The right words are words of adoration, of thanksgiving, of love and devotion, prayer and petition.

201. *How long does Jesus remain present in the Eucharist?*

Jesus remains present in the Eucharist as long as the Sacred Species remain, i.e., the form of bread and the form of wine.

When the Sacred Species cease to be, Christ's presence also ceases. Review Question 155.

202. *Where is the Blessed Sacrament kept?*

Left-over consecrated hosts are kept in a ciborium or other suitable receptacle and placed in the tabernacle.

In the first centuries, when persecutions prevented the building of churches, the faithful brought the Holy Eucharist home in a napkin or small basket so that they might administer Holy Communion to themselves. With the passing of the age of persecution and the ensuing construction of churches, the Blessed Sacrament was preserved in the sacristy (so named from the Sacrament). The custom also developed of keeping it in a pyx (Greek for "box") placed on the altar or suspended over it. The pyx was a flat-bottomed receptacle with a cover. In the 13th century it was given a stem, and so began to resemble the present-day ciborium.

Earlier, in the 12th century, a new development had appeared: hollows formed into the sanctuary wall to serve as little "tabernacles" for the Sacrament. Free-standing tabernacles—little "houses" for the Sacrament—also came into use. Indeed, the free-standing tabernacles we see today have had a long history. The new Missal of Pius V (d. 1572) did not require the tabernacle to be set on the altar, and in fact the Ceremonial for bishops in use in 1600 expressed a preference for celebrating Mass on an altar where the Blessed Sacrament was not reserved.

Still, one finds as early as the 14th century instances of tabernacles resting on the altar. After the Council of Trent, concluded in 1563, this practice became more common and was finally prescribed in the 1918 *Code of Canon Law.* However, in the *Constitution on the Sacred Liturgy* (no. 128), Vatican II ordered a revision of the canons governing, among other things, altars and tabernacles.

Accordingly, the new *Rite of Holy Communion and Worship of the Eucharist outside Mass* (issued by the Holy See in 1973 and approved in English translation in 1976) says:

"Therefore, to express the sign of the eucharist, it is more in harmony with the nature of the celebration that, at the altar where Mass is celebrated, there should if possible be no reservation of the sacrament in the tabernacle from the beginning of Mass. The eucharistic presence of Christ is the fruit of the consecration and should appear to be such.

"The consecrated hosts are to be frequently renewed and reserved in a ciborium or other vessel, in a number sufficient for the communion of the sick and others outside Mass.

"Pastors should see that churches and public oratories where, according to law, the holy eucharist is reserved, are open every day at least for some hours, . . . so that the faithful may easily pray in the presence of the blessed sacrament.

"The place for the reservation of the eucharist should be truly preeminent. It is highly recommended that the place be suitable also for private adoration and prayer so that the faithful may easily, fruitfully, and constantly honor the Lord, present in the sacrament, through personal worship.

"This will be achieved more easily if the chapel is separate from the body of the church, especially in churches where marriages and funerals are celebrated frequently. . . .

"The holy eucharist is to be reserved in a solid tabernacle. It must be opaque and unbreakable. Ordinarily there should be only one tabernacle in a church; this may be placed on an altar or, at the discretion of the local Ordinary, in some other noble and properly ornamented part of the church other than an altar" (General Instruction, nos. 6-10).

203.   What is the vigil or sanctuary lamp?

The vigil or sanctuary lamp is the lamp that burns day and night near the tabernacle to call attention to Christ's abiding presence in the Blessed Sacrament.

The lamp for the Blessed Sacrament came into use about the 11th or 12th century. The *Roman Ritual* of 1604 took note of the practice and recommended its general adoption. Initially only pure beeswax was used for this lamp, but in the course of time olive oil and other vegetable oils found acceptance. Present regulation (Canon 1271) prescribes either beeswax or the aforesaid oils. In 1916, and again in 1942, the Sacred Congregation of Rites granted bishops the faculty to permit electric lights, but clearly this faculty was for exceptional circumstances only.

204. What do we owe the Blessed Sacrament?

We owe the Blessed Sacrament deepest reverence and adoration.

"Let no one eat this Flesh without first worshiping it" (St. Augustine).

As a means of honoring the Blessed Sacrament the Church removes it from the tabernacle, places it on the altar for public adoration, then raises it in blessing—hence the name "Benediction of the Blessed Sacrament." The Benediction service can be conducted with the ciborium (simple form) or the monstrance (more solemn form). The monstrance (from the Latin *monstrare,* to show) is the sacred vessel into which the large consecrated Host is inserted for the adoration service.

Periods of exposition are sometime expanded to "Holy Hours," with prayers, hymns, and quiet meditation. In the *Forty Hours Devotion,* the Sacrament is exposed continuously for a period of one to three days. (Mention should also be made of Eucharistic Congresses held periodically around the world to give God thanks and praise for His Son's presence among us in the Blessed Sacrament.)

In recent years, especially since the Second Vatican Council, there has been a tendency to restrain enthusiasm for devotion to the Blessed Sacrament. Consequently, on September 3, 1965, Pope Paul VI issued an encyclical *(Mysterium fidei,* Mystery of Faith) reiterating Catholic doctrine and worship as regards the Eucharist. Concerning worship he said: "The Catholic Church worships the Holy Eucharist not only during Mass but also apart from Mass, by preserving the consecrated Host with greatest care, and exhibiting it for solemn adoration by the faithful and carrying it in festive procession with the people.... The faithful should not neglect visits to the Blessed Sacrament; such visits are evidence of thankfulness and a sign of the love and honor we owe to Christ the Lord, present in the Sacrament."

Likewise, the new Rite of Holy Communion and Worship of the Eucharist outside Mass *states: "When the faithful honor Christ present in the sacrament, they should remember that this presence is derived from the sacrifice and is directed toward sacramental and spiritual communion.*

"The same piety which moves the faithful to eucharistic adoration attracts them to a deeper participation in the paschal mystery. It makes them respond gratefully to the gifts of Christ who by his humanity continues to pour divine life upon the members of his body. Living with Christ the Lord, they achieve a close familiarity with him and in his presence pour our their hearts for themselves and for those dear to them; they pray for peace and for the salvation of the world. Offering their entire lives with Christ to the Father in the Holy Spirit, they draw from this wondrous exchange an increase of faith, hope, and love. Thus they nourish the proper disposition to celebrate the memorial of the Lord as devoutly as possible and to receive frequently the bread given to us by the Father" (no. 80).

Priests in particular have need of this devotion, as the Church constantly reminds them. In the Decree on the Ministry and Life of Priests, *Vatican II states: "In order that they may carry out their ministry with fidelity, [priests] should prize daily conversation with Christ the Lord in visits of personal devotion to the most Holy Eucharist" (no. 18).*

205. *What do we celebrate on the feast of the Body of Christ (Corpus Christi)?*

On the feast of the Body of Christ we celebrate and give thanks for the institution of the Holy Eucharist, the Sacrament of the Altar.

The immediate impetus for this feast came from the visions of the Augustinian nun St. Juliana of Lüttich (d. 1258), where it was first celebrated in 1246. When the Archdeacon of Lüttich, who had investigated the visions, became Pope Urban IV, he extended the feast to the whole Church in 1264. But not until some fifty years later, under Pope John XII, was it universally observed. The Mass and the Divine Office for the feast were written by St. Thomas Aquinas (d. 1274).

Soon added to the feast was a procession with the Blessed Sacrament, first in Cologne as early as 1277, and everywhere else from the 14th century on.

206. What is the purpose of devotion to the Sacred Heart of Jesus?

The purpose of devotion to the Sacred Heart of Jesus is to honor the human and divine love of our Redeemer, and all His work and all His Person.

"The venerable devotion to the Sacred Heart, based on the symbol of the human heart as a center of love and on the reality of God's love (1Jn 4:7), considers the heart of Christ as the special meeting place of the divine and the human. Encouraged by several papal documents in this century, devotion to the Sacred Heart has inspired many to respond to Jesus' invitation: 'Learn from me, for I am gentle and humble of heart' (Mt 11:29)" *(National Catholic Directory,* no. 143).

The Heart of our Lord is a symbol of all that Jesus as Savior came for and did. According to the Fathers, the Church was born from the wounded side of Christ. In his encyclical on the Sacred Heart *(Miserentissimus Redemptor)* of May 8, 1928, Pope Pius XI said: "This symbol of our redemption, together with the devotion attaching to it, goes to the core of all our worship of God and all our striving after perfection. For devotion to the Sacred Heart hastens the way to deeper knowledge of Christ the Lord and moves our hearts to love Him more fervently and follow Him more perfectly."

Devotion to the Sacred Heart has Scriptural basis, as the early Fathers of the Church already pointed out. The Heart of Jesus is not worshiped in isolation from His Person but always in conjunction with His Person. In fact, the object of this devotion is not the physical heart of Jesus but the love of which His Heart is a symbol while Christians always honored the Heart of Jesus as symbol of His human and divine love, devotion proper to the Sacred Heart as we speak of it today is first met in the writings of St. Gertrude the Great (d. 1302). These, however, did not become widely known until the 16th century, through the efforts of the Carthusian monk John the Just (d. 1539). St. Peter Canisius (d. 1597) reveals in his "Testament," written shortly before his death, that as a young man of 28 he was granted a vision in which the Heart of Jesus appeared for him to contemplate and worship.

The introduction of a distinct feast of the Sacred Heart goes back to revelations made to St. Margaret Mary Alacoque (d. 1690). In the revelation of mid-June, 1675, our Lord instructed her to work for the creation of such a feast: "I ask you that on the first Friday following the octave of Corpus Christi (feast of the Body of Christ) a feast honoring My Heart be celebrated. On that day Holy Communion should be received and public reparation made for the indignities suffered by Me during exposition on the altar." Church officials made a long, critical study of these private revelations. Finally, in 1697 Margaret Mary's Order (the Visitation Nuns) was granted permission by the Pope for a feast of the Sacred Heart but with the Mass of the Five Sacred Wounds. In 1765 some countries obtained permission to celebrate the feast with a Mass of its own, and in 1856 Pope Pius IX prescribed the feast for the universal Church.

In addition to the feast are First Friday observances, with Mass and devotions of the Sacred Heart.

The Sacrament of Penance (Reconciliation)

207. *What is the Sacrament of Penance?*

Our Savior Jesus Christ, when He gave to His Apostles and their successors power to forgive sins, instituted in His Church the Sacrament of Penance. Thus the faithful who fall into sin after Baptism may be reconciled with God and renewed in grace.

The Son of God made man came to dwell among human beings in order to free them from the bondage of sin and call them out of darkness into His marvelous light. And for this, He inaugurated His earthly mission by preaching repentance with the words: "Reform your lives and believe in the Gospel" (Mk 1:15).

However, Jesus not only exhorted people to repentance —to turn their back on sin and turn to God wholeheartedly. He also welcomed sinners and reconciled them with the Father. In addition, as a sign of His power to forgive sins, He cured the sick of their infirmities. Finally, He Himself "was handed over to death for our sins and raised up for our salvation" (Rom 4:25).

Therefore, on the very night that He was betrayed and began His saving Passion, He instituted the sacrifice of the New Covenant in His Blood shed for the forgiveness of sins. Then, after His Resurrection, He sent the Holy Spirit to the Apostles so that they might possess the power to forgive or to retain sins (Jn 20:19f) and receive the mission to proclaim to all peoples conversion in His Name and the forgiveness of sins (Lk 24:47).

From that time, the Church has never ceased both to exhort all people to conversion to God from sin and to show forth through the celebration of Penance Christ's victory over sin. The Church manifests this victory over sin first of all by means of the Sacrament of Baptism. Here our fallen nature is crucified with Christ, so that our personality as sinners is destroyed and freed from sin we rise with Christ and live for God. Hence, the Church proclaims in the Creed: "We acknowledge one Baptism for the forgiveness of sins."

In the Sacrifice of the Mass, the Passion of Christ is made present anew and the Church offers again to the Father, for the salvation of the whole world, the Body that was given for us and the Blood that was shed for the forgiveness of sins. For in the Eucharist, Christ is present and offers Himself as the Victim through Whom God has made peace with us so that by means of this Sacrifice the Holy Spirit might gather us together in peace.

208. Why do we have a Sacrament of Penance?

In the Sacrament of Penance the faithful obtain from the mercy of God pardon for their sins against Him; at the same time they are reconciled with the Church which they wounded by their sins and which works for their conversion by charity, example, and prayer.

The people of God lives a continual penitential life and brings it to perfection in many and varied ways. In sharing the sufferings of Christ and carrying out works of mercy and charity, the Church adopts ever more fully the outlook of the Gospel of Jesus Christ, thus becoming in the world a sign of conversion to God. She expresses this in her life and celebrates it in her Liturgy, when the faithful confess their sinfulness and ask forgiveness of God and their brothers and sisters in penitential services, in the proclamation of the Word of God, in prayer, and in the penitential parts of the Eucharistic celebration.

Effects of the Sacrament of Penance

In this Sacrament we attain a personal encounter with Christ Who, through the priest, brings about the following in us: (1) restoration or increase of sanctifying grace and loving union with God; (2) forgiveness of sins; (3) remission of the eternal punishment (if necessary) and also of at least part of the temporal punishment due to our sins; (4) help to avoid sin in the future; (5) restoration of the merits of our good works, if they have been lost by mortal sin; and (6) reconciliation with the Church.

209. Why does Penance include reconciliation with God and Church?

Sin affects the life of the whole Church, not just the sinner's; so the Sacrament of Penance reconciles us not only to God but also to one another.

Since every sin is an offense committed against God which disrupts our friendship with Him, the ultimate purpose of Penance consists in enabling us to love God deeply and consecrate ourselves to Him. The sinner who is moved by the grace of a merciful God and sets out on the path of conversion returns to the Father Who "first loved us" (1 Jn 4:19), to Christ Who "gave himself for us" (Gal 2:20), and to the Holy Spirit Who has been "lavished on us" (Ti 3:6).

Even more, by the hidden and loving mystery of the Divine will, human beings are joined together by a supernatural solidarity whereby the sin of one injures the others just as the holiness of one benefits the others. Accordingly, Penance always entails reconciliation with our brothers and sisters who have been injured by our sins.

210. What do sinners have to do?

Followers of Christ, the baptized Catholics, who sinned but who have been moved by the Holy Spirit to the Sacrament of Penance, should above all be converted to God with their whole heart.

This conversion of heart carries with it sorrow for sin and the firm resolve to lead a new life. It is expressed through confession made to the Church, due satisfaction, and an amendment of one's life. God grants forgiveness of sins through the Church, working through the ministry of priests.

The acts by which penitents participate in the Sacrament are of the greatest importance. When they make a proper preparation before approaching this saving remedy instituted by Christ and confess their sins, their acts form part of the Sacrament itself. And the Sacrament is fully accomplished with the words of absolution pronounced by the minister in the Name of Christ.

211. What are the principal parts of the Rite of Reconciliation?

The principal parts of the rite and also the key elements in the whole aspect of forgiveness are: (a) contrition, (b) confession, (c) act of penance or satisfaction, and (d) absolution.

212. What is contrition?

Contrition, the most important act of the penitent, is heartfelt sorrow and aversion for the sin committed along with the intention of sinning no more.

Contrition is sorrow of the heart and a turning away from sin as the greatest evil. Mere recitation of an Act of Contrition is not yet contrition. We must repent inwardly and wish that we had not offended God (see Ps 51:19).

To be sorry for sins for human reasons, such as shame or loss of job, is *natural* contrition, which does not suffice for forgiveness from God. *Supernatural* contrition must be based on motives of faith; the goodness of God that was offended and the justice of God to which we are liable for our sins.

Supernatural contrition is "perfect" if the motive of sorrow is true love of God as the highest Good and our greatest Benefactor, Whom we have offended by our sins and to Whom we have shown ourselves ungrateful. It is called perfect because love of God is the highest and most perfect motive of repentance. As the traditional Act of Contrition states: "... because they [my sins] offend You, my God, Who are all-good and deserving of all my love."

Supernatural contrition is "imperfect" when it is based on motives still of faith but not love of God for His own sake. (This also is contained in the traditional Act of Contrition: "... because I dread the loss of heaven and the pains of hell.") Such motives are acknowledgment of God's justice and fear of His just punishment (here or hereafter) if we do not turn from our sins and strive to serve Him. Imperfect contrition with sacramental Confession suffices for forgiveness of sin.

In practice, our contrition often is mixed. We love God but our love leaves something to be desired. And we fear God but not without trust in His mercy and love. As love grows, it drives out fear.

213. *What is confession?*

Confession is the acknowledging of our sins which comes from true knowledge of self before God and from contrition for those sins.

The inner examination of heart and the exterior accusation should be made in the light of God's mercy. On the part of penitents, confession requires the will to open their hearts to the minister of God; and on the part of ministers, it requires a spiritual judgment by which—acting in the person of Christ and in virtue of the power of the keys—they pronounce their decisions of forgiveness or retention of sins.

214. *What does satisfaction mean?*

Through contrition and confession true conversion takes place, and the penitents demonstrate this conversion by acts of penance or satisfaction for the sins committed. We can do this by amendment of conduct and by the reparation of injury.

The type and quantity of the satisfaction must be suited to the personal condition of penitents, so that they may repair the order they have destroyed and be cured by a remedy corresponding to the infirmity that afflicted them. Accordingly, the penance imposed by the minister must really be a remedy for the sins committed and constitute in some way a renewal of life. Thus, penitents may "give no thought to what lies behind" (Phil 3:13), and again become part of the Mystery of Salvation with their eyes steadfastly on the future.

215. What is absolution?

God uses visible signs to give salvation and to renew the broken covenant. Through the sign of absolution, the imposition of hands and/or the Sign of the Cross of the priest, God grants pardon to sinners who in sacramental Confession manifest their change of heart to the Church's minister.

By means of the Sacrament of Penance, the Father welcomes the child who comes back to Him, Christ places the lost sheep on His shoulders and brings it back to the sheepfold, and the Holy Spirit returns to sanctify His temple or dwells more fully in it. All this is manifested by a renewed sharing, or a fuller sharing, in the Lord's table, and there is great joy at the banquet of God's Church over the return of the child who was far off.

The sacramental form of absolution indicates that reconciliation of the penitent originates with the mercy of God the Father. It manifests the connection between the reconciliation of the sinner and the Paschal Mystery of Christ. It stresses the role of the Holy Spirit in the forgiveness of sins. Finally, it highlights the ecclesial aspect of the Sacrament because reconciliation with God is requested and given through the ministry of the Church.

216. *Who forgives sins?*

Through His mercy God alone forgives sins.

217. *How does God forgive sins?*

The Church becomes the instrument of the conversion and absolution of the penitent through the ministry entrusted by Christ to the Apostles and their successors.

The entire Church, as a priestly people, acts in different ways to carry out the task of reconciliation that has been entrusted to her by Almighty God. The Church calls sinners to repentance by proclaiming the Word of God. She also intercedes for them and helps penitents with maternal attentiveness and solicitude to recognize and confess their sins and thus obtain the mercy of God, since it is He alone Who forgives sins.

218. *How does the Church grant God's forgiveness?*

The Church exercises the ministry of the Sacrament of Penance through bishops and priests.

By the proclamation of the Word of God, the bishops and priests call the faithful to conversion. In the Name of Christ and through the power of the Holy Spirit, they declare and impart the forgiveness of sins.

Priests exercise this ministry in communion with the bishop and share in his power and office of regulating the penitential discipline.

219. *Who can absolve the sinner?*

The competent minister of the Sacrament of Penance is a priest who has the faculty to absolve in accordance with the Church's discipline or canon law.

All priests, however, even those not approved to hear confessions, absolve validly and licitly all penitents who are in danger of death.

220. What is the role of the priest?

The priest's role is to fulfill his office of judge wisely. He should acquire the knowledge and prudence necessary for this task by serious study, guided by the teaching authority of the Church and especially by fervent prayer to God.

The confessor should learn to recognize the disorders of souls and apply suitable remedies to them. This is done by the discernment of spirits, an intimate knowledge of God's action in human hearts, which is a gift of the Holy Spirit and the fruit of charity.

By welcoming repentant sinners and guiding them to the light of truth, the confessor carries out his paternal function —he lays bare the heart of the Father to his children and recalls to them the image of Christ the Good Shepherd.

221. How is the Sacrament of Penance received (that is, celebrated)?

The Sacrament of Penance has a rite, that is, a format in which the Sacrament is celebrated by use of various signs or symbols, gestures, words, and the like. It consists of the following: (1) reception of the penitent, (2) reading of the Word of God, (3) confession of sins and acceptance of satisfaction, (4) prayer of the penitent and absolution, and (5) proclamation of praise of God and dismissal.

Before celebrating the Sacrament, both confessors and penitents should prepare themselves above all by prayer. Priests should have recourse to the Holy Spirit for light and charity. Penitents should examine their lives in the light of Christ's example and commandments and then pray to God for forgiveness.

1) Welcoming the Penitents. Priests should welcome penitents with love and speak to them in friendship. Then the penitents make the Sign of the Cross and the priests—by a short formula—urge them to have confidence in God. Penitents who are not known to the confessors should indicate their state in life, the time of their last Confession, their difficulties in leading a Christian life, and any other particulars that may help the confessors to carry out their ministry.

2) Reading of the Word of God. Next the priests or penitents may read a text from Sacred Scripture (if it has not already been done as a preparation for the Sacrament). Through the Word of God Christians are illumined to recognize their sins and summoned to conversion and confidence in God's mercy.

3) Confession of Sins and Acceptance of Satisfaction. The penitents now confess their sins. If need be, the confessors help them make an integral confession and to have sincere sorrow for their sins. Finally, they offer the penitents suitable advice for beginning a new life and may even instruct them in the duties of the Christian life.

If the penitents have harmed or scandalized others, the confessors should exact from them a resolve to make restitution.

Then the confessors impose an act of penance or satisfaction which serves not only to expiate the penitents' sins but also aids them to begin a new life. The penance should correspond as far as possible to the gravity and nature of the sins committed. It may be a prayer, an act of self-denial, some service rendered to a neighbor, or a work of mercy—stressing the social aspect of sin and forgiveness.

4) The Prayer of the Penitents and Absolution. A prayer for God's forgiveness manifests the penitents' contrition and resolve to begin a new life. Then the priests extend their hands (or at least one hand) on the head of the penitents and pronounce the formula of absolution.

God, the Father of mercies,
through the death and resurrection of his Son
has reconciled the world to himself
and sent the Holy Spirit among us
for the forgiveness of sins;
through the ministry of the Church
may God give you pardon and peace,
and I absolve you from your sins
in the name of the Father,
and of the Son, ✠
and of the Holy Spirit.

The essential words are: "I absolve you from your sins in the name of the Father and of the Son and of the Holy Spirit."

5) Proclamation of Praise and Dismissal. After receiving forgiveness, the penitents praise God's mercy and give Him thanks by means of a short text taken from Sacred Scripture. Then the confessors tell them to go in peace.

Penitents continue their conversion and express it by a life renewed in accord with the Gospel and steeped in God's love, for "love covers a multitude of sins"(1 Pt 4:8).

In accord with pastoral needs, some parts of this rite may be shortened or even omitted. However, confession of sins and the acceptance of the act of penance as well as the invitation to contrition and the form of absolution and dismissal must be retained in their entirety. When there is imminent danger of death, the essential words of the form of absolution suffice: "I absolve you from your sins in the name of the Father, and of the Son, and of the Holy Spirit."

222. *Is there a general confession of sins?*

In addition to the rite between penitent and priest alone there are two other rites: (1) rite for reconciliation of several penitents with individual confession and absolution and (2) rite of reconcilia-

tion of penitents with general confession and absolution.

1) Communal celebration more clearly manifests the ecclesial nature of Penance. Together the faithful listen to God's Word which proclaims the divine mercy and summons them to conversion. Together they also examine their lives in the light of the Word of God and help one another with prayer. After they have individually confessed and received absolution, all praise God at the same time for the wondrous deeds He has accomplished on behalf of His people whom He purchased by the Blood of His Son.

At such celebrations, several priests are available in suitable places for individual confession and reconciliation of penitents.

2) Individual, integral confession and absolution continue to be the sole ordinary way in which Christians can achieve reconciliation with God and the Church, unless physical or moral impossibility excuses from this manner of confession. Particular circumstances may arise, however, when it is licit and even fitting to impart absolution in a general way to many penitents without previous individual confession.

In addition to cases when there is a danger of death, it is licit to give sacramental absolution to many penitents simultaneously who have made only a general confession (although they have been summoned to repentance) when there is grave need. This is the case when on account of the great number of penitents there are not enough confessors to hear individual confessions according to the new rite in a reasonable period of time—resulting in the fact that penitents will be deprived, through no fault of their own, of the sacramental grace or Holy Communion for a long period of time. This may take place principally in mission countries but it can also be the case in other places and in gatherings of people when the need is genuine.

Those who have received forgiveness for grave sins by general absolution are strictly bound to go to confession within a year unless they are impeded by some moral impossibility.

223. *What are penitential celebrations?*

Penitential celebrations are gatherings of the people of God to hear the proclamation of God's Word which summons them to conversion and renewal of life and announces our freedom from sin through the Death and Resurrection of Christ. They especially bring out the community aspects and significance of Penance.

Penitential celebrations must not be confused with the Sacrament of Penance. However, they are very useful to promote conversion of life and purification of heart. They are used especially (a) to foster the spirit of repentance in the Christian community; (b) to help the faithful prepare for the confession which can then be made individually later; (c) to teach children about sin in human life and the freedom from sin that comes through Christ; and (d) to help catechumens during their period of conversion.

In addition, penitential services are most useful where no priest is available to give individual absolution. They foster perfect contrition based on charity, through which the faithful can attain God's grace by a desire to receive the Sacrament of Penance.

224. *What is an examination of conscience?*

An examination of conscience is a sincere effort to recall the sins we have committed.

If we examine our conscience for a few moments at the end of each day, it will be easier to do so at the time of confession. A practical method of examination is to go through the Ten Commandments and the Precepts of the Church. The greatest Commandment, however, is love of God and its inseparable companion, love of neighbor. All other Commandments presuppose the observance of this twofold one.

In the examination of conscience we should remember that we are in God's presence, to Whom nothing is secret.

But the examination ought not to become an agony. An honest effort is all that is required. God is not only just but also merciful, our heavenly Father. What is left out unintentionally does not affect the validity of the Confession. Attention, however, should be paid not only to sins of commission but also of omission, i.e., both to the evil to be avoided and to the good to be done according to our state in life, and with the gifts God has given us.

The Ten Commandments and the Precepts of the Church are treated in Part Three, below, pp. 285-395.

225. What type of sins must we confess?

We must confess each and every grave sin which is remembered upon examination of conscience. Venial sins may also be confessed.

To those who by grave sin have cut themselves off from communion with God's love, the Sacrament of Penance restores the life they have lost. To those who daily experience their weakness by falling into venial sins, the repeated celebration of Penance imparts renewed strength to attain the full freedom of the children of God.

The frequent and diligent celebration of the Sacrament is very useful as a remedy for venial sins. However, we are not speaking of a mere ritual repetition or psychological exercise. We are speaking about a continual concern to perfect the grace of Baptism, so that as we bear in ourselves the death of Christ the life of Jesus may also be manifested in us. In their confessions, the faithful must make sure that in accusing themselves of venial faults they also try to be conformed closely to Christ and remain docile to the voice of the Spirit.

226. What are the words of the Act of Contrition?

O my God, I am heartily sorry for having offended You. I detest all my sins because I dread the loss

of heaven and the pains of hell, but most of all because they offend You, my God, Who are all-good and deserving of all my love. I firmly resolve, with the help of Your grace, to confess my sins, to do penance, and to amend my life. Amen.

This is one of the possible prayers to say which has been used for years. An updated version is also provided in the Rite of Penance as well as other prayers. Tried and proven formulas have their place in tradition: for example, there are many psalms which we might pray as an Act of Contrition, like Psalm 51, David's prayer of repentance ("Have mercy on me, O God. . . ."), or Psalm 130, which the Jews prayed in their Babylonian Captivity (De Profundis: "Out of the depths I cry to you, O Lord . . .").

Also, we need not cling to set words but may express our sorrow and purpose of amendment more freely in our own fervent words.

227. *How do we know that Christ commands us to confess our sins to the priest?*

We know that Christ commands us to confess our sins to the priest

1. **from the words and teachings of our Lord to His Apostles and disciples about forgiveness and sin,**
2. **and from the constant belief and teaching of the Church.**

1) In the Name of Christ the priest is to forgive or not forgive sins. But the priest could not exercise this power in any reasonable way unless the penitent's sins and disposition were made known to him by Confession.

2) "Many who had become believers came forward and openly confessed their former practices" (Acts 19:18).

"No one can be loosed from sin unless it has been confessed" (St. Ambrose, d. 397). — "Let no one say: I confess in secret to God; God, Who knows me, knows what is in my heart. To what purpose then would be: What you loose on earth shall be loosed in heaven? Or was the power of the keys given to God's Church for no reason?" (St. Augustine, d. 430).

The history of the Sacrament of Penance falls into three principal periods: (1) From the beginning of the Church until the 6th century. During this period, when a member of the Church committed a grave sin after Baptism, reconciliation with the ecclesial community as a rule was granted once in life. (2) From the 6th to the 11th century. Under the influence of the Irish monks forgiveness even for grave sins was granted more frequently. In addition, private Confession for secret sins was permitted, and penance also ceased to be public. (3) From the Middle Ages to the present. This was a time when the accent shifted from the penance to be performed to other elements of the Sacrament: confession, contrition, and priestly absolution. Penance was seldom a burden, and the participation of the community in the sinner's reconciliation shrank to a minimum.

228. *Where and when can we go to Confession?*

We can go to Confession anywhere, given the necessity or advantage, and usually we can go at any time within reason.

Confession or the Sacrament of Penance may be celebrated in the confessional, in a room of reconciliation, hospital, rectory, home, etc.—almost any place. Penitents have the option of retaining their anonymity or confessing face to face.

The reconciliation of penitents can be celebrated any time and on any day. However, the faithful should approach this Sacrament when Mass is not being celebrated and especially during the periods regularly assigned to the imparting of Penance.

229. *What is the Seal of Confession?*

The Seal of Confession is the sacred obligation of the confessor never to reveal anything made known to him in Confession.

The Seal of Confession arose with the practice of private Confession. It has existed ever since,' and always will. There is, for that matter, no known instance of a priest violating the seal, not even a priest who had renounced his faith and defected from the Church. On the other hand, there are many cases on record where a priest went to death rather than reveal what had been told him in confession.

The Seal of Confession is absolute; it applies under all circumstances, even when the Confession is invalid or absolution is denied. The confessor is not allowed to say anything to anybody, including the penitent outside of Confession. No one, not even the Pope, can dispense from the Seal of Confession, and it remains in effect after the penitent has died. Nor may the confessor treat the penitent any differently because of what he has learned from the penitent in Confession. Clearly, God watches in a special way over the Seal and its scrupulous observance, so that the faithful can go to Confession certain that nothing will be revealed.

230. *What is an indulgence?*

An indulgence is a remission of temporal punishment of sin which remains after sins are forgiven.

An indulgence is not a pardon for sins. Nevertheless, the practice of indulgences rests on the Church's power to bind and to loose. Christ said to St. Peter, without restriction: "Whatever you declare bound on earth shall be bound in heaven; whatever you declare loosed on earth shall be loosed in heaven" (Mt 16:19). Penitential practice of the early Church shows that already the concept of indulgence was sometimes applied, as it was when for weighty reasons the public penance imposed by the Church was replaced, in whole or in part, by useful good works. The Church forgave the penance and, by implication, the temporal punishment which the penance might have satisfied. St. Paul himself released a public sinner in Corinth from the remainder of his penance (2 Cor 2:10).

Indulgences draw on the merits of Christ and those of His Saints. These merits, which constitute an inexhaustible spiritual resource, have been placed at the disposal of the Church, which relies on them to provide an exchange for all or some of the temporal punishment we owe to God for our sins. "In an indulgence in fact, the Church, making use of its power as minister of the Redemption of Christ, not only prays but by an authoritative intervention dispenses to the faithful suitably disposed the treasury of satisfaction which Christ and the Saints won for the remission of temporal punishment" (Paul VI: Apostolic Constitution on *The Doctrine of Indulgences*, January 1, 1967, no. 8).

231. *What is the temporal punishment due to sin?*

The temporal punishment due to sin is that punishment which we must satisfy on earth or in purgatory.

Examples of such punishment are found in the Bible: Adam and Eve committed a grave sin of pride and disobedience; God forgave them their sin but as punishment they were cast out of Paradise. The Israelites in the wilderness worshiped the golden calf; for punishment they all died before they could enter the Promised Land. David's adultery was a grave sin; through the prophet Nathan God announced forgiveness of the sin but in punishment took the child of the sinful union, causing inconsolable grief to David.

232. *What is a partial and what is a plenary indulgence?*

A partial indulgence is release from some of the temporal punishment due to sin, whereas a plenary indulgence is release from all such punishment.

Until recently, it was common practice of the Church to attach a certain number of days or years or other time reference to prayers with partial indulgences. Because these numbers led to misunderstanding, the new *Enchiridion of Indulgences* (June 29, 1968) no longer uses them. People erroneously thought that an indulgence say of 300 days meant a lessening of purgatorial punishment by that many days. The true meaning was that such an indulgence remitted as much temporal punishment of sin as was remitted in the past by fulfilling a Church-imposed public penance of 300 days. To avoid misconceptions of this sort indications of time are now omitted from indulgences.

In addition to prayers to which partial indulgences are attached, the Church points out other ways of getting such an indulgence: (1) by turning to God in humble prayer, even inwardly, when beset by the demands and vexations of daily life; (2) by giving of ourselves or our goods, in the spirit of Christian faith and charity, to those in need; (3) by depriving ourselves, in the spirit of penance, of some permissible gratification.

For a plenary indulgence, which now can be gained only once a day, the following conditions are set down: (a) performing the prescribed works (e.g., visiting a church, the Our Father, the Creed); (b) Confession, before or after the prescribed works or on the day itself; (c) Holy Communion (as for Confession); (d) prayer for the intention of the Holy Father; (e) detachment from all sin, including venial sin.

The Anointing of the Sick

233. *What is the Anointing of the Sick?*

The Anointing of the Sick is a special Sacrament for Christians seriously ill as a result of sickness or old age. Through the Sacrament of Anointing Christ strengthens the faithful who are afflicted by illness, providing them with the strongest means of support.

Suffering and illness have always been among the greatest problems to challenge the human spirit. Christians feel and experience pain as do all other people; yet their faith helps them to grasp more deeply the mystery of suffering and to bear their pain more bravely. From Christ's words they know that sickness has meaning and value for their own salvation and for the salvation of the world. They also know that Christ loves the sick and that during His life He often visited the sick and healed them.

It is part of the plan laid down by God's providence that we should fight strenuously against all sickness and carefully seek the blessings of good health, so that we may fulfill our role in human society and in the Church. Yet we should always be prepared to fill up what is lacking in Christ's sufferings for the salvation of the world as we look forward to creation being set free in the glory of the children of God.

Moreover, the role of the sick in the Church is to be a reminder to others of the essential or higher things. By their witness the sick show that our mortal life is to be redeemed through the Mystery of Christ's Death and Resurrection.

The Lord Himself showed great concern for the bodily and spiritual welfare of the sick and commanded His followers to do likewise. This is clear from the Gospels, and above all from the existence of the Sacrament of Anointing which he instituted and which is made known in the Epistle of James.

Since then the Church has never ceased to celebrate this Sacrament for her members by the anointing and the prayer of her priests, commanding those who are ill to the suffering and glorified Lord, that He may raise them up and save them (see Jas 5:14-16). Moreover, the Church exhorts them to associate themselves freely with the Passion and Death of Christ, and thus contribute to the welfare of the people of God.

Those who are seriously ill need the special help of God's grace in this time of anxiety, lest they be broken in spirit and, under the pressure of temptation, perhaps weaken in their faith.

234.   *How is the Anointing of the Sick celebrated?*

There are three distinct and integral aspects to the celebration of this Sacrament: the prayer of faith, the laying on of hands, and the anointing with oil.

Prayer of faith. The community, asking God's help for the sick, makes its prayer of faith in response to God's Word and in a spirit of trust. In the rites for the sick, it is the people of God who pray in faith. The entire Church is made present in this community—represented by at least the priest, family, friends, and others—assembled to pray for those to be anointed. If they are able, the sick persons should also join in this prayer.

Laying on of hands. The Gospels contain a number of instances in which Jesus healed the sick by the laying on of hands or even by the simple gesture of touch. With this gesture the priest indicates that this particular person is the object of the Church's prayer of faith. The laying on of hands is clearly a *sign of blessing,* as we pray that by the power of God's healing grace the sick person may be restored to health or at least strengthened in time of illness. The laying on of hands is also an *invocation:* the Church prays for the coming of the Holy Spirit upon the sick person. Above all, it is the biblical *gesture of healing.*

Anointing with oil. The practice of anointing the sick with oil signifies healing (Mk 6:13), strengthening (Jas 5:14), and the presence of the Spirit *(Prayer for Blessing the Oil of the Sick).*

The sick person is anointed on the forehead and on the hands. In case of necessity, however, it is sufficient that a single anointing be given on the forehead or on another suitable part of the body.

The following is the sacramental form with which the anointing of the sick is given in the Latin Rite:

**Through this holy anointing
may the Lord in his love and mercy help you
with the grace of the Holy Spirit.
May the Lord who frees you from sin
save you and raise you up.**

Anointing of the Sick with a Large Congregation

The rites for anointing outside Mass and anointing during Mass may be used to anoint a number of people during the same celebration. These rites are appropriate for large gatherings of a diocese, parish, or society for the sick, or for pilgrimages. These celebrations should take place in a church, chapel, or other appropriate place where the sick and others can easily gather. On occasion, they may also take place in hospitals and other institutions.

The full participation of those present must be fostered by every means, especially through the use of appropriate songs, so that the celebration manifests the Easter joy which is proper to this Sacrament.

Continuous Rite

For special cases, when sudden illness or some other cause has unexpectedly placed one of the faithful in proximate danger of death, a *continuous rite* is provided by which the sick person may be given the Sacraments of Penance, Anointing, and the Eucharist as Viaticum in a single celebration.

If death is imminent and there is not enough time to celebrate the three Sacraments in the manner described above, the sick person should be given an opportunity to make a sacramental Confession, even if it has to be a generic Confession. After this the person should be given Viaticum, since all the faithful are bound to receive this Sacrament if they are in danger of death. Then, if there is sufficient time, the sick person should be anointed.

235. *Who should receive the Sacrament of Anointing of the Sick?*

The Epistle of James states that the sick are to be anointed in order to raise them up and save them. Great care and concern should be taken to see that those of the faithful whose health is seriously impaired by sickness or old age receive this Sacrament.

A prudent or probable judgment about the seriousness of the sickness is sufficient; in such a case there is no reason for scruples, but if necessary a doctor may be consulted.

The Sacrament may be repeated if the sick person recovers after being anointed or if during the same illness the person's condition becomes more serious. A sick person may be anointed before surgery whenever a serious illness is the reason for the surgery. Elderly people may be anointed if they have become notably weakened even though no serious illness is present. Sick children may be anointed as soon as they have sufficient use of reason to be strengthened by this Sacrament.

236. *How should the sick prepare for the Anointing?*

The faithful should clearly understand the meaning of the anointing of the sick so that this Sacrament may nourish, strengthen, and express faith.

The prayer of faith which accompanies the celebration of the Sacrament is supported by the profession of this faith.

The sick person will be saved by personal faith and the faith of the Church which looks back to the Death and Resurrection of Christ, the source of the Sacrament's power (see Jas 5:15), and looks ahead to the future Kingdom which is pledged in the Sacraments.

The faithful should recall two complementary aspects of the Sacrament of Anointing: during their suffering they find support in their struggle against illness, and in the Sacrament of Anointing the Church continues Christ's Messianic work of healing. All who are united in the bond of a common Baptism and a common faith are joined together in the Body of Christ since what happens to one member affects all. The Sacrament of Anointing effectively expresses the share that each one has in the sufferings of others.

Holy Orders

237. *What is Holy Orders?*

Holy Orders is the Sacrament by which the office of bishop, priest, or deacon, together with its power and grace, is conferred.

The outward sign of the Sacrament of Holy Orders is the laying on of hands and the accompanying prayer by the bishop.

In the *Decree on the Ministry and Life of Priests,* Vatican II says: "The office of priests, since it is connected with the episcopal order, also, in its own degree, shares the authority by which Christ builds up, sanctifies, and rules His Body. Wherefore the priesthood, while indeed it presupposes the Sacraments of Christian initiation, is conferred by that special Sacrament; through it priests, by the anointing of the Holy Spirit, are signed with a special character and are conformed to Christ the Priest in such a way that they can act in the person of Christ the Head" (no. 2).

238. How do we know that Jesus Christ instituted the Sacrament of Holy Orders?

That Jesus Christ instituted the Sacrament of Holy Orders we know
1. from Sacred Scripture,
2. and from the teaching of the Church throughout her history.

The New Testament shows that Christ bestowed on the Apostles the power and grace of priesthood (e.g., at the Last Supper, and after His Resurrection) and that the Apostles handed on this power to others.

1) "I remind you to stir into flame the gift of God bestowed when my hands were laid on you" (2 Tm 1:6).

2) "Both [Baptism and Holy Orders] are Sacraments, and no one questions it" (St. Augustine).

Vatican II, in the Dogmatic Constitution on the Church, *says: "Christ, Whom the Father has sanctified and sent into the world, has through His Apostles made their successors, the bishops, partakers of His consecration and His mission. They have legitimately handed on to different individuals in the Church various degrees of participation in this ministry. Thus the divinely established ecclesiastical ministry is exercised on different levels by those who from antiquity have been called bishops, priests, and deacons. Priests, although they do not possess the highest degree of the priesthood, and although they are dependent on the bishops in the exercise of their power, nevertheless are united with the bishops in sacerdotal dignity. By the power of the Sacrament of Orders, in the image of Christ the eternal High Priest, they are consecrated to preach the Gospel and shepherd the faithful and to celebrate divine worship, so that they are true priests of the New Testament"* (no. 28).

The Apostles understood their office as a priestly one, as participation in the priesthood of Jesus Christ. Primarily, the office of the priest consists in building up the Church, by continuing the priestly mission of Christ in word, Sacrament and living example. In this sense the priest is a representative of Christ, and this position as representative has great significance exactly for the Eucharistic celebration.

239.   What does priestly ordination do?

1. **Priestly ordination imprints the soul with the indelible mark of the priesthood;**
2. **it bestows the powers of the priesthood;**
3. **it increases sanctifying grace;**
4. **it strengthens the priest to live a good priestly life and fulfill his priestly mission.**

The notion of "indelible mark" is not expressly given in Revelation. But the New Testament points to it in speaking of the "seal" with which Christians are sealed (Eph 1:13; 4:30; 2 Cor 1:22; see also Rv 7:2-8). Beginning with these scriptural indications the Church Fathers, St. Augustine in particular (d. 430), developed the concept of the seal and associated it with the three Sacraments of Baptism, Confirmation, and Holy Orders. The permanence of the seal, or character, was taught by the Council of Florence and reaffirmed by the Council of Trent. "In recent times the Second Vatican Council more than once mentioned it, and the Second General Assembly of the Synod of Bishops rightly considered the enduring nature of the priestly character throughout life as pertaining to the teaching of faith" *(Sacred Congregation for the Doctrine of the Faith*, June 24, 1973).

In our day, discussion about the permanence of the priesthood is sometimes raised. Is the priesthood for life or can one be priest "for a time"? By nature the priesthood is a permanent vocation: "You are a priest forever" (Ps 110:4). If the character or mark which ordination produces is permanent, so is the priesthood—just as one is baptized or confirmed forever, and can never undo it. Christ did not ordain the Apostles "for a time." The priest, by accepting ordination, binds himself whole and entire to Christ, perpetually. For his revolution Lenin wanted only people who would give their whole life to it, not just their free time. One hesitates to paint the moral, but a "temporary" dedication is inconsistent with the call to the Catholic priesthood. This is not to say that the Church may not grant an individual priest permission to cease living as a priest, "laicize" him, as we say, though in reality a priest can never become a layman, i.e., shed his priesthood: "The special participation in Christ's priesthood does not disappear even if a priest for ecclesial or personal reasons is dispensed or removed from the exercise of his ministry" *(Second General Assembly of the Synod of Bishops*, The Ministerial Priesthood, 1971).

Many of our brothers in the priesthood are hard pressed, they say, to find a fulfilled life in priestly ministry and speak of a frustrated priesthood. Such a feeling may have many causes but certainly frustration sets in where the ministerial service demanded of us is not fulfilled, or poorly. This danger is not averted by reduction but by intensification of our personal dedication. . . . From the priest is expected not just a round of activities, each with carefully measured expenditure of time and energy; not just individual functions but engagement of the person in unstinted self-commitment. Our priestly activity is not properly performed without such oblation and investment of the total person. The reason lies in the Christological structure of our priestly office, as appears from the priestly work of Christ Himself, which reached its peak in His self-offering in death on the Cross. . . .

As long as there are human beings on earth, the spiritual ministry for which the priest is ordained will never be superfluous or meaningless. Indeed, there is scarcely a more meaningful, more satisfying, and more important work to which we can dedicate ourselves than the work of proclaiming the Lord.

240. *What powers does ordination to the priesthood confer?*

Ordination to the priesthood confers the powers
1. to offer the Holy Sacrifice of the Mass for the living and the dead,
2. to administer the Holy Sacraments,
3. to preach, to bless, and to sanctify.

Catholics honor their priests, not for themselves but for their priesthood, which is a participation in the priesthood of Christ. They call them "father," because priests are spiritual fathers of their people. "Nothing in this life is more blessed and in the eyes of the faithful more precious than the office of the priest" (St. Augustine, (d. 430).

"You are now made a priest and are consecrated to celebrate Mass. Take heed, therefore, to offer your sacrifice to God in due time faithfully and devoutly and to keep yourself without reproof. You have not made your burden more light, but you are now bound by a stricter bond of discipline and of higher perfection than you were before. A priest ought to be adorned with all virtues and to give others the example of a good life" (Imitation of Christ, *IV, 5).*

God's people believe that Christ is present in the ordained priest. This conviction must not be lost. The priest therefore must not only fulfill this representation of Christ in his official capacity but also exemplify and make it belief-worthy in his personal life.

241. *Why does the Catholic priest live a celibate life?*

A Catholic priest lives a celibate life to give himself, his time and effort, more fully to God's people.

"I should like you to be free of all worries. The unmarried man is busy with the Lord's affairs, concerned with pleasing the Lord; but the married man is busy with this world's demands and occupied with pleasing his wife" (1 Cor 7:32-33). Celibacy was not always a general requirement for priests, even in the West. Yet from the beginning there were celibate priests, who did not marry so they could give themselves undividedly to the service of Christ (see Pauline quotation above, and 1 Cor 9:5). Different practices arose in the Church. One of the first regulations in the matter is found in the Synod of Elvira in Spain, about the year 300. The First General Council of Nicaea in 325 declared that anyone unmarried at ordination could not marry afterward, and noted that this was a long-standing tradition. But anyone married before ordination was free to continue his married life. This practice still prevails in the Catholic Churches of the Eastern Rite, i.e., married men are ordained but ordained men may not marry.

In the Western Church celibacy more and more became the rule. Pope Leo the Great (d. 461) extended it to subdeacons, an office now abolished. After him, Popes continued to promote celibacy and eventually, at the Second Lateran Council in 1139, it was made binding for all priests of the Latin Rite. This was reiterated by the Council of Trent in 1563. In our time suggestions that the Church relax its stand prompted Pope Paul VI on June 24, 1967, to issue an encyclical upholding the traditional requirement. In 1971 the Second General Assembly of the Synod of Bishops returned to the question and concluded: "The rule of celibacy existing in the Latin Church is to be kept in its entirety" (*Ministerial Priesthood,* Part II, no. 4). The Synod's finding was confirmed by the Pope.

In a 1979 letter to all the priests of the Church, entitled Celibacy and Priestly Life, *Pope John Paul II called celibacy a "treasure" and noted: "The essential, proper, and adequate reason for celibacy is to be found in the truth which Christ revealed when speaking of the renunciation of marriage for the sake of God's Reign and which St. Paul proclaimed when he wrote that each person has his or her own gift from God. Celibacy is precisely such a 'gift of the Spirit.' ...*

"Celibacy 'for the sake of God's Reign' not only is an eschatological sign but also has great social importance in our present life for the service of God's people. The priest's celibacy makes him a 'man for others,' although in a way different from that of the man who through conjugal union with a woman becomes husband and father, a 'man for others,' that is, for his wife and, with her, for the children to whom he gives life.

"The priest renounces the kind of fatherhood proper to married men and seeks another kind of fatherhood and even another kind of motherhood, for he is mindful of the Apostle's words about the children whom he begot and brought to birth. These are his spiritual children, the persons whom the Good Shepherd has entrusted to his care, and they are many, more numerous than any ordinary family could comprise. The pastoral vocation of priests is great indeed, since it embraces the entire Church, and is, therefore, missionary as well."

Bishop Tenhumberg of Münster (Herder Correspondence, Sept. 1973) noted that even ecumenically-minded theologians among Protestants had repeatedly expressed the hope that the Catholic Church would retain the "charism of celibacy." He continued: "The abandonment of celibacy would not automatically solve the shortage of priests. The lack of clerical ministers in other Churches is in some ways even greater than in the Catholic Church with its requirement of celibacy. This shows that what is in question is the spiritual ministry itself, and as a whole. Basically, it comes down to a question of faith. ... Moreover, given the pleasure psychosis of our day, I fear that dissociating the priestly office from celibacy would lead to a still greater temptation, namely complete secularization of the priest's lifestyle, which already has gone far enough. In the present phase of our civilization, much more even than formerly, celibacy is a prophetic sign of protest. This sign, I might add, is still understood, despite protestations to the contrary."

Recent Popes have made occasional exceptions to the rule of celibacy, like permitting, in a few instances, a married non-Catholic minister to be ordained and serve as a priest after coming into the Church. Whether, in case of continuing shortage of vocations, a broader waiver of the rule can be expected, no one knows. At present it does not seem likely. In any case, it would be up to the Holy Father, Vicar of Christ, under the guidance of the Spirit to make whatever decisions were in order.

242. *Who can ordain priests?*

Only a bishop can ordain priests.

In the *Decree on the Pastoral Office of Bishops in the Church,* Vatican II says: "Bishops enjoy the fullness of the Sacrament of Orders and both presbyters and deacons are dependent upon them in the exercise of their authority. For the presbyters are the prudent fellow workers of the episcopal order and are themselves consecrated as true priests of the New Testament, just as deacons are ordained for the ministry and serve the people of God in communion with the bishop and his presbytery. Therefore bishops are the principal dispensers of the Mysteries of God, as well as the governors, promoters, and guardians of the entire liturgical life in the church committed to them" (no. 15).

243. *What is the common priesthood of the faithful?*

The common (universal) priesthood of the faithful is their way of participating in the priesthood of Christ for the salvation of all. It is different in essence and not only in degree from the ministerial priesthood.

Through Baptism the faithful are incorporated in the Church and become the new People of God, chosen to offer prayer and sacrifice through the ordained priest. Not only this, but everything they do, all their work and activity, can be made a spiritual sacrifice to God. In the Old Testament, God also had a chosen people, which He made His special

LIKE A GOOD SHEPHERD, JESUS SOUGHT OUT LOST SOULS
"I am the good shepherd; the good shepherd lays down his life for the sheep. . . . I know my sheep and my sheep know me in the same way that the Father knows me and I know the Father; for these sheep I will give my life" (Jn 10:11, 14f).

possession. By hearkening to His voice and keeping His covenant-law they were to be to Him "a kingdom of priests, a holy nation" (Ex 19:6). In the New Testament, St. Peter takes up this thought when he writes: "You too are living stones, built as an edifice of spirit, into a holy priesthood, offering spiritual sacrifices acceptable to God through Jesus Christ. . . . You are a chosen race, a royal priesthood, a holy nation, a people he claims for his own to proclaim the glorious works of the One who called you from darkness into his marvelous light" (1 Pt 2:5-9).

With these words of St. Peter's Epistle in mind the Church always has held to the idea of a common priesthood of the faithful, distinct from the priesthood of the ordained priest yet being in its way a participation in the royal priesthood of Christ. Even at the time of the Protestant Reformation with its denial of the special priesthood of the ordained priest, the Church did not retreat from teaching the common priesthood. The Roman Catechism *published in 1566 under Pope Pius V affirmed it, and in our own day the Second Vatican Council in its* Dogmatic Constitution on the Church *reaffirmed it.*

The Council states: "Though they differ from one another in essence and not only in degree, the common priesthood of the faithful and the ministerial or hierarchical priesthood are nonetheless interrelated: each of them in its own special way is a participation in the one priesthood of Christ. The ministerial priest, by the sacred power he enjoys, teaches and rules the priestly people; acting in the person of Christ, he makes present the Eucharistic Sacrifice, and offers it to God in the name of all the people. But the faithful, in virtue of their royal priesthood, join in the offering of the Eucharist. They likewise exercise that priesthood in receiving the Sacraments, in prayer and thanksgiving, in the witness of a holy life, and by self-denial and active charity" (no. 10).

Matrimony

244. *Who instituted marriage and who raised it to a Sacrament?*

God instituted marriage in Paradise and Christ raised it to a Sacrament called Matrimony.

"For this reason a man shall leave his father and mother, and shall cling to his wife, and the two shall be made into one. This is a great foreshadowing: I mean that it refers to Christ and the Church" (Eph 5:31-32).

The Council of Trent declared that marriage in the Church is one of the seven Sacraments instituted by Christ. The Council was not teaching new doctrine but affirming the constant, universal belief of the Church.

Christian marriage sanctifies family life. Moreover, the Christian family should be a house of God in its own right, a little church where father and mother exercise the priesthood of the faithful. There is indeed a priesthood of the family that serves the Church. Families build the parish, parishes build the diocese, and dioceses build the Church. Humanly speaking, the whole Church rests on the church in the home. Not for nothing did Christ spend the greater part of his life on earth within the family circle; he wanted to sanctify this church in miniature. It is the family most of all that must save the faith and pass it on. St. John Chrysostom said: "Prayer and instruction in church are not enough; with them must go prayer and reading in the home, which forms a little church."

245. *What does Christ do in the Sacrament of Matrimony?*

In the Sacrament of Matrimony, Christ joins man and woman in a holy and indissoluble union,

enables them to signify and share in the mystery of that unity and fruitful love which exists between Christ and His Church, and gives them grace to fulfill their tasks as husband and wife and as parents.

"[Jesus] replied, 'Have you not read that at the beginning the Creator made them male and female and declared, "For this reason a man shall leave his father and mother and cling to his wife, and the two shall become as one"? Thus they are no longer two but one flesh' " (Mt 19:4-6).

"[God] created man in love to share [his] divine life. / We see his high destiny in the love of husband and wife, / which bears the imprint of [God's] own divine love. / Love is man's origin, / love is his constant calling, / love is his fulfillment in heaven. / The love of man and woman / is made holy in the sacrament of marriage, / and becomes the mirror of [God's] everlasting love" (Preface of Nuptial Mass).

246. *How do the bride and groom enter upon the Sacrament of Matrimony?*

The bride and groom declare in the presence of the authorized priest and two witnesses that they take each other as husband and wife.

Generally speaking, the couple must obtain a marriage license from the civil authorities. Some countries also require a civil marriage, but this does not exempt the couple from the grave obligation to be married in the Church. In the eyes of the Church, Catholics are not married until they are married "in the Church," i.e., in the presence of an authorized priest of the Church.

Although the *Rite of Marriage* makes provision for marriage apart from Mass, a Catholic marriage is most fittingly celebrated with Mass, where the ceremony takes place after the Liturgy of the Word.

247. *What are the graces received from the Sacrament of Matrimony?*

1. **The Sacrament of Matrimony increases sanctifying grace;**
2. **it gives the married couple the special grace to remain true to their marriage until death and to fulfill the duties of married life.**

In the *Pastoral Constitution on the Church in the Modern World,* Vatican II says: "The intimate partnership of married life and love has been established by the Creator and qualified by His laws, and is rooted in the conjugal covenant of irrevocable personal consent.... As God of old made Himself present to His people through a covenant of love and fidelity, so now the Savior of human beings and the Spouse of the Church comes into the lives of married Christians through the Sacrament of Matrimony. He abides with them thereafter so that just as He loved the Church and handed Himself over on her behalf, the spouses may love each other with perpetual fidelity through mutual self-bestowal.

"Authentic married love is caught up into divine love and is governed and enriched by Christ's redeeming power and the saving activity of the Church, so that this love may lead the spouses to God with powerful effect and may aid and strengthen them in the sublime office of being a father or a mother" (no. 48.)

248. *What are the duties of married persons?*

Married persons should

1. **live in love and harmony and be true to each other until death,**
2. **strengthen and encourage each other by living a good Catholic life,**
3. **and bring up their children in the love and fear of God.**

Parents should also prepare their children for life in the world. They should help them with obtaining the training or education to get started in the world.

Vatican II (ibid., *see Question 247) says: "With their parents leading the way by example and family prayer, children and indeed everyone gathered around the family hearth will find a readier path to human maturity, salvation, and holiness. Graced with the dignity and office of fatherhood and motherhood, parents will energetically acquit themselves of a duty which devolves primarily on them, namely, education and especially religious education."*

249.   Can marriage be dissolved?

A valid marriage cannot be dissolved.

Let no man separate what God has joined" (Mt 19:6). — "Everyone who divorces his wife and marries another commits adultery. The man who marries a woman divorced from her husband likewise commits adultery" (Lk 16:18).

When the state or civil law "breaks" a valid marriage and permits the divorced persons to marry again, this has no validity in the eyes of God and the Church. For grave reasons the Church may permit a Catholic married couple to live apart, but they are not free to enter upon another marriage.

It is also possible that a marriage was invalid from the beginning because of an impediment, which may or may not have been known to the couple when they took the marriage vows. In such cases, after due process (which may require much time because it must be thorough), the Church can declare an annulment. To outsiders this may seem like a divorce, but it is not a divorce, only a juridical finding that no marriage existed.

Concerning married love, Vatican II in the Pastoral Constitution on the Church in the Modern World *says, "Sealed by mutual faithfulness and hallowed above all by Christ's Sacrament, this love remains steadfastly true in body and in mind, in bright days or dark. It will never be profaned by adultery or divorce. Firmly established by the Lord, the unity of marriage will radiate from the equal personal dignity of wife and husband, a dignity acknowledged by mutual and total love. The constant fulfillment of the duties of this Christian vocation demands notable virtue. For this reason, strengthened by grace for holiness of life, the couple will painstakingly cultivate and pray for steadiness of love, large-heartedness, and the spirit of sacrifice" (no. 49).*

250. *What is expected of those who want to enter into marriage?*

Those who want to enter into marriage are expected to

1. **be free of impediments to marriage,**
2. **become engaged only after due acquaintance with each other,**
3. **live chastely during the engagement,**
4. **and go to Confession and receive Holy Communion in view of marriage.**

When the Church—as, for that matter, the State—sets up impediments to marriage, it is for the good of marriage, which redounds to the good of the parties and the social structure. Pius XI remarked: "By matrimony the souls of the contracting parties are joined and knit together more directly and more intimately than are their bodies, and that not by any passing affection of sense or spirit, but by a deliberate and firm act of the will; and from this union of souls by God's decree, a sacred and inviolate bond arises.

"Hence the nature of this contract, which is proper and peculiar to it alone, makes it entirely different both from the union of animals entered into by the blind instinct of nature alone in which neither reason nor free will plays a part, and also from the haphazard unions of human beings, which are far removed from all true and honorable unions of will and enjoy none of the rights of family life.

"From this it is clear that legitimately constituted authority has the right and therefore the duty to restrict, to prevent, and to punish those base unions which are opposed to reason and to nature" *(Encyclical on Christian Marriage, nos. 7-8).*

Examples of impediments are: a prior valid marriage, too close a degree of blood relationship, lack of age, and a difference of religion. Some, known as "impeding"impediments, can be waived by the Church if there is sufficient reason. Others, known as "diriment" impediments, are incompatible with the very nature of marriage and are never set aside, e.g., being validly married already.

Because of the general disintegration of the marriage bond, sadly among Catholics too, the American Bishops have adopted the policy of a "waiting period" (from three to six months or longer depending of the diocese) before two people can be married. The policy is designed above all, but not exclusively, for the younger age group, who are prone to marry in haste and "split" almost at will. During the waiting period prospective couples are to be thoroughly instructed in the Catholic teaching on marriage and imbued with the seriousness of the step they are taking: what it demands, what and what not to expect from marriage, how to deal with the problems that arise, how Catholic marriage differs from other marriage and with God's grace can keep them happily together till death—and after.

251. *What is to be said about mixed marriages?*

Mixed marriages—generally between a Catholic and a non-Catholic Christian—are permitted with a dispensation by the Church but nevertheless are to be discouraged because in many cases they give rise to grave, if not insoluble, difficulties, especially in regard to the upbringing of children.

"Mixed marriages, that is to say, marriages in which one party is a Catholic and the other a non-Catholic, whether baptized or not, have always been given careful attention by the Church in pursuance of her duty. Today the Church is constrained to give even greater attention to them, owing to the conditions of present times. In the past Catholics were separated from members of other Christian confessions and from non-Christians, by their situation in their community or even by physical boundaries.

"In more recent times, however, not only has this separation been reduced, but communication between people of different regions and religions has greatly developed, and as a result there has been a great increase in the number of mixed marriages. Also a great influence in this regard has been exercised by the growth and spread of civilization and industry, urbanization and consequent rural depopulation, migrations in great numbers and the increase in numbers of exiles of every kind.

"The Church is indeed aware that mixed marriages, precisely because they admit differences of religion and are a consequence of the division among Christians, do not, except in some cases, help in reestablishing unity among Christians. There are many difficulties inherent in a mixed marriage, since a certain division is introduced into the living cell of the Church, as the Christian family is rightly called, and in the family itself the fulfillment of the Gospel teachings is more difficult because of diversities in matters of religion, especially with regard to those matters which concern Christian worship and the education of the children.

"For these reasons the Church, conscious of her duty, discourages the contracting of mixed marriages, for she is most desirous that Catholics be able in matrimony to attain to perfect union of mind and full communion of life. However, since human beings have the natural right to marry and beget children, the Church, by her laws, which clearly show her pastoral concern, makes such arrangements that on the one hand the principles of Divine law be scrupulously observed and that on the other the said right to contract marriage be respected" (Paul VI: *Apostolic Letter on Mixed Marriages*).

The early Church was faced with mixed marriages, at that time between a Christian convert and a pagan. In such marriages the pagan partner often took exception to the Christian practices of the other, like making the Sign of the Cross or going out for celebration of the Eucharist. In contrast, Tertullian extols the beauty of a marriage in which both parties have the same Christian faith. He dedicated a little book on the subject to his wife in the belief that he would die first and she would marry again. He concludes:

"Who can describe the happiness of a marriage which is ratified by the Church, sealed by her blessing, and strengthened by the Father in heaven. Both are servants of the same Lord. They pray together, fast together, are together in church, together at the Table of the Lord. Leaving the house to attend the Eucharist arouses no suspicion and daily devotions at home encounter no displeasure. Here there is no need to make the Sign of the Cross on the sly, or to bless oneself in silence. Pleased to see and hear such things, Christ sends them His peace. Remember this, just in case, because Christians ought not to marry differently" (Tertullian, Christian writer, d. ca. 220).

Sacramentals

252. *What are Sacramentals?*

Sacramentals are sacred signs which bear a resemblance to the Sacraments: they signify effects, particularly of a spiritual kind, which are obtained through the intercession of the Church. By them people are disposed to receive the chief effect of the Sacraments, and various occasions in life are rendered holy.

"Ever since Christ's Incarnation, Passion, and Resurrection, the redeemed world belongs to a sacramental world. The effects of what the Son of God once accomplished for us in history are now transmitted by Him to His members in the way of sacramental rites. Christ has brought sacramental life into operation. The Infinite condescends to live in the finite by grace; the finite has by Him been elevated to experience living union with the Uncreated. Between the life of the Deity and the life of humanity lies the field of sacramental activity where Infinite and finite meet and are united. After man is first initiated into the sacramental system through Baptism, his new life is exercised and developed by the other Sacraments, but primarily by the Eucharist, the Sacrament-Sacrifice and the Sacrament-Banquet. . . .

"Just as the Sacraments are radiations of being from the Eucharist as their center, so also the Sacramentals can be said to form an outer circle around the Sacraments, all of them converging toward the Eucharist as the center. Eucharistic worship is the consecration of all time and all matter. A Christian's every and entire day is sanctified by it. 'Go into the world, and be light-bearers,' is the meaning of the dismissal at the end of the Sacrifice" (Philip T. Weller, *The Roman Ritual, Vol. III: The Blessings,* pp. vii and xii–xiii).

253. *How do Sacramentals differ from the Sacraments?*

Sacramentals differ from the Sacraments in that they were not directly instituted by Christ, do not produce grace of themselves, and are not signs of His direct action on our souls. They were instituted by the Church and obtain graces for us indirectly by arousing us to those acts of virtue which draw down God's graces on us.

"The consecrations and blessings [that is, Sacramentals] of the Church are extensions and radiations of the Sacraments. Their purpose, too, is Christ-life—building up of the

Mystical Body into perfect stones to fit into the perfection of the Corner-Stone. They continue the work of the Sacraments or prepare for their reception.

"Baptism is followed up by the Sacramentals of holy water, the Sunday morning Asperges, the blessing of infants, of children. Confirmation is extended in the blessings of a school, of a library, an archive, a typewriter, or in those Sacramentals which have a relation to the functioning of the Spirit's gifts. The consecration of a monk or of a nun is patterned on Holy Orders. Matrimony is followed by the blessing of a bridal-chamber, the blessing of an expectant mother, the act of churching, the blessing of a home, and the profusion of blessings for material things which are used in family life. The Sacrament of Penance is extended in the Sacramentals of the Confiteor, absolutions, the papal blessing in the hour of a Christian's departure from this world, and exorcisms. The Anointing of the Sick has for its radiations the blessings for the sick, the blessing of sick pilgrims, blessing of wine, medicine, linens. the blessing of a corpse, of a grave.

"Thus the Sacramentals either lead up to or continue the grace of the Sacraments. The various circumstances and conditions and materials of life are consecrated, lest by their unsanctified state they prove to be obstacles in the way of sanctified humanity" (Weller, *op. cit.*, p. xii).

254. *What are the chief benefits obtained by the use of Sacramentals?*

The chief benefits obtained by the use of Sacramentals are:

1. **actual graces,**
2. **forgiveness of venial sins,**
3. **remission of temporal punishment due to sin,**
4. **health of body and material blessings,**
5. **and protection from evil spirits.**

In the *Constitution on the Sacred Liturgy*, the Second Vatican Council says: "Thus, for well-disposed members of the faithful, the liturgy of the Sacraments and Sacramentals sanctifies almost every event in their lives; they are given access to the stream of divine grace which flows from the Paschal Mystery of the Passion, Death, and Resurrection of Christ, the fountain from which all Sacraments and Sacramentals draw their power. There is hardly any proper use of material things which cannot be directed toward the sanctification of human beings and the praise of God" (no. 61).

255. What are the chief kinds of Sacramentals?

The chief kinds of Sacramentals are:

1. **blessings,**
2. **exorcisms,**
3. **and blessed objects of devotion.**

The most used objects are: holy water, candles, ashes, palms, crucifixes, medals, rosaries, scapulars, and images of Jesus, Mary, and the Saints.

Blessings provide an opportunity for catechizing the faithful. For example, the primary place occupied in them by the Bible is a pressing invitation to read the Scriptural passages to which allusion is made and consequently to render understandable the formula and the gesture by placing them within the framework of the whole of Revelation.

In this connection, the Sacred Congregation for Divine Worship discussed blessings in 1972 and concluded among other things: (1) A blessing obtains certain spiritual effects, consecrating people or things to God's service or praying for people and their needs. (2) The first element in a blessing is praise and gratitude toward God Who made everything. (3) A blessing reminds us that all creation is good and that God watches over every part of it. When we give thanks to God, we profess that He made all things and gives us all things. (4) The use of blessings should increase in the lives of Christians. We should continue to be conscious of God and His

Providence over the universe. Accordingly, it is good for lay people to make use of blessings, especially those which refer to their daily lives and activities, as indicated by Vatican II: "Let provision be made that some Sacramentals, at least in special circumstances and at the discretion of the Ordinary, may be administered by qualified lay persons" (no. 79).

256. From whom has the Church this power to bless, to consecrate, and to perform exorcisms?

The Church has this power to bless, to consecrate, and to perform exorcisms from Christ.

"[Jesus] summoned his twelve disciples and gave them authority to expel unclean spirits and to cure sickness and disease of every kind" (Mt 10:1). — "They will use my name to expel demons . . . and the sick upon whom they lay their hands will recover" (Mk 16:17-18).

The Church prays to ward off God's judgment; she prays for protection from the devil, for peace, for blessing, for the spiritual and temporal welfare of her people and the world. Powerful as the Church's invocation may be, it is not without fail, because the effect also depends on the worthiness of the recipient.

257. What is the purpose of the Church's blessings?

The purpose of the Church's blessings is to invoke God's favor on persons, places, and things.

For example: Benediction of the Blessed Sacrament, blessing of the sick, of fields and harvests, blessing of children by their parents.

The 1979 German Interim Book of Blessings, which has the approval of the Sacred Congregation for the Sacraments and Divine Worship, states:

"God, source of blessing. *Human beings need blessings. They seek salvation, protection, happiness, and fulfillment in their lives. Therefore, they mutually bless one another: they wish each other well. Above all, they aspire to and implore the blessing that comes from God.*

"God is the source of all good and all blessing (Gn 1:22, 28). Israel experienced and acknowledged this fact more clearly than other peoples. According to the affirmations of the Old Testament, a blessing increases life to the same extent that a malediction decreases it. God's blessing is manifested first of all in creation, which is a gift of God, above all for human beings (cfr. Gn 1:26). . . .

"In Jesus Christ, the Revelation of God's salvation reached its culminating point in the story of humankind. Christ is the 'Yes' of God; 'all the promises of God have been fulfilled in Him' (2 Cor 1:20). Since the Son of God relies on the Spirit of God in fullness (cfr. Lk 1:30-36). He establishes the Kingdom of God through the medium of His word and His deeds with the language of signs (cfr. Acts 10:37ff; Lk 4:18ff; 11:20) and communicates God's grace and blessing to all in Israel. Through His Death and Resurrection, the saving power of Christ is made accessible to all human beings and is communicated in the Holy Spirit, principally by means of the Sacraments, but also by means of blessings" (Introduction, nos. 1, 2, 5: Notitiae 153, pp. 219-220).

258. What is the further purpose of the Church's blessings?

The further purpose of the Church's blessings is to set apart certain things for God's service or the pious use of the faithful.

"Everything . . . is made holy by God's word and by prayer" (1 Tm 4:5). — Some blessings of this type are: blessing of churches, altars and cemeteries, sacred vessels and vestments. Various blessings in the course of the liturgical year: blessing of the new fire of Easter, the Easter candle, the baptismal water.

Blessed articles should be treated and used with proper reverence, in a spirit of humble faith and trust in God's mercy.

In addition to places and things, persons are blessed or consecrated for exclusive service to God: bishops, priests and deacons, and members of religious orders when they take their vows.

The use of Sacramentals (e.g., wearing a blessed religious medal) is not superstition. We do not ascribe special power to the medal itself, which is only a material object of a certain size, shape, color, and such. Rather, the medal, or any Sacramental, is an outward sign of what is in our heart: faith and trust in God, and trust in the intercessory power of the Saint depicted on the medal. It is from God, not from the medal, that we seek help, and it is the Saint whom we beseech to intercede for us with God. The medal helps bring our thought back to God and what He has wrought for us, and back to the Saint or Saints through whom He has wrought it.

259. Why do we use holy water?

We use holy water to ask God's blessing and to ward off the devil and all evil of body and soul.

Washing with water, sometimes mixed with salt, was a sign of spiritual cleansing in the Old Testament (Ps 51:9; Ez 16:4; 36:25). These biblical precedents no doubt influenced the Christian practice of using holy water against sickness and evil spirits. The practice is first found in Egypt, in the 4th century. From there it spread to Rome, where the blessing of water included the addition of salt in imitation of 2 Kgs 2:19-21. At first priests would bless water in individual homes, but by the 7th century the blessing had moved to church.

Holy water is a reminder of baptismal water and therefore of our Baptism and baptismal promises. We should think of this whenever we use holy water and make the Sign of the Cross, as on entering a church. A Catholic home should keep and make devout use of holy water, one of the Sacramentals that identify the Catholic family.

Prayer

260. *What is prayer?*

Prayer is lifting our heart and mind to God so as to praise Him, to thank Him, or to ask Him for something.

More simply, prayer is talking with God. The Second Vatican Council says in the *Dogmatic Constitution on the Church:* "All disciples of Christ, persevering in prayer and praising God, should present themselves as a living sacrifice, holy and pleasing to God" (no. 10).

261. *Why do we pray?*

We pray:
1. because God is Lord and Father to us,
2. because without prayer we cannot be saved.

"[Jesus] told them a parable on the necessity of praying always and not losing heart" (Lk 18:1). "Ask and you shall receive; seek and you shall find; knock and it shall be opened to you" (Lk 11:9).

"All the blessed in heaven (infants excepted) were saved through prayer; all the damned were lost because they did not pray" (St. Alphonsus of Ligouri, d. 1787).

262. *What especially should we pray for?*

We should pray especially that God may be glorified and that all people may gain eternal salvation.

In the *Decree on the Apostolate of the Laity,* Vatican II says: "All should remember that they can reach all human

JESUS LEFT US THE GREATEST EXAMPLE OF PRAYER
Jesus lived his entire life in communion with his Father, so that the attitude of prayer was for him a permanent one. Among other times he prayed especially in the Garden of Gethsemani, before his passion and death (Lk 23:39-46).

beings and contribute to the salvation of the whole world by public worship and prayer as well as by penance and voluntary acceptance of the labors and hardships of life whereby they become like the suffering Christ (2 Cor 4:10; Col 1:24)" (no. 16).

263. How should we pray?

We should pray with (1) devotion, (2) humility, (3) resignation, (4) confidence, and (5) perseverance.

Devotion: this means praying from the heart, avoiding distractions. Only voluntary distractions are culpable. But persons who indulge in distraction at prayer should remember our Lord's reproof, citing Isaiah: "This people pays me lip service, but their heart is far from me" (Mt 15:8).

Humility: we acknowledge our sinfulness and need for help. The tax collector in the temple prayed with humility: "O God, be merciful to me, a sinner" (Lk 18:13).

Resignation: we leave it to God's will as to when and how He will hear us. Our Lord prayed in this way on the Mount of Olives: "Let it be as you would have it, not as I" (Mt 26:39).

Confidence: we trust that God will hear us. Christ said: "Whatever you ask the Father, he will give you in my name" (Jn 16:23). One of the criminals crucified with Jesus had this confidence. Though by his own admission a wrongdoer, he yet prayed and said to Jesus: "Remember me when you enter upon your reign" (Lk 23:42).

Perseverance: we continue to pray even though our prayer is not heard at once or as soon as we would like. St. James writes: "The fervent petition of a holy man is powerful indeed" (5:16). An example of persevering prayer is the Canaanite woman (Mt 15:21-28).

Models of prayer are numerous, in and out of the Bible. Moses spoke with God forty days and nights on the mountain (Ex 24:18). — Daniel, despite the king's prohibition, betook himself to prayer three times daily (Dn 6:11). — Our Lord Himself, though Son of God, prayed often (Mk 1:35; Lk

5:16; 6:12). — Because he prayed much to God, the centurion Cornelius became the first Gentile to be received into the Church (Acts 10:1ff). — All the Saints were much in prayer. St. Monica (d. 387) prayed eighteen years so that her son Augustine might mend his ways and turn to God.

264. What does prayer do?

Prayer brings many graces; it unites us with God, strengthens us against evil, and help us to persevere and lead a good Catholic life.

Vatican II, in the *Dogmatic Constitution on the Church,* says: "In order that love, like good seed, may grow and bring forth fruit in the soul, the faithful must . . . complete what God has begun by their own actions with the help of God's grace." Among these actions are "application of oneself to prayer, self-abnegation, lively fraternal service and the constant exercise of all virtues" (no. 42).

265. When should we pray?

We should pray often, especially in the morning and at night, before and after meals, at worship services in church, in every need and temptation.

Concerning the many ways of prayer the New (Dutch) Catechism says:

"Those who love God will sometimes interrupt their day to say a short word to Him. Just as there are many who curse unthinkingly, there are many (or perhaps the same?) who often turn deliberately to God to say 'Help me' or 'Give me patience' or 'Thanks.' They are all ways of expressing briefly the great basic attitudes of faith, hope and love. Some men have a quick sense of God's peace in the midst of a fierce rush of business, in a traffic jam or at a party. — And it can also happen that those who have not really spoken to God for a long time, suddenly find words during the repose of their holidays.

"A very simple and common way to create a space of peace is to recite set prayers. We must not despise this form of prayer. In a busy life, fixed forms can be a help and an inspiration, as when we say the Our Father and the Hail Mary to ourselves. . . . Obviously we cannot think of each word during vocal prayer at such times. . . . But the whole gesture is a little pause for peace, an indication of the Other who is among us, an act of thanksgiving.

"A greater inward peace is brought about by a longer vocal prayer, as when we use a prayerbook, or recite one or more psalms. Here too one cannot always think of all the words. But they create an atmosphere of peace, so that we can let God's light in our lives, or say how sad or how grateful our existence makes us. . . .

"Early morning is a privileged time for prayer. Many of us would be happier if we got up half an hour earlier and went more quietly about everything each day. The morning hours are golden. And prayer is part of that gold. . . . Many have the habit of offering each day to God expressly each morning, and this can in fact be a very good thing. . . . Very often evening prayers well said fit in better than morning prayers in the rhythm of our life. Night-fall is the time of recollection. It is the hour to give thanks, to reflect, to ask pardon, to read some Scripture or some other book. What reason can there be for married people not to pray together to Him in whose name they have been married? It can be a very good practice to make night prayers consist in part of a fixed form of words . . . and in part of one's own words, even though very few. Set prayers, as we have seen, form a haven of peace for busy men, while one's own words do much to make prayer real.

"As well as morning and night prayers, there is grace at meals. We bless our food before eating and give thanks afterward. It is one of the ways by which human eating is distinguished from that of the animals. We should not let ourselves grow slovenly at this good family custom. And if it has become slipshod or even disappeared, we should restore it" (Herder and Herder, New York, 1967, pp. 314-315).

266. *For whom should we pray?*

We should pray for all people, particularly for those most dear to us or most in need of our prayer, and also for the dead.

St. Paul's Letters often appeal for prayer. He prays for his readers and ask their prayer for him: "We have been praying for you unceasingly. . . . Pray for us, too" (Col 1:9; 4:3). To Timothy his pupil he writes: "I urge that petitions, prayers, intercessions, and thanksgiving be offered for all men, especially for kings and those in authority" (1 Tm 2:1).

In the *Constitution on the Sacred Liturgy,* Vatican II says: "Especially on Sundays and feasts of obligation, there is to be restored, after the Gospel and the homily, 'the common prayer' or 'the prayer of the faithful.' By this prayer, in which the people are to take part, intercession will be made for holy Church, for the civil authorities, for those oppressed by various needs, for all mankind, and for the salvation of the entire world" (no. 53).

Some Catholic Prayers that We Should Often Pray

Our Father (Lord's Prayer)

The commonly used form of the Our Father occurs in Matthew 6:9-13. A shorter rendering is Luke 11:2-4. Taught by Christ Himself to His disciples, it is truly the Lord's Prayer, preeminently sacred. Already in the first century Christians prayed it three times a day, as we learn from the *Didache,* one of the earliest Christian writings. Tertullian (d. ca. 220) called it "an abstract or summary of the whole Gospel."

The *Didache* subjoined the doxology: "For Yours are the power and the glory forever." To this the Liturgy of St. John

Chrysostom in the 4th century added a third motif: *the kingdom* (to "the power and the glory"). In this form it was long in use in Protestant services. In an updated form it is now embodied also in the Roman Catholic liturgy of the Mass ("For the kingdom, the power, and the glory are Yours now and for ever"). Hence, it is suitable for private recitation of the Our Father, if one so desires.

O UR Father, Who art in heaven,
  hallowed be Thy Name;
Thy kingdom come;
Thy will be done on earth as it is in heaven.
Give us this day our daily bread;
and forgive us our trespasses
as we forgive those who trespass against us;
and lead us not into temptation,
but deliver us from evil. Amen.

Another (Ecumenical) version of the Our Father is as follows:

O UR Father in heaven.
  hallowed be Your Name,
Your kingdom come,
Your will be done,
  on earth as in heaven.
Give us today our daily bread.
Forgive us our sins
  as we forgive those who sin against us.
Save us from the time of trial
  and deliver us from evil.
For the kingdom, the power, and the glory are Yours
  now and for ever.

Sign of the Cross

This prayer, simple and profound, expresses our belief in the Blessed Trinity. It recalls Christ's words when sending His Apostles to teach and baptize all nations (Mt 28:19). It can be used at the beginning and end of almost anything: prayer, work, study, play, whatever.

IN the Name of the Father,
and of the Son,
and of the Holy Spirit.   Amen.

Glory to the Father (Gloria Patri)

Like the Sign of the Cross, this is a simple little prayer in honor of the Blessed Trinity. In the Divine Office (Liturgy of the Hours) it is said at the end of each psalm. It is used in many other liturgical settings, as well as in popular devotions.

GLORY be to the Father,
and to the Son,
and to the Holy Spirit.
As it was in the beginning,
is now, and ever shall be,
world without end. Amen.

Another (Ecumenical) version is used in the Liturgy of the Hours:

GLORY to the Father,
and to the Son.
and to the Holy Spirit:
as it was in the beginning,
is now,
and will be for ever. Amen.

Hail Mary

Also known as "Ave Maria" (its first words in Latin) and the Angelic Salutation, the Hail Mary was inspired by St. Luke's Gospel. It consists of three parts: the words of the Archangel Gabriel to Mary at the Annunciation (Lk 1:28), the words of Elizabeth to Mary visiting her (Lk 1:42), and a prayer of supplication to Mary (not in Luke). The first two parts formed a devotional prayer as early as the 6th century in Antioch, somewhat later in the West (7th/8th cent.). The supplication to Mary was first introduced by St. Bernardine of Siena, about the year 1440. In 1568, Pius V inserted the Hail Mary in the new Breviary.

HAIL Mary, full of grace,
  the Lord is with you;
blessed are you among women,
and blessed is the fruit of your womb, Jesus.
Holy Mary, Mother of God,
pray for us sinners,
now and at the hour of our death. Amen.

Hail, Holy Queen

Of uncertain origin, this prayer (Latin: *Salve Regina)* dates at least from the 11th century. It became very popular, and still is. The monks of Cluny often used it as a processional hymn, and the Cistercians prayed it three times daily. The 14th century saw its inclusion in the Breviary, where in present practice it is one of several Marian anthems at the end of Compline or Night Prayer. Many of the faithful add it to their Rosary.

HAIL, Holy Queen, Mother of Mercy, our life, our sweetness, and our hope! To you do we cry, poor banished children of Eve. To you do we send up our sighs, mourning and weeping in this valley of tears. Turn, then, most gracious Advocate, your eyes of mercy toward us. And after this our exile show unto us the blessed fruit of your womb, Jesus. O clement, O loving, O sweet Virgin Mary.

We Fly to Your Patronage (Sub tuum praesidium)

This is the oldest prayer of petition to Mary. What is perhaps its original version was discovered on an Egyptian papyrus in 1917. Experts say that the papyrus goes back to the 3rd century, an indication that the prayer already was in use in Egypt at that time, hence even before the Council of Nicaea (325). From Egypt, where Mary and Joseph fled with Jesus (Mt 2:13-15), its use spread to other parts of the Christian world, to Europe in particular. The prayer is like a cry out of the distant past, the Age of Persecution. As such it is always relevant, even as persecution somehow or somewhere is always occurring (Cf. *Osservatore Romano,* Oct. 9, 1954).

W E fly to your patronage, O holy Mother of God. Despise not our petitions in our necessities, but deliver us always from all dangers, O glorious and blessed Virgin.

Angelus (Angel of the Lord)

It is a holy tradition to pray at morning, noon, and night. The Angelus is part of this tradition and seems to have been inspired, indirectly, by the Liturgy of the Hours. The church bells were rung when the monks prayed the hours of Lauds (Morning Prayer) and Vespers (Evening Prayer). At each ringing the people of the countryside, wanting to join in the prayer of the monks, prayed something at home. The beginnings of this custom can be traced to the early 14th century, but the present form of the Angelus dates to the 17th. During the Easter season, instead of the Angelus the Regina Caeli or Queen of Heaven is said (see below).

V. The angel of the Lord declared unto Mary.

R. And she conceived of the Holy Spirit.

Hail Mary, etc.

V. Behold the handmaid of the Lord.

R. Be it done to me according to your word.

Hail Mary, etc.

V. And the Word was made flesh.

R. And dwelt among us.

Hail Mary, etc.

V. Pray for us, O holy Mother of God.

R. That we may be made worthy of the promises of Christ.

Let us pray. Pour forth, we beg You, O Lord, Your grace into our hearts: that we, to whom the Incarnation of Christ Your Son was made known by the message of an Angel, may by His Passion and Cross be brought to the glory of His Resurrection. Through the same Christ our Lord. **R.** Amen.

Regina Caeli (Queen of Heaven)

This Marian anthem celebrates the joy of Christ's Resurrection. Its substitution for the Angelus dates from 1742, though the prayer itself is much older, appearing in the Franciscan Breviary as early as 1235 or thereabouts.

O QUEEN of heaven, rejoice, alleluia.
For He Whom you merited to bear, alleluia,
Has risen, as He said, alleluia.
Pray for us to God, alleluia.

V. Rejoice and be glad, O Virgin Mary, alleluia.
R. Because the Lord is truly risen, alleluia.

Let us pray. O God, Who by the Resurrection of Your Son, our Lord Jesus Christ, granted joy to the whole world: grant, we beg You, that through the intercession of the Virgin Mary, His Mother, we may lay hold of the joys of eternal life. Through the same Christ our Lord. Amen.

The Rosary

Popular tradition associates the origin of the Rosary with St. Dominic (d. 1221). Its first appearance, as a matter of fact, dates from his lifetime, and there is no doubt that his influence contributed to its popularization. Moreover, people generally could not read; so instead of 150 psalms from a book (manuscript), they prayed 150 Hail Marys, a prayer everyone knew. The practice of combining the Hail Marys with meditation on the Mysteries of the Catholic Faith was introduced by two Carthusian monks in the early 15th century. Toward the end of that century the list of mysteries had become standardized. The list has remained the same ever since.

The victory of the Christian forces at the battle of Lepanto, October 7, 1571, was attributed to the Rosary, which Pope Pius V had asked all Christendom to pray for the successful protection of Christian borders. Pope Leo XIII issued 16 documents on the Rosary—encyclicals and other Apostolic

Letters. He is known as the "Pope of the Rosary." He also prescribed the Rosary for the month of October, which then became the "month of the Rosary."

The name "Rosary" was given currency by a Cistercian monk of the 13th century, who described devotional prayers in honor of Mary as a "garland of spiritual roses." The Rosary as a whole consists of 15 decades (10 beads each). To "say a Rosary" generally means to pray five of the 15 decades, while meditating on the Mysteries assigned to the decades.

In praying the Rosary it is not necessary to think of each word we say, It is enough, indeed better, to focus attention on the general theme of a given Mystery as we tell our beads. Whoever prays the Rosary in this way, and as the Church intends (devoutly, meditatively), will not find it monotonous but a source of spiritual comfort and renewal. The Rosary has given many people a deeper appreciation of the great Mysteries of our faith. It is the Gospel relived, the life and work of our Lord reenacted in our hearts and minds.

The Joyful Mysteries

1. **The Annunciation of the Archangel Gabriel to Mary.**
2. **The Visitation of Mary to Elizabeth.**
3. **The Birth of Jesus at Bethlehem.**
4. **The Presentation of Jesus in the Temple.**
5. **The Finding of Jesus in the Temple.**

The Sorrowful Mysteries

1. **The Agony of Jesus in the Garden.**
2. **The Scourging at the Pillar.**
3. **The Crowning of Jesus with Thorns.**
4. **The Carrying of the Cross by Jesus to Calvary.**
5. **The Crucifixion and Death of Jesus.**

The Glorious Mysteries

1. **The Resurrection of Jesus from the Dead.**
2. **The Ascension of Jesus into Heaven.**
3. **The Descent of the Holy Spirit upon the Apostles.**
4. **The Assumption of Mary into Heaven.**
5. **The Coronation of Mary as Queen of Heaven.**

The Te Deum

This celebrated hymn of the Western Church is at once a prayer, a song of thanksgiving and praise, a plea for a blessing, and a profession of faith. It is still used today on Sundays and major feasts in the Liturgy of the Hours after Morning Prayer. It is also used outside liturgical celebrations to give thanks to God. The first part calls upon God the Father. The second part addresses God the Son. The third part, which does not really belong to the prayer itself, offers a series of petitions that are based on psalm verses.

Since the 9th century tradition has assigned the composition of this hymn to Sts. Ambrose and Augustine at the latter's Baptism. However, this attribution is now almost universally rejected by modern scholars. Today, the *Te Deum* is widely thought to be the work of St. Nicetas of Remesiana. (d. 414).

YOU are God: we praise You;
   You are the Lord: we acclaim You;
You are the eternal Father:
All creation worships You.

To You all angels, all the powers of heaven,
Cherubim and Seraphim, sing in endless praise:
   Holy, holy, holy, Lord, God of power and might,
   heaven and earth are full of Your glory.

The glorious company of Apostles praise You.
The noble fellowship of Prophets praise You.
The white-robed army of Martyrs praise You.

Throughout the world the holy Church acclaims You:
   Father, of majesty unbounded,
   Your true and only Son, worthy of all worship,
   and the Holy Spirit, advocate and guide.

You, Christ, are the King of glory,
the eternal Son of the Father.

When You became Man to set us free
You did not spurn the Virgin's womb.

You overcame the sting of death,
and opened the kingdom of heaven to all believers.

You are seated at God's right hand in glory.
We believe that you will come, and be our judge.
　Come then, Lord, and help Your people,
　bought with the price of Your own Blood,
　and bring us with Your Saints
　to glory everlasting.

V. Save Your people, Lord, and bless Your inheritance.
R. Govern and uphold them now and always.
V. Day by day we bless You.
R. We praise Your name for ever.
V. Keep us today, Lord, from all sin.
R. Have mercy on us, Lord, have mercy.
V. Lord, show us Your love and mercy;
R. for we put our trust in You.
V. In You, Lord, is our hope:
R. and we shall never hope in vain.

Canticle of Mary (Magnificat)

Shortly after the Blessed Virgin Mary learned from the Angel that she was to be the Mother of God, she visited her cousin Elizabeth. Upon being greeted by Elizabeth, Mary chanted a song of praise (Lk 1:46-55). This hymn praising the Divine power and mercy resembles the canticles sung by Hannah in the Old Testament when she learned that her prayer for a child had been answered (1 Sm 2:1-10). This canticle is recited each day at Evening Prayer in the Liturgy of the Hours and as an expression of joy on occasions of solemn thanksgiving.

M Y being proclaims the greatness of the Lord,
　my spirit finds joy in God my savior.
For He has looked upon His servant in her lowliness;
　all ages to come shall call me blessed.
God Who is mighty has done great things for me,
　holy is His name;
His mercy is from age to age
　on those who fear Him.
He has shown might with His arm;
　He has confused the proud in their inmost thoughts.

He has deposed the mighty from their thrones
  and raised the lowly to high places.
The hungry He has given every good thing,
  while the rich He has sent empty away.
He has upheld Israel His servant,
  ever mindful of His mercy;
Even as He promised our fathers,
  promised Abraham and His descendants forever.

Canticle of Zechariah (Benedictus)

When John the Baptist was born, his father Zechariah uttered a song of thanksgiving (Lk 1:68-79). The hymn is addressed to God in gratitude for the fulfillment of the Messianic hopes and to the child who will be the forerunner of the Messiah. This canticle is recited each day at Morning Prayer in the Liturgy of the Hours.

BLESSED be the Lord the God of Israel
  because He has visited and ransomed His people.
He has raised a horn of saving strength for us
  in the house of David His servant,
As He promised through the mouths of His holy ones,
  the Prophets of ancient times:
Salvation from our enemies
  and from the hands of all our foes.

He has dealt mercifully with our fathers
  and remembered the holy covenant He made,
the oath He swore to Abraham our father
  He would grant us:
    that, rid of fear and delivered from the enemy,
We should serve Him devoutly and through all our days
  be holy in His sight.
And you, O child, shall be called
  prophet of the Most High;
For you shall go before the Lord
  to prepare straight paths for Him,
Giving His people a knowledge of salvation
  in freedom from their sins.

All this is the work of the kindness of our God;
He, the Dayspring, shall visit us in His mercy
To shine on those who sit in darkness
    and in the shadow of death,
    to guide our feet into the way of peace.

Canticle of Simeon (Nunc Dimittis)

When the aged Simeon caught sight of the child Jesus in the Temple, he burst out in a short hymn (Lk 2:29-32). It is an expression of joy and thanksgiving for God's special blessing and lends itself to use as a night prayer. It is recited at Night Prayer in the Liturgy of the Hours.

NOW, Master, You can dismiss Your servant in peace; You have fulfilled Your word.
For my eyes have witnessed Your saving deed
    displayed for all the peoples to see:
A revealing light to the Gentiles,
    the glory of Your people Israel.

Prayers at Meals

Our Lord prayed at meals, as did the Apostles (Jn 6:11; Acts 27:35). We can pray in our own words, or say the traditional prayers here given. Prayer at table should make us mindful also of the spiritual Eucharistic food in Holy Communion.

Before Meals

BLESS us, O Lord, and these Your gifts, which we are about to receive from Your bounty. Through Christ our Lord. Amen.

After Meals

WE give You thanks, almighty God, for these and all the gifts we have received from Your bounty. Through Christ our Lord. Amen.
(May the souls of all the faithful departed by the mercy of God rest in peace. Amen.)

Morning and Evening Prayers

Though we can pray any time, for most people morning and evening are most convenient for private prayer, the prayer "to the Father in secret" (Mt 6:6).

Morning Offering

MOST holy and adorable Trinity, one God in three Persons, I praise You and give You thanks for all the favors You have bestowed upon me. Your goodness has preserved me until now. I offer You my whole being and in particular all my thoughts, words, and deeds, together with all the trials I may undergo this day. Give them Your blessing. May Your Divine Love animate them and may they serve Your greater glory.

I make this morning offering in union with the Divine intentions of Jesus Christ Who offers Himself daily in the holy Sacrifice of the Mass, and in union with Mary, His Virgin Mother and our Mother, who was always the faithful handmaid of the Lord.

Another Morning Offering

O JESUS, through the Immaculate Heart of Mary, I offer You my prayers, works, joys, and sufferings of this day in union with the Holy Sacrifice of the Mass throughout the world. I offer them for all the intentions of Your Sacred Heart: the salvation of souls, reparation for sins, the reunion of all Christians. I offer them for the intentions of our Bishops and of all the Apostles of Prayer, and in particular for those recommended by our Holy Father for this month.

Evening Prayer

I ADORE You, my God, and thank You for having created me, for having made me a Christian and preserved me this day. I love You with all my heart and I am sorry for having sinned against You, because You are infinite Love and infinite Goodness. Protect me during my rest and may Your love be always with me. Amen.

Eternal Father, I offer You the Precious Blood of Jesus Christ in atonement for my sins and for all the intentions of our Holy Church.

Holy Spirit, Love of the Father and the Son, purify my heart and fill it with the fire of Your Love, so that I may be a chaste Temple of the Holy Trinity and be always pleasing to You in all things. Amen.

Acts of the Theological Virtues

These virtues have God for their direct object. Faith is belief in God's infallible teaching. Hope is confidence in the Divine assistance. Love is love of God. They are given us in the first instance through Baptism and incorporation into Christ, and they can be increased through the different "Acts."

An Act of Faith

O MY God, I firmly believe that You are one God in three Divine Persons, Father, Son, and Holy Spirit; I believe that Your Divine Son became man, and died for our sins, and that He will come to judge the living and the dead. I believe these and all the truths which the Holy Catholic Church teaches, because You have revealed them, Who can neither deceive nor be deceived.

An Act of Hope

O MY God, relying on Your almighty power and infinite mercy and promises, I hope to obtain pardon of my sins, the help of Your grace, and life everlasting, through the merits of Jesus Christ, my Lord and Redeemer.

An Act of Love

O MY God, I love You above all things, with my whole heart and soul, because You are all-good and worthy of all love. I love my neighbor as myself for the love of You. I forgive all who have injured me, and ask pardon of all whom I have injured.

Prayer to the Holy Spirit

COME, Holy Spirit, fill the hearts of Your faithful, and kindle in them the fire of Your love.

V. Send forth Your Spirit and they shall be created.

R. And You shall renew the face of the earth.

Let us pray. O God, You instructed the hearts of the faithful by the light of the Holy Spirit. Grant us, by the same Spirit, to have a right judgment in all things and ever to rejoice in His consolation. Through Christ our Lord. **R.** Amen.

267. *What is the Liturgy of the Hours?*

The Liturgy of the Hours is the prayer of Christ and the whole Church (priests and laity) which prepares for or prolongs the Eucharistic Sacrifice.

As we have seen, the Eucharist is the prayer and offering of Christ and of the Church and helps Catholics be united with God in Christ through the Holy Spirit. However, there is also a second prayer of Christ and of the Church, His Mystical Body. This is called the Liturgy of the Hours and constitutes a way in which the entire day can be made holy by the praises of God.

Hence, this prayer is part of the priesthood of Christ. In the Holy Spirit, Jesus carries out through the Church the work of humankind's redemption and God's perfect glorification.

It also achieves human sanctification. Worship is offered to God in an exchange or dialogue between God and human beings in which God speaks to His people and they respond to Him in song and prayer. Those who take part in the Liturgy of the Hours have access to holiness of the richest kind through the life-giving Word of God, to which it gives such great importance. God's Words in the Psalms are sung in His presence, and the intercessions, prayers, and hymns are steeped in the inspired language of Scripture.

Since the Liturgy of the Hours is the prayer of the Mystical Body, it is also the prayer of the faithful. According to St.

Paul, the community of Christians constitutes the temple of God. Each Christian is personally this temple, yet all form one single temple, with faith as its foundation and the Christians as its living stones.

In this temple the new priesthood is exercised. As we have seen, this priesthood devolves on all Christians as a royal priesthood. In the Divine Office they offer to the Father —through the lips of the priest and insofar as they belong to the Mystical Body—a filial prayer of obedience and adoration.

The Liturgy of the Hours has the same relationship to our lives that the Eucharist has. It enables us to pray with the sentiments willed by God and His Church. In so doing, it helps us become less concerned with self and more other-oriented. And if we participate fully, actively, and consciously in the Hours, we can integrate our whole lives and petitions into it.

268. *In what do the ceremonies of the Church consist?*

The ceremonies of the Church consist in meaningful signs (objects) and actions adopted by the Church for the enhancement of her worship and the spiritual edification of the faithful.

In the Old Testament God prescribed many ceremonies of Jewish life and worship. Our Lord, too, adopted a certain ritual whenever He healed someone.

The burning candle is a sign of Christ as light of the world. It also represents faith, which enlightens; and hope, which tends upward; and love, which kindles. The Easter candle denotes the Risen Lord, Who delivers us from bondage to sin and the devil, just as the pillar of fire led the Israelites out of Egyptian servitude. Incense symbolizes prayer and worship: "Let my prayer come like incense before You" (Ps 141:2).

Ceremonies are not a superfluous component of worship, excess baggage as it were. They are, in a way, expressions of proper behavior in things divine. If in secular life there are occasions for ceremonial comportment, we should allow as much for Catholic worship of God. Performed reverently and from the heart, ceremonies not only foster devotion but impress outsiders.

For example, we have processions (1) to proclaim our faith to the world, (2) to praise and thank God publicly, and (3) to pray collectively for God's blessing and the averting of deserved punishment.

269. Why does the Church encourage pilgrimages?

The Church encourages pilgrimages
1. **because they are an age-old Christian practice,**
2. **and because they bring much blessing if made in the right spirit.**

The early Christians traveled frequently to places where Jesus lived and suffered, and to the graves of the Apostles and Martyrs. Doubtless God is everywhere and can hear us anywhere. Still, it is possible for Him to hear us more at certain places, even as at certain times. Besides, places of pilgrimage can inspire and augment devotion.

A proper pilgrimage is one that is compatible with one's duties in life, is spiritually motivated and is infused with a desire to pray and worship. It should also be an occasion for receiving the Sacraments (Confession and Holy Communion). St. Gregory of Nyssa (d. 394) wrote: "If you are a child of the world filled with base thoughts, you will remain far from Christ even if you journey to Golgotha, to the Mount of Olives, or to the place where Christ arose."

270. Why does the Church support and encourage religious societies, sodalities, and other organizations?

The Church supports and encourages these various groups as forms of apostolic activity which promote the life of prayer, the frequent reception of the Sacraments, and many other good works.

There are numerous religious societies and associations of this kind within the Church, some old, some of more recent origin. Guided by the Hierarchy, all have their place, their scope, and their importance in the framework of the Church's mission. Far from discouraging these forms of activity, Vatican II as it were renewed and enlarged their charter, addressing itself to them especially in the Decree on the Apostolate of the Laity and saying in part:

"The laity can engage in their apostolic activity either as individuals or together as members of various groups or associations.... They should remember, nevertheless, that human beings are naturally social and that it has pleased God to unite those who believe in Christ into the people of God (1 Pt 2:5-10) and into one body (1 Cor 12:12). Hence, the group apostolate of Christian believers happily corresponds to a human and Christian need....

"In the present circumstances, it is quite necessary that, in the area of lay activity, the united and organized form of the apostolate be strengthened. In fact, only the pooling of resources is capable of fully achieving all the aims of the modern apostolate and firmly protecting its interests.... There is a great variety of associations in the apostolate. Some set before themselves the broad apostolic purpose of the Church; others aim to evangelize and sanctify in a special way. Some propose to infuse a Christian spirit into the temporal order; others bear witness to Christ in a special way through works of mercy and charity.

"Among these associations, those which promote and encourage closer unity between the concrete life of the members and their faith must be given primary consideration. Associations are not ends unto themselves; rather they should serve the mission of the Church to the world. Their apostolic dynamism depends on their conformity with the goals of the Church as well as on the Christian witness and evangelical spirit of every member and of the whole association....

"*Maintaining the proper relationship to Church authorities, the laity have the right to found and control such associations and to join those already existing. Yet dispersion of efforts must be avoided. This happens when new associations and projects are promoted without a sufficient reason, or if antiquated associations or methods are retained beyond their period of usefulness. . . .*

"*Whether the lay apostolate is exercised by the faithful as individuals or as members of organizations, it should be incorporated into the apostolate of the whole Church according to a right system of relationships. Indeed, union with those whom the Holy Spirit has assigned to rule His Church (Acts 20:28) is an essential element of the Christian apostolate. No less necessary is cooperation among various projects of the apostolate which must be suitably directed by the Hierarchy*" *(nos. 15, 18, 19, 23).*

JESUS ASKED FOR OBEDIENCE TO HIS COMMANDMENTS

"If you love me ... obey the commands I give. ... He who obeys the commandments he has from me is the man who loves me; and he who loves me will be loved by my Father. I too will love him and reveal myself to him" (Jn 14:15, 21).

PART THREE: THE COMMANDMENTS

The Law of God (Ten Commandments)

271. *What is the highest norm by which we must govern our lives?*

The highest norm by which we must govern our lives is the law of God.

In the *Declaration on Religious Freedom,* Vatican II says: "The highest norm of human life is the divine law—eternal, objective and universal—whereby God orders, directs, and governs the entire universe and all the ways of the human community by a plan conceived in wisdom and love. Human beings have been made by God to participate in this law, with the result that, under the gentle disposition of divine Providence, they can come to perceive ever more fully the truth that is unchanging" (no. 3).

In the *Decree on the Media of Social Communication* we read: "The Council proclaims that all must hold to the absolute primacy of the objective moral order, that is, this order by itself surpasses and fittingly coordinates all other spheres of human affairs. ... For human beings who are endowed by God with the gift of reason and summoned to pursue a lofty destiny are alone affected by the moral order in their entire being. And likewise, if human beings resolutely and faithfully uphold this order, they will be brought to the attainment of complete perfection and happiness" (no. 6).

272. *What is conscience?*

Conscience is a judgment of human reason declaring the moral goodness or the moral evil of a human act.

Conscience is sometimes called the "voice of God," insofar as it reflects the moral law of God. Moreover, in the larger sense the name "conscience" applies not only to individual acts of moral judgment but to the faculty itself that makes the judgments. This faculty is human reason exercising its natural function of recognizing moral good and moral evil. In addition, conscience as faculty of moral judgment admits of greater or lesser development, depending on the individual. But no one with the use of reason can be ignorant of the basic moral precepts, e.g., that murder is morally wrong and love and respect for parents is morally good.

In the Pastoral Constitution on the Church in the Modern World, *Vatican II says concerning conscience: "In the depths of their conscience, human beings detect a law which they do not impose upon themselves, but which holds them to obedience. Always summoning them to love good and avoid evil, the voice of conscience when necessary speaks to their heart: do this, shun that.... Conscience is the most secret core and sanctuary of human beings. There they are alone with God, Whose voice echoes in their depths. In a wonderful manner conscience reveals that law which is fulfilled by love of God and neighbor....*

"Hence the more right conscience holds sway, the more persons and groups turn aside from blind choice and strive to be guided by the objective norms of morality. Conscience frequently errs from invincible ignorance without losing its dignity. The same cannot be said for a person who cares but little for truth and goodness, or for a conscience which by degrees grows practically sightless as a result of habitual sin" (no. 16).

273. *Must we follow our conscience?*

We must follow our conscience, but we also have a continuing obligation to conform our conscience to the moral law of God as expressed in Sacred Scripture and taught by His Church.

Even as we adjust our clocks to solar time, so must we adjust our conscience again and again to what God expects and demands of us. The reason is that conscience is not infallible—it can err—but there is an infallible truth which God teaches us through the Church and to which we must constantly conform our life. Many times God's voice in us is drowned out by other voices, and only by having an informed and well-trained conscience can we be sure that the voice we hear is the voice of God.

If we ignore the Catholic teaching of faith and morality, in whole or in part, or never listen to a sermon, never read a Catholic book or the Catholic press, conscience becomes a deceitful voice, a faithless guide. In such circumstances, to say that we are following our conscience likely means that we are simply yielding to instinct and desire—the blind leading the blind. True conscience then, for all practical purposes, is dead or dying.

Vatican II, in the Declaration on Religious Freedom, says: "*The human person perceives and acknowledges the imperatives of the divine law through the mediation of conscience. In all activity a person is bound to follow his or her conscience in order to come to God, the end and purpose of life. It follows that a person is not to be forced to act in a manner contrary to conscience. . . . In the exercise of their rights, individual persons and social groups are bound by the moral law to have respect both for the rights of others and for their own duties toward others and for the common welfare. . . .*

"*Many pressures are brought to bear upon the people of our day, to the point where the danger arises lest they lose the possibility of acting on their own judgment. On the other hand, not a few can be found who seem inclined to use the name of freedom as the pretext for refusing to submit to authority and for making light of the duty of obedience. Wherefore this Vatican Council urges all, especially those who are charged with the task of educating others, to do their utmost to form persons who, on the one hand, will respect the moral order and be obedient to lawful authority, and, on the other hand, will be lovers of true freedom—persons, in other words, who will come to decisions on their own judgment and in the light of truth, govern their activities with a sense of responsibility, and strive after what is true and right, willing always to join with others in cooperative effort" (nos. 3, 7, 8).*

274. Which is the greatest commandment?

The greatest commandment is: " 'You shall love the Lord your God with your whole heart, with your whole soul, and with all your mind.' This is the greatest and first commandment. The second is like it: 'You shall love your neighbor as yourself.' There is no other commandment greater than these" (Mt 22:37-39, Mk 12:30-31).

Already in the Old Testament God enjoined the commandment of love. In Dt 6:4-5, it is written: "Hear, O Israel! The Lord is our God, the Lord alone! Therefore, you shall love the Lord, your God, with all your heart, and with all your soul, and with all your strength." By His example and teaching, Christ perfected the commandment of love in regard to both God and neighbor.

Vatican II, in the *Decree on the Apostolate of the Laity*, says: "The greatest commandment in the law is to love God with one's whole heart and one's neighbor as oneself. Christ made this commandment of love of neighbor His own and enriched it with a new meaning. For He wanted to equate Himself with His brothers and sisters as the object of this love when He said: 'As long as you did it for one of My least brothers and sisters, you did it for Me' (Mt 25:40). Assuming human nature, He bound the whole human race to Himself as a family through a certain supernatural solidarity and established charity as the mark of His disciples, saying, 'This is how all will know that you are My disciples: by your love for one another (Jn 13:35)' " (no. 8).

275. When do we love God above everything?

We love God above everything when we value Him higher than anything in the world and are prepared to lose everything rather than offend Him by grave sin.

Our love of God is more perfect if we also strive to avoid venial sin. — "I am certain that neither death nor life, neither angels nor principalities, neither the present nor the future, nor powers, neither height nor depth nor any other creature, will be able to separate us from the love of God that comes to us in Christ Jesus, our Lord" (Rom 8:38-39).

"Love does not consist in tasting the sweetness of God. Humility, patience, suffering, self-denial—this is true love" (St. Jane Frances de Chantel, d. 1641). Since we cannot see God, our feelings for persons we can see, such as parents, may be stronger than our feelings for God. But, as St. Jane Frances points out, love of God—or any true love, for that matter—is not primarily a matter of feelings. With regard to God, love means that in our mind we acknowledge Him as the highest good and in our will are prepared to forsake everything else in order to adhere to Him. It is in this sense that our Lord said: "Whoever loves father or mother, son or daughter, more than me is not worthy of me"(Mt 10:37). With God's grace and true faith in us, all can meet this test, or Christ would not have demanded it.

Doubtless, there are moments when we also experience strong feelings for God, but we should not make them the touchstone of our love: "He who obeys the commandments he has from me is the man who loves me" (Jn 14:21). Some of the greatest Saints went through life, or much of it, without sensory consolation from their love of God.

"My Lord and my God, take everything that keeps me from You. My Lord and my God, grant everything that brings me to You. My Lord and my God, strip me of myself and make me all Your own" (Prayer of St. Nicholas of Flüe).

"All that is in the world is vanity (Eccl 1:2), except to love God and to serve Him only" (Imitation of Christ, I, 1).

276. *When do we love ourselves correctly?*

We love ourselves correctly when our first concern is the salvation of our soul.

With due regard to our spiritual welfare, we must also be concerned with the body and things of this world: health, possessions, good name, job security. But we should always remember our Lord's words: "What profit would a man show if he were to gain the whole world and destroy himself in the process?" (Mt 16:26). "Those habitually guilty of sin are their own worst enemies" (Tb 12:10).

Wrong self-love is egotism, the spirit of self-aggrandizement, when we use everyone and everything for our own advantage. If others must suffer in the process, so be it. Egotism makes people boastful, brazen, heartless, and offensive. This is not the way of Christian self-love, or Christian love of neighbor.

277. *Who is our neighbor?*

Our neighbor is everyone, friend or enemy.

In the parable of the Good Samaritan our Lord gives a graphic example of love of neighbor as He taught it (Lk 10:30-38). And in Mt 7:12, He announced for all time the Golden Rule: "Treat others the way you would have them treat you." From this it follows that what we do *not* want done to us, we should not do to others.

Many a work of love of neighbor could be called "love in the distance." There are married couples who scarcely talk to each other anymore but are ever so helpful and friendly away from each other. Young people with banners take to the streets to demonstrate against injustice in the world and forget that at home there are parents who would be grateful for just a kind word from them. We need homes for the elderly, hospitals for the sick, and counseling centers. But we simply cannot default love of neighbor to an organization. We must make ourselves available. Love of neighbor in the spirit of Jesus demands ourselves, our money, our time, our efforts. Only those who are prepared for this love of neighbor can call themselves disciples of Jesus.

In the Pastoral Constitution on the Church in the Modern World, *Vatican II says: "This Council lays stress on reverence for the human person; all must consider every neighbor without exception as another self, taking into account first of all his or her life and the means necessary to living it with dignity, so as not to imitate the rich man who had no concern for the poor man Lazarus" (no. 27).* And in the Decree on the Missionary Activity of the Church, *it says: "Christian charity truly extends to all, without distinction of race, creed, or social condition: it looks for neither gain nor gratitude. For as God loved us with an unselfish love, so also the faithful should in their charity care for the human person, loving him or her with the same affection with which God sought out human beings" (no. 12).*

278. *Why should we love all people?*

We should love all people

1. because God commands it,

2. and because all people are children of God, redeemed by the blood of Christ and called to eternal happiness in heaven.

"This is my commandment: love one another as I have loved you" (Jn 15:12). — "Have we not all the one Father? Has not the one God created us? Why then do we break faith with each other. . .?" (Mal 2:10).

"Many pitiable souls have lost faith in God because they lost faith in people, in the humanity of people, and many have found faith in God again because they came in contact with a good person" (Cardinal Faulhaber, d. 1952).

Old Testament examples of true love of neighbor are Joseph in Egypt (Gn 43:15ff; 45:1ff) and the elder Tobit (Tb 2:1ff). In New Testament times: St. Martin of Tours (d. 397), St. Nicholas of Myra (4th cent.), St. Elizabeth of Hungary (d. 1231), and St. Charles Borromeo of Milan (d. 1584). More recent examples are Damien, apostle of the lepers on the Island of Molokai (d. 1880), and the saintly Anton Joseph Messmer of Switzerland (d. 1948), himself a partial cripple from 1915 who dedicated his life to the service of the handicapped and disabled, handling some 7,000 cases (not to mention his work as Catholic editor and educator). Second to none, however, is a contemporary, Mother Teresa of Calcutta together with her Missionaries of Charity.

279. How can we show love of neighbor?

We can show love of neighbor by practicing corporal and spiritual works of mercy.

"Little children [little: in spirit, humble, docile], let us love in deed and in truth and not merely talk about it" (1 Jn 3:18).

Corporal (material) works of mercy are:
1. To feed the hungry.
2. To give drink to the thirsty.
3. To clothe the naked.
4. To visit the imprisoned.
5. To shelter the homeless.
6. To visit the sick.
7. To bury the dead.

Spiritual works of mercy are:
1. To admonish the sinner (correct those who need it).
2. To instruct the ignorant (teach the ignorant).
3. To counsel the doubtful (give advice to those who need it).
4. To comfort the sorrowful (comfort those who suffer).
5. To bear wrongs patiently (be patient with others).
6. To forgive all injuries (forgive others who hurt you).
7. To pray for the living and the dead (pray for others).

Not everyone can practice all the corporal works of mercy, but even the poorest person can visit the sick or attend the funeral of a neighbor (bury the dead). Among spiritual works, everyone can suffer wrongs patiently, forgive others willingly, and pray for people, which sometimes is the best thing we can do for them.

280. *Why should we be devoted to the works of mercy?*

We should be devoted to the works of mercy because Christ demands them in the words:

1. **"I assure you, as often as you did it for one of my least brothers, you did it for me"** (Mt 25:40).
2. **"Blest are they who show mercy; mercy shall be theirs"** (Mt 5:7).

"Merciless is the judgment on the man who has not shown mercy" (Jas 2:13).

Many Catholic organizations are devoted to the works of mercy, e.g., the St. Vincent de Paul Society. The Bishops' annual appeal is designed to help the needy, a work of mercy. So is the annual clothing drive. Religious orders, of men and women, engage in works of charity, some exclusively. Mother Teresa of Calcutta and her Missionaries of Charity spend themselves worldwide for the poorest of the poor, for lepers and the terminally ill, for people whom no one else wants or bothers with.

Not only adults but growing children can perform works of mercy. They can be kind to less fortunate children, possibly run errands for the elderly and ailing, or contribute some of their allowance and incidental earnings to programs for the poor. Christian parents will instill in their children the spirit of self-sacrifice for the sake of others in need.

281. Why should we love our enemies?

We should love our enemies because Christ by word and example taught us to do so.

"My command to you is: love your enemies, pray for your persecutors. This will prove that you are sons of your heavenly Father, for his sun rises on the bad and the good, he rains on the just and the unjust" (Mt 5:44-45). — "Father, forgive them; they do not know what they are doing" (Lk 23:34)

Love of enemy was not foreign to the Old Testament. Read Ex 23:4-5 and Prv 25:21-22. A memorable display of such love is seen in David when he had Saul, who sought David's life, in his grasp but spared him (1 Sm 24:1ff). St. Stephen, the first Christian martyr, prayed for his stoners (Acts 7:59-60). St. Paul, too, had frequent occasion to practice love of enemy, and practiced it. In 1 Cor 4:12-13, he writes: "When we are insulted we respond with a blessing. Persecution comes our way; we bear it patiently. We are slandered, and we try conciliation." — When Pope Pius XII (d. 1959) was informed that the Russian dictator Stalin had suffered a stroke, he immediately went to his private chapel to pray for him. Yet next to Hitler, no modern dictator had done as much harm to the Church as Stalin (d. 1953).

282. *Which are the Ten Commandments?*

The Ten Commandments are:

1. I, the Lord, am your God. You shall not have other gods besides Me.
2. You shall not take the name of the Lord, your God, in vain.
3. Remember to keep holy the Sabbath day.
4. Honor your father and your mother.
5. You shall not kill.
6. You shall not commit adultery.
7. You shall not steal.
8. You shall not bear false witness against your neighbor.
9. You shall not covet your neighbor's wife.
10. You shall not covet your neighbor's goods.

The Ten Commandments are found in two places in the Old Testament, Exodus 20:1-17 and Deuteronomy 5:6-21. The formation which is given in the answer above is a distillation of the biblical reading (especially Deuteronomy). It is based on Origen (d. ca. 254), Clement of Alexandria (d. ca. 215), and Augustine (d. 430) and is followed by the Catholic lic and Lutheran Churches.

Another Christian formulation is based on the Jewish philosopher Philo (d. ca. 50 A.D.), the Jewish historian Flavius Josephus (d. 100 A.D.), and the Greek Fathers. It is followed by the Anglican and Reformed Churches as well as the Greek Orthodox. In this enumeration the Second Commandment is a prohibition of the use of images, and the prohibition of the use of the divine name drops one number to become the Third Commandment. All succeeding Commandments drop one number until the Ninth which is coupled with the Tenth (coveting wife *and* goods).

The modern Jewish enumeration differs from both as is shown by the Chart below.

Catholic and Lutheran	Anglican, Reformed, Greek	Jewish
1. False gods (images sometimes included	1. False gods	1. Introduction: "I am . . ."
2. Divine name	2. Images	2. False gods and images
3. Sabbath	3. Divine name	3. Divine name
4. Parents	4. Sabbath	4. Sabbath
5. Killing	5. Parents	5. Parents
6. Adultery	6. Killing	6. Killing
7. Stealing	7. Adultery	7. Adultery
8. Bearing false witness	8. Stealing	8. Stealing
9. Coveting wife	9. Bearing false witness	9. Bearing false witness
10. Coveting goods	10. Coveting wife and goods	10. Coveting wife and goods

Another name for the Commandments is the Decalogue (from the Greek meaning "the ten words"). They were given by God to Moses on Mount Sinai and were written on two tablets of stone (Dt 4:13). The Israelites kept the tablets with great care and reverence in the ark of the covenant as they journeyed through the wilderness to the Promised Land.

For the Israelites, the Decalogue represented the terms of the Covenant which Yahweh had chosen to establish with His People. If this People kept the Commandments faithfully, they could count on God's special providence in their behalf. On the other hand, if they proved faithless—and often they did—God's corrective punishment awaited them. Their history shows that God is not mocked without paying the consequences.

Christ said He came not to abolish the law—especially the Commandments—but to perfect it. Indeed, the Commandments could not have been abolished even by Christ, because in general they simply transcribe the basic moral precepts which God has written in the human heart (as St. Paul notes in Rom 2:14-16). No one with the use of reason can be ignorant of them. Nevertheless, as a consequence of sin, mankind had corrupted even these fundamental principles of morality and therefore, humanly speaking, it became necessary for God to proclaim them and to put His authority behind them in the unmistakable manner of Mount Sinai. Even so, the waywardness of the human heart requires an infallible guide, the Church, to declare again and again the authentic teaching of the Ten Commandments together with their ramifications in our life.

Anyone who disregards God's Commandments is his own worst enemy. Transgression of God's Commandments harms not God but the transgressor. God asks for our love, and even pleads for it, not because He needs it but because by loving Him we find our happiness. Here one touches on the heart of God's mystery, the love by which He loves us before we love Him. Much in our life would become easier if we did not view God's Commandments as road barriers but as signposts. God's Commandments are signs that point in the direction of His love. If we follow them willingly, we discover the good we seek, our happiness.

JESUS TAUGHT THE FIRST AND GREATEST COMMANDMENT

" 'Teacher, which commandment of the law is the greatest?' Jesus said . . . : 'You shall love the Lord your God with your whole heart, with your whole soul, and with all your mind. This is the greatest and first commandment' " (Mt 22:36f).

FIRST COMMANDMENT OF GOD

"I, the Lord, am your God. You shall not have other gods besides Me."

283. What does the First Commandment require?

The First Commandment requires that we believe in the one true God, hope in Him steadfastly, love Him above everything, and worship Him alone.

Concerning the meaning of faith or belief, see Question 3.

In the *Pastoral Constitution on the Church in the Modern World,* Vatican II says: "The basic source of the dignity of human beings lies in their call to communion with God. From the very circumstance of their origin people are already invited to converse with God. For people would not exist were they not created by God's love and constantly perserved by it. And they cannot live fully according to truth unless they freely acknowledge that love and devote themselves to their Creator.

"Yet many of our contemporaries have never recognized this intimate and vital link with God, or have explicitly rejected it. Thus atheism must be accounted among the most serious problems of this age and is deserving of closer examination" (no. 19).

284. What is atheism?

Atheism is the philosphy of life that denies God's existence.

The word derives from the Greek *atheos,* meaning no God, godless.

In the same *Pastoral Constitution* above, the Council continues: "The word atheism is applied to phenomena which are quite distinct from one another. For while God is expressly denied by some, others believe that one can assert absolutely nothing about Him. Still others use such a method to scrutinize the question of God as to make it seem devoid of meaning. Many, unduly transgressing the limits of the positive sciences, contend that everything can be explained by this kind of scientific reasoning alone, or by contrast, they altogether disallow that there is any absolute truth.

"Some laud the human so extravagantly that their faith in God lapses into a kind of anemia, though they seem more inclined to affirm humanity than to deny God. Again some form for themselves such a fallacious idea of God that when they repudiate this figment they are by no means rejecting the God of the Gospel. Some never get to the point of raising questions about God, since they seem to experience no religious stirrings nor do they see why they should trouble themselves about religion. Moreover, atheism results not rarely from a violent protest against the evil in this world. . . . Modern civilization itself often complicates the approach to God not for any essential reason but because it is so heavily engrossed in earthly affairs" (no. 19).

285. *Do Christians bear some responsibility for the existence of atheism?*

Christians bear some responsibility for the existence of atheism if they do not live according to the teachings of the Christian faith.

Vatican II, in the same Constitution, says: "Undeniably, those who willfully shut out God from their hearts and try to dodge religious questions are not following the dictates of their consciences, and hence are not free of blame; yet believers themselves frequently bear some responsibility for this situation. For, taken as a whole, atheism is not a spontaneous development but stems from a variety of causes, including a critical reaction against religious beliefs, and in some places against the Christian religion in particular. Hence believers can have more than a little to do with the birth of atheism. To the extent that they neglect their own training in the faith, or teach erroneous doctrine, or are deficient in their religious, moral, or social life, they must be said to conceal rather than reveal the authentic face of God and religion" (no. 19).

After the Second Vatican Council a Secretariat for Unbelievers (= Atheists) was created. One of its first steps was the publication, in 1968, of a document titled "On Dialogue with Unbelievers," which set forth the Church's readiness to enter into discussion with nonbelievers as well as the guidelines to be followed, especially in countries under totalitarian regimes. In 1970 the Secretariat issued another document asking that the study of atheism be included in the seminary curriculum as part of the training for dealing with a secularized world. Priests already ordained were also to acquire an adequate knowledge of contemporary atheism.

286. *When do we sin against faith?*

We sin against faith:

1. **when we do not believe in God and His revealed truth (unbelief), or through our own fault lapse into false belief (heresy);**

2. **when we deny our faith or renounce the faith altogether (apostasy);**

3. **when we think it does not matter what one believes (religious indifferentism);**

4. **when we entertain doubts of faith instead of dismissing them;**

5. **when we do not practice our faith;**

6. **when we talk against the faith or like to listen to such talk;**

7. **when we read or spread writings against the faith unnecessarily, or habitually associate**

with people without any faith, or join societies and groups that are hostile to the faith.

1) Pride and sinful living are what usually lead to unbelief.

2) Denying our faith (declaring that we are not a Catholic) and apostasy (giving up our faith entirely) are among the greatest sins, because through them the very foundation of our salvation is imperiled (by denial) or destroyed (by apostasy).

3) Religious indifferentism, the attitude that one religion is as good or as true as another, is self-contradictory. If one religion says that Christ is truly present in the Eucharist with His flesh and blood and another says He is only symbolically present, or if one says that Christ is God and another says He is only man, both cannot be true, any more than something can be black and white at the same time. If in fact all religions were equally acceptable to God, it would mean that God Himself makes no distinction between truth and error, not even between His truth and the error of human beings. The insult in this to God need not be pointed out. The indifferentist, however, is not likely to be swayed by such considerations; to him religion simply does not matter all that much. What is important to the true believer is not to fall into such sophistry, and to pray for those who have allowed themselves to fall victim to it.

The Second Vatican Council, while supporting ecumenical efforts, also warned against the spirit of religious indifferentism, insisting that the full truth of faith be maintained and asserted, e.g., in the *Pastoral Constitution on the Church in the Modern World* (nos. 7, 28) and in the *Decree on the Missionary Activity of the Church* (nos. 15, 20).

4) A difficulty is not a doubt. A person may have trouble understanding a truth of faith and seek further knowledge, as one should. Nor is every doubt sinful, only such as we consciously keep alive in our minds or use as excuse to justify our neglect of the faith. Moses doubted God in the

wilderness and forfeited his personal entrance into the Promised Land (Nm 20:8-13). Zechariah doubted God's messenger, the angel Gabriel, and suffered the loss of speech (Lk 1:18).

5) There are, one notes with sadness, many negligent Catholics. They neglect prayer, Mass, the Sacraments, Catholic reading and activities. They come close to being practical atheists, people who live as though God and the Church did not exist. Such a way of life is fraught with great spiritual danger, threatening complete loss of faith—through one's own fault.

6) Criticizing or even vilifying the Pope, the Church, the bishop, the pastor, and things Catholic is a favorite pastime even among some Catholics. This can be a sin not only against faith but against charity as well. Doubtless, there is a place for criticism in the Church, but not in the presence of children or the weak of faith, who are scandalized in the true sense of the word. One can always take constructive criticism directly to the pastor or anyone in a position to deal with it. To have nothing but faultfinding or dispraise for the Church is not the way to recommend oneself to Christ, founder of the Church.

7) Some will say they are not harmed by anti-Church reading or association and godless atmosphere. Experience proves otherwise, as little by little they lose interest in the faith and then give it up entirely. Even a small dose of poison taken often enough can be deadly. It is one thing to have no choice in the matter because our work requires us to mingle with irreligious or dissolute individuals, but unnecessary association or friendship with them is not in the spirit of the Gospel because it exposes us to great spiritual danger.

In the Decree on Ecumenism, *Vatican II says: "Before the whole world let all Christians . . . bear witness to our common hope which does not play us false. In these days when cooperation in social matters is so widespread, all human beings without exception are called to work together. Those who believe in God have a stronger summons, but the strongest claims are laid on Christians since they bear the name of Christ. Cooperation among Christians vividly expresses the relationship which in fact already unites them. . . .*

"This cooperation . . . should be developed more and more, particularly in regions where a social and technical evolution is taking place. It should contribute to a just evaluation of the dignity of the human person, the establishment of the blessings of peace, the application of Gospel principles to social life,• and the advancement of the arts and sciences in a truly Christian spirit. Christians should also collaborate in the use of all possible means to relieve the afflictions of our times such as famine and natural disasters, illiteracy and poverty, housing shortage and the unequal distribution of wealth. All believers in Christ can, through this cooperation, be led to acquire a better knowledge and appreciation of one another, and so pave the way to Christian unity" (no. 12).

287. How do children sin against faith?

Children sin against faith when they do not take part in religious instruction and Holy Mass, or when they do not learn their Catechism and lessons from the Bible

That this is a sin against faith can be seen from the importance which the Second Vatican Council attaches to catechetical instruction in its *Declaration on Christian Education:* "In fulfilling its educational role, the Church, eager to employ all suitable aids, is concerned especially about those which are her very own. Foremost among these is catechetical instruction, which enlightens and strengthens the faith, nourishes life according to the spirit of Christ, leads to intelligent and active participation in the liturgical mystery and gives motivation for apostolic activity" (no. 4).

In the same Declaration the Council says: "Feeling very keenly the weighty responsibility of diligently caring for the moral and religious education of all her children, the Church must be present with her own special affection and help for the great number who are being trained in schools that are not Catholic. This is possible by the witness of the lives of those who teach and direct them, by the apostolic action of their fellow-students, but especially by the ministry of priests and lay people who give them the doctrine of salvation in a way suited to their age and circumstances . . ." (no. 7).

288. What must we do to protect and preserve our faith?

To protect and preserve our faith we must pray regularly, participate in church services faithfully (Holy Mass and homily), and at least now and then read a good spiritual book.

Also important, of course, is that Catholics read the authentic Catholic press: newspapers, magazines, periodicals, and pamphlets. To this should be added Catholic radio and television programs where available. By these means our faith grows and strengthens. As children, we received a child's introduction to the teachings of Catholic faith and morality. As adults, we need an adult understanding, one that keeps pace with our mental and moral awakening as we pass from adolescence to manhood and womanhood. Precisely here, in the explication and fortification of the Faith, Catechisms such as this one have a role, ours perhaps uniquely because it features numerous presentations from the Second Vatican Council. These Conciliar passages, even if too advanced for children, do have much to say to their elders.

JESUS OFFERED HOPE IN TIME OF TROUBLE
With the boat in danger of being swamped by the storm, the disciples implored Jesus: " 'Lord, save us! We are lost!' . . . He stood up and took the winds and the sea to task. Complete calm ensued" (Mt 8:25f).

289. *What is meant by hope in God?*

By hope in God is meant trust in all His promises, especially the assurance of His forgiveness of our sins and His promise of grace and eternal life.

We may and should look to God for temporal blessings as well, presupposing that they help us gain heaven or at least are not hindrances. Only God can know this in advance.

The following passages from the Bible can increase our trust in God: Is 50:2; Mt 6:25-32; Lk 15:7; Gal 5:5; 1 Pt 1:3. Often we are not heard because of some doubt that God will help us. And often we are not heard because God knows that what we ask would be against our best interest, and so He sends other blessings. Only in eternity will we see how good God was by not always giving us exactly what we prayed for.

290. *When do we sin against hope?*

We sin against hope

1. when we lack confidence in God or even give way to despair;
2. when our trust in Him is presumptuous.

1) Peter walking on water began to lose his confidence in the Lord (Mt 14:31). — Judas after his betrayal would have found pardon had he turned to Christ in confidence (Mt 27:3-5)

2) Our trust in God is presumptuous when without necessity we place ourselves in danger, with the attitude that God, since He is God, will save us. This is wanton trust and the sin of presumption. Read Sir 5:4-9; Mt 26:30-35, 69-75 (Peter's denial).

291. *What is meant by worship of God?*

By worship of God is meant acknowledging Him as Lord and Creator of all, and accepting His will in everything.

Jesus said: "An hour is coming... when authentic worshipers will worship the Father in Spirit and truth. Indeed it is just such worshipers the Father seeks. God is Spirit, and those who worship him must worship in Spirit and truth" (Jn 4:23-24).

Worship is an act of religion and consists of internal and external elements, private and social prayer as well as liturgical rites, including sacrifice. The highest type of worship is rendered to God alone and called *latria* to distinguish it from the honor given to the Blessed Virgin Mary *(hyperdulia)* and to the Saints *(dulia)*. Worship is also paid to the Blessed Sacrament which is really and truly Jesus Christ as God-Man.

292. *What are some outward signs of worship of God?*

Some outward signs of worship of God are vocal prayer, attendance and active participation in church services (especially Holy Mass), kneeling in honor of God, folded hands, and the Sign of the Cross.

We must worship God by outward sign as well as in spirit, because the body also was created to honor and serve God.

On prayer, see Questions 260ff. On Ceremonies, of which kneeling is one, see Question 268.

293. *How do we sin against the worship that we owe to God?*

We sin against the worship that we owe to God by

1. **neglecting prayer and church services, especially Holy Mass,**
2. **practicing superstition,**
3. **and committing a sacrilege.**

294. *How do we sin by practicing superstition?*

We sin by practicing superstition when we engage and believe in an occult power that God has not bestowed on human beings.

There are many forms of superstition. Some of them profess to tell one's fortune by reading the lines and marks of the palm or by interpreting one's dreams. Witchcraft implies a compact with evil spirits to inflict harm or produce marvels: "Should anyone turn to mediums and fortune-tellers and follow their wanton ways, I will turn against such a one and cut him off from his people" (Lv 20:6).

Astrological charts are followed by many individuals. For some, it may be an innocent pastime, good for an occasional chuckle. But to seriously plan one's life by the horoscope is superstition pure and simple, and sinful. In 1949 the German society of astronomers issued this statement: "The astronomical society, representing the science of astronomy in Germany, takes the occasion of its annual meeting to caution the public against the ever-growing influence of astrology. What passes for astrology today is nothing more than a combination of superstition, charlatanism, and commercialism." More recently, the American society of astronomers addressed a similar admonition to the American public.

Some persons wear a charm or keep a good-luck piece (rabbit's foot, horseshoe). As a rule, no doubt, these things are not taken seriously and only serve an ornamental purpose. Does anyone really believe that a horseshoe over the front door will keep the burglar from ransacking the house, or lightning from striking? Still, the possibility exists of letting such objects influence our lives unduly and leading us to risk the sin of superstition. (N.B. Wearing a blessed medal, for example, is not superstition. See earlier explanation in Question 258.)

Despite all efforts to stamp them out, chain letters keep cropping up. A person receives a letter and is warned to make copies and send them to other individuals. By breaking the chain, i.e., not sending copies to others, the person will suffer some (unspecified) harm. This is gross stupidity as well as outright superstition. In some states it is also liable to civil penalties.

295. *What is the sin of sacrilege?*

The sin of sacrilege is the misuse or mistreatment of persons, places, or things dedicated to God or the worship of God.

Examples: Unworthy reception of the Sacraments; physical assault of persons vowed to God (priests, religious, and others); profanation of a church by robbing from it or committing a crime on the premises.

In the Old Testament King Belshazzar committed sacrilege by profaning the sacred vessels he had plundered from the temple in Jerusalem (Dn 5:3-4). The sons of Eli were guilty of sacrilegious conduct by their contemptuous treatment of the offerings of the Lord (1 Sm 2:12-17)

Thefts of sacred art objects from churches, shrines, etc. have grown alarmingly, perhaps an ironic tribute to the general lawlessness of the age. In 1973 France reported the sacrilegious theft of 67 art objects, Bavaria 369. Churches in the United States have not been spared, either.

The consignment of people to concentration camps and the tortures inflicted upon them violate every law of God and man. In the case of persons consecrated to God, it is also a crime of sacrilege.

SECOND COMMANDMENT OF GOD

"You shall not take the name of the Lord, your God, in vain."

296. *When do we take the name of God in vain?*

We take the name of God in vain when we
1. **speak it irreverently,**
2. **utter blasphemy,**
3. **swear a false oath (perjury),**
4. **or fail to keep a vow made to God.**

297. *When do we speak the name of God irreverently?*

We speak the name of God irreverently when we speak it thoughtlessly or in anger (as a "cuss" word).

It is also sinful to use other sacred names disrespectfully, above all the name of Jesus, the Blessed Virgin Mary, and the Saints. Sacred words, too, should be treated with respect (words of Scripture, of Sacraments, of Holy Mass and the Cross). — "The Lord will not leave unpunished him who takes his name in vain" (Ex 20:7).

We ought also to avoid crude speech in regard to any person and any of God's creatures.

298.   *Who sin by blasphemy?*

They sin by blasphemy who by word or action insult or express contempt for God, or the Saints, or sacred things.

"Whoever blasphemes the name of the Lord shall be put to death. The whole community shall stone him" (Lv 24:16).

Also guilty of blasphemy are those who scoff at the teachings and practices of the Church. Scoffers of religion can do much harm. We should have the courage to rebuke them, when they carry on in our presence.

299.   *What is meant by taking an oath?*

By taking an oath is meant calling God to witness that we are speaking the truth or that we will keep a promise.

An oath is a solemn acknowledgment that God is all-knowing and all-just. Since this is what underlies an oath, swearing an oath is permitted. Christ did indeed say: "Do not swear at all. . . . Say, 'Yes' when you mean 'Yes' and 'No' when you mean 'No.' Anything beyond that is from the evil one" (Mt 5:34, 37). His meaning, however, is not that an oath is wrong but that among Christians perfect truth and honesty should prevail. Christ Himself spoke the equivalent of an oath, when He was charged by the high priest to tell whether He was the Messiah, the Son of God (Mt 26:63-64).

300.   *When is an oath a sin?*

An oath is a sin

1. **when we swear falsely or in doubt,**
2. **when we swear without necessity,**
3. **or when we swear to do something evil or not to do something good.**

A false oath is called perjury.

Not to keep an oath that could and should be kept is a grave sin. But if we have sworn to do an evil or not to do a good, keeping the oath not only is wrong but an additional sin. Example: Herod in regard to John the Baptist's death.
— Also guilty of sin is the person who prevails upon another to swear an oath without sufficient reason, i.e., in matters of little consequence. An oath is a serious matter and should not be trivialized.

301. Why is perjury one of the most grave sins?

Perjury is one of the most grave sins

1. **because we call upon the all-knowing God to certify a lie as the truth, and so make a mockery of Him;**
2. **because we withdraw ourselves from God in a formal way and call down His judgment upon us.**

"[My curse] shall come . . . into the house of him who perjures himself with my name; it shall lodge within his house, consuming it, timber and stone" (Zec 5:4).

302. What is meant by taking a vow?

By taking a vow is meant promising something to God that is pleasing to Him and binding ourselves to the promise under pain of sin.

A vow is more than a wish or intention.

Moses, among other legislation, left instruction concerning vows: "When you make a vow to the Lord, your God, you shall not delay in fulfilling it; otherwise you will be held guilty, for the Lord, your God, is strict in requiring it of you. Should you refrain from making a vow, you will not be held guilty. But you must keep your solemn word and fulfill the votive offering you have freely promised to the Lord" (Dt 23:22-24). Similarly Ecclesiastes: "Fulfill what you have vowed. You had better not make a vow than make it and not fulfill it" (5:3-4).

A vow, therefore, should be undertaken only after mature consideration and in consultation with one's confessor or spiritual director. Should circumstances change materially so that keeping a vow becomes impractical or overburdensome, release or commutation may be sought through one's pastor or confessor.

The most important vows in the Church are those taken by members of religious orders, men and women. Release from these vows is obtained through higher ecclesiastical authority. See also Question 383.

THIRD COMMANDMENT OF GOD

"Remember to keep holy the Sabbath day."

303. What does the Third Commandment require?

The Third Commandment requires that we keep holy the Lord's day.

Sabbath, literally, means rest. In the Old Testament the Lord's day was the Sabbath or Saturday, in remembrance of the six days of creation and God's "rest" on the seventh. In the New Testament the Lord's day is Sunday, because Christ rose from the dead on Sunday and sent the Holy Spirit on Sunday.

"God blessed the seventh day and made it holy because on it he rested from all the work he had done in creation" (Gn 2:3). — "On the first day of the week, when we gathered for the breaking of bread, Paul preached to them" (Acts 20:7). See also Question 346.

In the First Epistle to the Corinthians (16:2), the Apostle asks that "on the first day of the week [hence on Sunday, at the Eucharist] everyone should put aside whatever he has been able to save," for a collection for the Church in Jerusalem. Likewise the *Didache,* one of the earliest Christian writings, takes for granted the Sunday celebration of the Eucharist.

The expression "Lord's day" for the first day of the week occurs in the Book of Revelation (1:10). As for the name Sunday or Day of the Sun, St. Justin Martyr (d. ca. 165) seems to have been the first one to apply it to the Lord's day of Christians. The name was not his invention, since pagans also had called the first day of the week Day of the Sun. The reference, however, was not the same in both cases. For pagans it meant the physical sun. For Christians it was Christ, the "sun of justice" foretold by the prophet Malachi (3:20). The Lord's day, therefore, is the Day of the Sun - Sunday, day of Christ true Sun of the world.

How devoted the early Christians were to the Sunday celebration is attested, for example, by the martyr-priest St. Saturninus and his companions, who were put to cruel death in the year 303/304 under the Emperor Diocletian. Their crime? Offering the Eucharist on Sunday. Despite relentless torture they stood firm, Saturninus repeatedly declaring that the Sunday celebration was a sacred rule and could not be omitted.

Occasionally, in the course of history, attempts have been made to do away with Sunday. The French Revolutionists in 1789 introduced a ten-day week. Sunday disappeared from the calendar, its place taken by the tenth day called Décadi. The invocation, like the Revolution, soon collapsed.

304. *How is Sunday kept holy?*

Sunday is kept holy through Sunday rest, Holy Mass, and pious works.

Saturday evening Mass, where authorized, substitutes for Sunday worship. But the obligation remains to keep Sunday holy in all other respects.

Sunday rest is violated through unnecessary work and commercial activity, which disturb the spirit of holy leisure and joyful observance that ought to pervade the Lord's day. Business should close and buying and selling be restricted to the essential. Even housework that can be postponed should generally be avoided on Sunday.

"Six days you may labor and do all your work, but the seventh day is the sabbath of the Lord, your God. No work may be done then either by you, or your son or daughter, or your male or female slave, or your beast" (Ex 20:9-10).

"God gives you six days and keeps only one day of the week for Himself, and you have so little respect for the Lord that you do not let Him have even this day but profane it through secular activity. You do not shrink from becoming like a church robber who plunders sacred treasure, inasmuch as you steal from God this consecrated day and misuse it for earthly affairs" (St. John Chrysostom).

305. *When is work on Sunday permitted?*

Work on Sunday is permitted when there is compelling need for it.

Compelling need includes chores that must be done daily, e.g., around the house, on the farm, in some types of manufacturing. It includes essential services for public health and safety (hospitals, transportation facilities, electric utilities, police work, and the like). Farmers may bring in a harvest already overdue because of bad weather. In time of calamity (tragic loss to a neighbor, earthquakes, floods, epidemics) Sunday work not only is permitted but may be required by the law of charity, i.e., love of neighbor. In these and like instances, however, a person still should participate at Mass, if possible.

306. *Is Sunday profaned only through work?*

Sunday is also profaned through wild and excessive recreation.

We need and are entitled to relaxation and recreation. But Sunday is not sanctified nor is Sunday rest observed if the whole day is regularly given to a type of activity that leaves the body too exhausted to properly perform its work on Monday, or the soul spiritually worse instead of better.

Besides attending Holy Mass, we ought also to make time on Sunday for things like reading a good book, or visiting a sick or lonely neighbor. It should be a day when the family spends more time together and gets to listen to each other on matters weighing on the mind of parents and children. It should not be a day of selfish indulgence, when we plan only for our interests and expect others in the family to fall in line.

Vatican II took note of the use of leisure time in the Pastoral Constitution on the Church in the Modern World: *"With the more or less generalized reduction of working hours, the leisure time of most people has increased. May this leisure be used properly to relax, to fortify the health of soul and body through spontaneous study and activity, through tourism which refines people's character and enriches them with understanding of others, through sports activity which helps preserve equilibrium of spirit even in the community, and to establish fraternal relations among persons of all conditions, nations, and races. Let Christians cooperate so that the cultural manifestations and collective activity characteristic of our time may be imbued with a human and a Christian spirit. . . .*

"Applying their time and strength to their employment with a due sense of responsibility, workers should also all enjoy sufficient rest and leisure to cultivate their familial, cultural, social, and religious life. They should also have the opportunity freely to develop the energies and potentialities which perhaps they cannot bring to much fruition in their professional work" (nos. 61, 67).

307. *What harm do we bring upon ourselves by not keeping Sunday holy?*

By not keeping Sunday holy we deprive ourselves of God's blessing now and risk the loss of heaven hereafter.

"My sabbaths, too, they desecrated grievously. Then I thought of pouring out my fury on them in the desert to put an end to them" (Ez 20:13).

An old saying is: Like Sunday, like dying day. If, that is, we come to God on Sunday, participate at Holy Mass regularly, we shall not die without God, without the Sacraments.

FOURTH COMMANDMENT OF GOD

"Honor your father and your mother."

308. *What does the Fourth Commandment require?*

The Fourth Commandment requires that we love, respect, and obey our parents and lawful superiors.

The Fourth Commandment begins the second part of the Ten Commandments. The first three have referred to our relationship with God. The next seven will concern our relationship with one another. They prescribe honor for one's parents and forbid the arbitrary taking of human life, adultery, stealing, perjury, and covetousness. They thus insure the human rights to life, marriage, justice and freedom, reputation, and property.

309. *Why must children love, respect, and obey their parents?*

Children must love, respect, and obey their parents

1. because parents speak for God in regard to their children;
2. because next to God parents are the children's greatest benefactors.

According to Matthew 23:9, we should not call anyone on earth father. The context shows, however, that Jesus does not condemn this or any other title but the failure to live up to what the title demands. He really condemns the use of one's position of trust or authority for one's own ends instead of for service to God and fellow humans—in the case of father and mother, for the good of their children.

By God's design parents are cooperators with Him in bringing children into the world and ruling over them in His name. They are therefore God's representatives in regard to their children.

"How much your mother endured for you, how many sleepless nights she spent for you, what anxiety she suffered when you were endangered. How much toil and trouble your father went through to provide you with food and clothing. Since your parents did so much for you, how could you ever be ungrateful to them?" (St. Ambrose, d. 397).

310. *How do children show parents love, respect, and obedience?*

Children show parents love, respect, and obedience

1. by obeying them gladly and promptly,
2. by being a credit and a joy to them,
3. and by praying for them and taking care of them in their old age.

JESUS GAVE HIS PARENTS LOVE, OBEDIENCE, AND RESPECT
Jesus, after being found by his parents in the temple, "went
down with them . . . and came to Nazareth, and was obedient to
them. . . . [He] progressed steadily in wisdom and age and
grace before God and men" (Lk 2:51f).

"With your whole heart honor your father; your mother's birthpangs forget not. Remember, of these parents you were born; what can you give them for all they gave you?" (Sir 7:27-28).—[Tobit tells his son Tobiah:] "My son, when I die, give me a decent burial. Honor your mother, and do not abandon her as long as she lives" (Tb 4:3).

The most beautiful example for children to follow is the boy Jesus at Nazareth.

The Book of Sirach, 3:1-16, speaks at length of duties toward parents, as well as of blessings dutiful children can expect. And in the Pastoral Constitution on the Church in the Modern World, *Vatican II says: "As living members of the family, children contribute in their own way to making their parents holy. For they will respond to the kindness of their parents with sentiments of gratitude, with love and trust. They will stand by them as children should when hardships overtake their parents and old age brings its loneliness" (no. 48).*

311. *When do children sin against their parents?*

Children sin against their parents when they

1. **obey them poorly or not at all,**
2. **are ungrateful or rude and stubborn toward them, and sadden them,**
3. **regard them with contempt or wish them evil,**
4. **or do not pray for them or do not help them in need.**

Just as children can be a great pride and joy to parents, they can also be a source of intense grief and agony. Many a mother or father has been brought to a premature grave by ingratitude or ill-treatment on the part of children.

The Bible gives examples of exemplary obedience, and other examples which are a warning to all disobedient children. Joseph was prompt and cheerful in obedience to his

father (Gn 37); so was Tobiah, son of Tobit (Tb 4:3ff). Dis-
obedient and ungrateful were Ham (Gn 9:22), Hophni, and
Phinehas, sons of the high priest Eli (1 Sm 2:12ff), and
Absalom toward his father David (2 Sm 13:23ff; 15:1ff;
18:1ff). — Among the curses Moses ordered the Levites to
proclaim to all the people was: "Cursed be he who dishonors
his father or mother. And all the people shall answer
'Amen' " (Dt 27:16).

312. *Besides parents, to whom do we owe respect and obedience?*

Besides parents, we owe respect and obedience to lawful superiors, i.e., to spiritual and temporal authorities, to foster parents, to teachers and employers, and to all who are rightfully over us.

Employees owe their employers loyalty on the job and an honest day's work. — "Obey your human masters perfectly, not with the purpose of attracting attention and pleasing men but in all sincerity and out of reverence for the Lord" (Col 3:22).

Employers also owe respect, namely, to the human dignity of employees, mindful that with God what counts is not industrial position but how we stand with Him.

313. *Why do we owe respect and obedience to spiritual and temporal authority?*

We owe respect and obedience to spiritual and temporal authority because their power comes from God.

"Let everyone obey the authorities that are over him, for there is no authority except from God, and all authority that exists is established by God" (Rom 13:1).

Christ acknowledged the authority of Pilate when the procurator said he had power to crucify Him and power to set Him free. Christ answered: "You would have no power over me whatever unless it were given you from above" (Jn 19:11). — Here a word should be said about criticism of authority. Leaving aside for the moment spiritual authority, in a democracy criticism of the government is part of the system. But criticism should be tempered by a sense of civic responsibility. Sometimes the government withholds information for what it deems the good of the nation. In such a case, in a democracy, we ought to give the government the benefit of the doubt. We have elected it, and if we want its policies changed, there is always a remedy: the next election.

Vatican II spoke at length on authority and civic obedience. In the *Pastoral Constitution on the Church in the Modern World,* it says: "Individuals, families, and the various groups which make up the civil community are aware that they cannot achieve a truly human life by their own unaided efforts. They see the need for a wider community. . . . Yet the people who come together in the political community are many and diverse, and they have every right to prefer divergent solutions. If the political community is not to be torn apart while everyone follows his own opinion, there must be an authority to direct the energies of all citizens toward the common good, not in . . . despotic fashion, but by acting above all as a moral force which appeals to each one's freedom and sense of responsibility.

"It is clear, therefore, that the political community and public authority are founded on human nature and hence belong to the order designed by God, even though the choice of a political regime and the appointment of rulers are left to the free will of citizens. It follows also that political authority . . . must always be exercised within the limits of the moral order and directed toward the common good. . . . When authority is so exercised, citizens are bound in conscience to obey. Accordingly, the responsibility, dignity, and importance of leaders are indeed clear. . . .

"Citizens must cultivate a generous and loyal spirit of patriotism, but without being narrow-minded. This means that they will always direct their attention to the good of the whole human family. . . . (nos. 74, 75).

In the *Decree on the Apostolate of the Laity,* the Council speaks to Catholics in particular: "In loyalty to their country and in faithful fulfillment of their civic obligations, Catholics should feel themselves obliged to promote the true common good. Thus they should make the weight of their opinion felt in order that civil authority may act with justice and that legislation may conform to moral precepts and the common good. Catholics skilled in public affairs and adequately enlightened in faith and Christian doctrine should not refuse to administer public affairs since by doing this in a worthy manner they can both further the common good and at the same time prepare the way for the Gospel" (no. 14).

Duties to the State include payment of taxes. St. Paul, writing to the Romans, impresses upon them this civic obligation (Rom 13:6-7).

314. *What is the basic duty of parents toward their children?*

The basic duty of parents toward their children is to provide for their spiritual and temporal welfare.

Not only parents but all persons in authority or in command over others must have regard for both the spiritual and the temporal good of subordinates, allowing them time for their religious duties and in general maintaining a wholesome atmosphere in the workplace. Employers owe their workers a just wage and humane treatment. "Deal justly and fairly," St. Paul tells employers, "realizing that you too have a master in heaven" (Col 4:17).

Concerning the duties of parents, Vatican II says in the Declaration on Christian Education: *"Since parents have given children their life, they are bound by the most serious obligation to educate their offspring and therefore must be recognized as the primary and principal educators. This role in education is so important that only with difficulty can it be supplied where it is lacking. Parents are the ones who must create a family atmosphere animated by love and respect for God and human beings, in which the well-rounded personal and social education of children is fostered. Hence the family is the first school of the social virtues that every society needs.*

"It is particularly in the Christian family, enriched by the grace and office of the Sacrament of Matrimony, that children should be taught from their early years to have a knowledge of God according to the faith received in Baptism, to worship Him, and to love their neighbor. Here, too, they find their first experience of a wholesome human society and of the Church. Finally, it is through the family that they are gradually led to a companionship with their fellow human beings and with the people of God. Let parents, then, recognize the inestimable importance a truly Christian family has for the life and progress of God's own people" (no. 3).

315. *When is it wrong to obey parents and superiors?*

It is wrong to obey parents and superiors when they command something forbidden by God.

"Better for us to obey God than men" (Acts 5:29).

In the Old Testament as well as in the New, we read of persons who obeyed God rather than human beings.

Recall the prophet Daniel, who despite the king's prohibition continued his custom of praying to God three times a day and for his defiance was thrown in the lions' den (Dn 6:11ff). Or the elderly scribe Eleazar, who chose to die rather than transgress the holy laws of God even in appearance (2 Mc 6:18ff). About the same time seven brothers and their mother were put to gruesome death for the same reason (2 Mc 7:1ff).

Christian martyrs throughout the centuries have not hesitated to obey God rather than humans, when the latter contravened the law of God. The Christian soldiers of the Theban legion commanded by St. Maurice objected to persecution of Christians and would not take part in ceremonies honoring the gods. For loyalty to Christ they were massacred by order of the Emperor Maximian in 297. In England Thomas More, chancellor of the realm, and John Cardinal Fisher opposed the divorce of Henry VIII and refused to take the oath of supremacy by which the king was installed as supreme head of the Church in England. As a result they were consigned to the Tower of London and soon after died a martyr's death on the scaffold, the Cardinal on June 22, Thomas More on July 7, 1534.

A phenomenon of our time is the concentration camp, where Christians, Jews, and others have suffered actual or virtual death for conscience's sake. Rather than yield to the impositions of a godless regime men and women, priests and lay people, have endured and still endure forced labor and other cruelties equivalent to slow martyrdom.

Most celebrated, perhaps, though by no means unique is the ordeal of Josef Cardinal Mindszenty, primate of Hungary. Because of his resistance to the oppression of the Church in Hungary, he was made to run the gamut of the most advanced brainwashing techniques and sentenced to life-long imprisonment. In October, 1956, when the Hungarian people rose in revolt, he was set free but not for long. Russian troops invaded the country and Mindszenty took refuge in the American embassy in Budapest. There he remained, a voluntary exile, until 1971, when he took up residence in Vienna for what were to be the last years of his life. He died in 1975.

We ought to pray daily for all the Mindszentys, all the martyrs who are suffering heroically for their faith, in camps, jails, dungeons, and other incarceration. And while we are praying for them, we ought also to pray for ourselves, that we too may stand fast in the tests God sends us.

FIFTH COMMANDMENT OF GOD

"You shall not kill."

316. *What does the Fifth Commandment forbid?*

The Fifth Commandment forbids us to harm the body or soul of others or our own.

"You have heard the commandment imposed on your forefathers, 'You shall not commit murder; every murderer shall be liable to judgment.' What I say to you is: everyone who grows angry with his brother shall be liable to judgment" (Mt 5:21-22). — "Anyone who hates his brother is a murderer, and you know that eternal life abides in no murderer's heart" (1 Jn 3:15).

317. *When do we sin against the body of others?*

We sin against the body of others
1. **when we assault others physically, wound or kill them;**
2. **when through abuse and mistreatment we embitter or shorten their life.**

Drinking parties and brawling seem to go hand in hand. The result almost always is bodily harm, and death itself is not unheard-of. Brawling is not new but there is a "modern" sinning against the body of others that takes place on our streets and highways. A staggering number of traffic accidents are recorded every year, bringing death to thousands and reducing many more to cripples for life. If through careless driving or conscious violation of traffic laws (speeding, illegal passing, improper vehicle maintenance) we are the cause of bodily harm or death to others, we sin grievously against the Fifth Commandment of God. Most serious and sinful is to drive when drunk or drugged.

July 1968 saw the beginning of a heretofore unknown way of sinning against the life and body of others: the hijacking of airplanes. An airliner was commandeered and ordered to land in Algeria. Since then, aerial piracy has grown alarmingly. Sometimes the hijackers are politically motivated, or they demand enormous ransoms. Always, innocent passengers, women and children among them, are subjected to physical and mental cruelty, wondering what will happen to them or whether they will come out alive.

Terrorists specializing in kidnapping and bombing represent another form of sinning against the life and body of other. Bombs are planted in public places (markets, theaters, airports, even in schools and churches). Innocent lives are lost or seriously damaged. Not only bomb explosions but bomb threats are grievous sins, because threats also imperil lives and cause mental and physical suffering, which is a violation of the Fifth Commandment.

One of the cruelest sins against the life of others is the killing of the unborn, the sin of abortion. The victims are not only innocent but utterly defenseless. Abortion, which is the direct killing of an unborn child, constitutes murder, notwithstanding that "respectable" organizations backed by generous contributions from "respectable" foundations repudiate the charge. The medical profession, for all its easy acquiescence in the practice of abortion, is hard put to deny that from its inception the unborn child differs biologically from the born child in degree, not in kind—in other words, is a human being in process of development. Only a people that has lost its moral direction and gone pleasure-mad would lend the majesty of its law to this crime that cries out to God for judgment.

318. *Is the killing of a human being never allowed?*

The killing of a human being is allowed

1. **to individuals in legitimate self-defense,**
2. **to the State when necessary as punishment for heinous crimes,**
3. **or to its soldiers acting in the name of the State in defense of its borders.**

1) *Legitimate self-defense.* In self-defense against an unjust aggressor the innocent party can use every appropriate means, killing included, to defend self and dear ones from grave harm. But the defender must guard against vengeance or excessive retaliation. If the aggressor can be subdued or warded off without killing, then killing no longer is an appropriate means and is strictly forbidden.

What I may do for myself or my family I may do for others who are unjustly attacked, whether they be neighbors or strangers, and I may come to their defense by every appropriate means, killing included. I may do this not only to save their life but to wrest them from the power of the unjust aggressor.

2) *Capital punishment.* Many countries have abolished capital punishment. In the United States, some states have it, some do not. The Supreme Court, while not outlawing it, has severely circumscribed its application. Basically, society has the moral right to capital punishment if it cannot properly protect itself in some other way. On this there is general agreement among Catholic moralists. At issue, therefore, is not the existence of the right but whether it should be used today.

On March 7, 1981, the Jesuit review *Civiltà Cattolica,* published in Rome, argued in a lengthy editorial that the death penalty is unjust and unacceptable in today's world. Society, it contended, has other means to ensure its safety and welfare. The American Hierarchy has taken a similar stand. To keep the matter in perspective it should be remembered that social conditions change. Society might need the death penalty at one time and not at another. Whether in the United States today society can fulfill its function just as well without the death penalty is really what is at issue.

On this point, the Fifth Commandment is not much help. The primitive text reads: You shall not *murder,* which is not the same as *kill.* If all killing were murder, how, to raise just one point, could killing in self-defense be justified, which it is?

3) *Defense of one's Country.* Vatican II speaks of the right of the State to defend itself. In the *Pastoral Constitution on the Church in the Modern World,* the Council says: "Insofar as people are sinful, the threat of war hangs over them, and hang over them it will until the return of Christ. . . . As long as the danger of war remains and there is no competent and sufficiently powerful authority at the international level, governments cannot be denied the right to legitimate defense once every means of peaceful settlement has been exhausted. State authorities and others who share public responsibility have the duty to conduct such grave matters soberly and to protect the welfare of the people entrusted to their care.

"But it is one thing to undertake military action for the just defense of the people, and something else again to seek the subjugation of other nations. Nor does . . . the fact that war has unhappily begun mean that all is fair between the warring parties. . . . Those too who devote themselves to the military service of their country should regard themselves as the agents of security and freedom of peoples. As long as they fulfill this role properly, they are making a genuine contribution to the establishment of peace" (nos. 78, 79).

Recent Popes, before and since the Council, have repeatedly turned their attention to the subject of war, a subject the more critical with the development of nuclear capabilities. Pope Paul VI told the United Nations: "No more war! War never again!" In *Pacem in Terris* (Peace on Earth) Pope John XXIII wrote: "It is hardly possible to imagine that in the atomic era war could be used as an instrument of justice." In 1944, viewing the massive destruction of World War II, Pius XII had said that war was "out of date" as a means of settling disputes. Visiting Hiroshima on February 25, 1981, Pope John Paul II declared that "peace or the survival of the human race is henceforth linked indissolubly with progress, development, and dignity for all peoples," rather than with the "balance of terror" or the arms race.

Offensive war, war of naked aggression, is wrong and morally condemned. But no one wants to deny States the right to legitimate self-defense. The problem is how to weigh this right against the horrendous prospects of a nuclear conflagration. In addition, in practice the line between offensive and defensive war is usually obfuscated by conflicting claims. It is a notorious fact, for example, that nations regularly plead self-defense for their aggressions.

Conscientious objection. In February, 1981, the Administrative Board of the United States Catholic Conference — in effect, the American Catholic Hierarchy—reaffirmed its support of the right of conscientious objection "as a valid moral position, derived from the Gospel and Catholic teaching." The Board also reaffirmed the right of selective conscientious objection, arguing that this right is "a valid moral conclusion from the classical Catholic moral teaching embodied in the just-war theory." The Board regretted that the principle of selective objection is not yet recognized in our (American) legal system and hoped that it will be.

General conscientious objection (objection to all war) is indeed a position that has been traditionally supported by Catholic moralists. Something of a departure from tradition, however, was the Bishops' espousal during the Vietnam conflict of selective objection (objection, not to all war but to a particular one). The Bishops, speaking through their Administrative Board, have no doubt as to the moral validity of this form of conscientious objection. Whether, as they propose, it will be accorded legal status remains to be seen.

319. Is everything in the Sermon on the Mount (Mt 5—7) to be taken literally?

Not everything in the Sermon on the Mount is to be taken literally, since this would lead to manifestly impossible consequences in private and public life.

Christ often spoke in hyperbole and other figures of speech which cannot be taken literally (cp. Mt 5:18, Mk 11:23, Jn 16:23). By His own example He showed that not everything in the Sermon on the Mount is literal teaching. When He stood before the high priest Annas and was struck in the face by one of the guards, He did not—as the Sermon requires—turn the other cheek but said to the guard: "If I said anything wrong produce the evidence, but if I spoke the truth why hit me?" (Jn 18:22-23).

What a literal interpretation of everything in the Sermon on the Mount would lead to in practice has been spelled out by the editor of a Protestant journal: "Were the Sermon on the Mount to be taken as a charter for a Christian social order, not only military defense of a country would go by the board. Every savings account and every bank would be un-Christian ('Do not lay up for yourselves an earthly treasure'). Every insurance policy, every pension plan, every road sign and traffic light would be un-Christian ('Do not worry about your livelihood,' or your life). Every labor contract, all medical coverage, all locks on doors and all refrigerators would be un-Christian ('Let tomorrow take care of itself'). All police protection, all criminal and penal law, indeed the whole judicial system would be un-Christian, since in the Sermon on the Mount Jesus takes exception to every form, however just, of punishment and reprisal. Even schools would be un-Christian since they look to tomorrow and compare unfavorably with the lilies of the field ('They do not work; they do not spin. . . Stop worrying, then . . .').

"Clearly, then, in the Sermon on the Mount Jesus could not have been propounding a philosophy of government or a juridical order, which in fact would be neither juridical nor orderly. What He was talking about is the kingdom of God, not a utopian dream. He is not an anarchist, a nullifier of law Who thought it was possible among imperfect human beings to build with love alone a sort of paradise on earth, after first destroying the existent social order. . . . The Sermon on the Mount shows us how and why the Gospel gives us the strength to live in this world without fear and anxiety, without anger, without revenge, and how through love of Christ we can make the world around us better."— Read also Rom 13:1-6.

320. Does the Fifth Commandment forbid only evil deeds against others?

The Fifth Commandment forbids not only evil deeds but also thoughts, desires, and words that lead to evil deeds, e.g., hatred, anger, desire for revenge, quarreling, abusive language, and wishing ill to others.

Wishing ill to others (or to ourselves) and cursing them is a violation of Christian love. In the process God is often blasphemed and His name taken in vain. In that case there is also a sin against the Second Commandment. — "Anyone who hates his brother is a murderer" (1 Jn 3:15).

There is such a thing as righteous anger. The Bible shows this in the case of Moses (Ex 32:19ff), and in the life of Jesus Himself (Jn 2:15-16). The extremes to which sinful anger can go are also manifest in the Bible in the conduct of Cain (Gn

4:3-8, Esau (Gn 27:41ff), the brothers of Joseph (Gn 37:11ff), and Herodias (Mk 6:17ff). — Read Paul's exhortation, Rom 12:14-21.

321. *When do we sin against our own life?*

We sin against our own life when we

1. **shorten it through excess of any kind, through anger, unchaste living, and other addiction to the appetites of the flesh,**
2. **needlessly endanger our life or health,**
3. **or take our own life (suicide).**

1) Read Proverbs 14:30 and Sirach 6:2, 4. — Fleshly appetite is a killer spider, First it traps its victim, then paralyzes and devours it. The moral and bodily devastation of licentious living is not unlike the devastation of an explosion, deluge, avalanche, or hurricane—it is complete.

2) Overindulgence in food or drink endangers health. So does smoking in proportion to the indulgence, at least statistically, and drug addiction. If we engage in dangerous sports, we are morally obligated to have proper training and regard for the rules of safety. Otherwise we needlessly, hence sinfully, put life and limb at risk.

3) "No persons may intentionally seek their own death to escape temporal burdens, for in fact they are only exchanging them for everlasting ones. Nor may we do so seeing the sins of others, and fearing we will fall into sins of our own, when in fact the sins of others are theirs and need not be our own. Nor because of past sins, which make it the more necessary that we live in order to atone for them. Nor, finally, from a desire for a better life after death, since a better life after death is not in store for real suicides" (St. Augustine, d. 430, *City of God*).

Suicides. — *Canon Law states that suicides are not to receive Church burial if they killed themselves deliberately, i.e., in full possession of their faculties, realizing and intending what they were doing. In practice, suicides almost always are given the benefit of the doubt, since many factors can and most often do render such an act less then fully responsible, if indeed responsible at all. Example: severe depression, temporary insanity, mental illness (unsuspected). The case is different if a person is known to have professed suicide as his or her philosophy of life, rationally planned for it, and carried it through on a day of choice. Such a person, however, is not likely to have been a Catholic; so the question of Church burial would scarcely arise. In any case, ultimate judgment of responsibility rests with God.*

In a study on suicide covering the years 1900-1955, the World Health Organization found that the incidence of suicide is higher in good times than in bad. This is in line with what we read daily in the papers, namely, suicide by persons who seem to have everything to live for: affluence, position, celebrity, health. Alarming also is the growing rate of suicide among young people.

Perhaps the key to the prevalence of suicide can be found in another statistic, supplied by a European journal of psychology (1974), which showed that predominantly Catholic countries of Europe have a considerably lower rate of suicide than others. Evidently, strong belief in God and the hereafter works against suicide. Not unexpectedly, it has also been found that where the divorce rate is higher the suicide rate is higher. Other groups more apt to commit suicide are confirmed alcoholics and drug addicts.

322.   When do we harm the soul of others?

We harm the soul of others when we give scandal, i.e., when by word or deed we are an occasion of sin to them, and still more when we intentionally lead them into sin.

323. *What are the words of Jesus that warn us against giving scandal?*

Jesus said: "It would be better for anyone who leads astray [by scandal] one of these little ones who believe in me, to be drowned by a millstone around his neck, in the depths of the sea. What terrible things will come on the world through scandal. . . . Woe to that man through whom scandal comes!"(Mt 18:6, 7).

By giving scandal we help the devil to destroy souls for whom Christ died. We also share in the sins that grow out of the scandal.

"He [the devil] brought death to man from the beginning. . . . He is a liar and the father of lies" (Jn 8:44). — Example: Jeroboam (1 Kgs 12:28-32).

Shun bad companions. Do not become a soul-destroyer. Heed Mt 5:29-30, Rom 14:13ff, and 1 Cor 8:13.

324. *What must we do when we have harmed the body or soul of others.*

When we have harmed the body or soul of others, we must repair the harm as far as possible.

"This is how all will know you for my disciples: by your love for one another" (Jn 13:35).

325. *How should we treat animals?*

We should treat animals as creatures of God and not vent our anger or cruelty on them.

The Bible teaches that we should treat animals as God's creatures. The Third Commandment, in the expanded version of Ex 20:10, states that beasts of burden also should be rested on the Sabbath. Subsequently, Moses gave the following instruction to his people, which again underscores the treatment we owe to animals as God's creatures: "When you come upon your enemy's ox or ass going astray, see to it that it is returned to him. When you notice the ass of one who hates you lying prostrate under its burden, by no means desert him; help him, rather, to raise it up" (Ex 23:4-5).

Care of animals is called for in Dt 25:4: "You shall not muzzle an ox when it is treading out grain." In Prv 12:10 it is said: "The just man takes care of his beast, but the heart of the wicked is merciless." In other words, animals should be properly fed and sheltered.

When Mary laid Jesus in a manger, we may assume that animals were about and that Is 1:3 came to pass: "An ox know its owner, and an ass, its master's manger." Concerning Christ's forty days in the desert, Mark says: "He stayed in the wasteland forty days, put to the test there by Satan. He was with wild beasts, and angels waited on him" (Mk 1:13). Jesus' staying with "wild beasts" may have reference to Is 11:6-9, where the idyllic harmony of paradise (the wolf a guest of the lamb, etc.) is used as symbol for the universal peace and justice of Messianic times.

On one occasion when Jesus, to the displeasure of the Pharisees, healed a man on the Sabbath he said to them: "If one of you has . . . an ox and he falls into a pit, will he not immediately rescue him on the sabbath day?" (Lk 14:5). Christ came to save human beings, but he could feel for the animal world too.

God gave human beings dominion over animals (Gn 1:26), but ultimate dominion He kept for Himself: "Mine are all the animals of the forests, beasts by the thousand on my mountains. I know all the birds of the air, and whatever stirs in the plains, belongs to me" (Ps 50:10-11). Human beings, therefore, may use animals but they may not abuse them. They may also kill animals for their needs so long as it is

done humanely, without prolonged or unnecessary pain to
them.

*A perfect friend of animals was St. Francis of Assisi (d.
1226), patron of kindness to animals. He moved among them
as though they were his brothers and sisters. Efforts to ensure kindness to animals are doubly necessary today because we have learned to use them like machines. We have
industrialized them to get the most from them. Pope Pius
XII said: "The animal world . . . shows God's power, wisdom
and goodness and therefore deserves considerate treatment
from humans. Every inhumane procedure in the slaughter-
ing of animals, every unnecessary roughness and callous
cruelty, must be condemned. Such treatment is incompatible with healthy human feelings and necessarily leads to
human brutality" (Nov. 1952).*

*The Pope's words should stir our interest in the proper
treatment of animals. At the least, we ought not to become
part of the problem by our own mistreatment of them. Let
us not forget: in the long run kindness to animals is also
kindness to humans. (And yet how ironic, and truly sad,
that so many people who could not stand to "hurt a flea"
can stand by or nod approval when the far worse slaughter
of human life in the womb confronts them.*

SIXTH AND NINTH COMMANDMENTS OF GOD

"You shall not commit adultery."
"You shall not covet your neighbor's wife."

326. *What does God forbid in the Sixth and Ninth
Commandments?*

**In the Sixth and Ninth Commandments God for-
bids immodesty and unchastity and everything
that leads to such sins.**

JESUS ENDORSED MARRIAGE AND DENOUNCED ADULTERY

"A man shall leave his father and mother and cling to his wife, and the two shall become as one. . . . Therefore, let no man separate what God has joined. . . . Whoever divorces his wife and marries another commits adultery" (Mt 19:5f, 9).

The Sixth Commandment refers to words and deeds, and the Ninth Commandment to thoughts and desires.

God created the body as the abode of the soul. He sanctifies it through Baptism, Confirmation, and Holy Communion, and destines it for glorious resurrection and eternal happiness. The body is a temple of God. God dwells in it by His grace. Therefore we must keep the body holy.

We may rightfully be glad that our body is healthy, robust, and beautiful, a work of art fashioned and created by God and a temple of the Holy Spirit. This is a legitimate rejoicing in the body. We may also do for the body whatever is necessary to keep it clean and healthy.

We sin against *modesty* when we expose the body wantonly or without need; or gaze at, talk about, or handle it in a lewd manner. We should preserve and practice modesty. It is the guardian of chastity.

We sin against *chastity* when we indulge in immoral sexual activity (e.g., between unmarried persons) or entertain thoughts and desires of such activity.

When we are in doubt about whether something is a sin against modesty or chastity, we should ask a person whom we can trust, preferably a priest or parent.

"As for lewd conduct or promiscuousness or lust of any sort, let them not even be mentioned among you; your holiness forbids this" (Eph 5:3).

327. *What does God require in the Sixth and Ninth Commandments?*

In the Sixth and Ninth Commandments God requires that we practice modesty and live chastely.

God requires us to be pure in thought and desire, in what we read and see and listen to, in our speech and all our conduct.

The Bible speaks in many places about sins against chastity, and also about inner purity of mind and heart. In Gn 38:8-10: sin of Onan (onanism); in Ex 22:15, 18: sin of the unmarried and bestiality (sin with animals); in Lv 18:6-23: incest and homosexuality; in Dt 22:22-24: rape; in Dt 23:2: castration; in Dt 23:18-19: prostitution; nor could money from prostitution be used for a votive offering in the Temple.

In the New Testament Christ calls attention to the importance of purity of heart and mind, as in Mt 5:8, 27-28 and Mk 7:20-23. In the Epistle to the Romans (1:23ff), St. Paul mentions a variety of sexual depravities which were a consequence of pagan idolatry, and in 1 Cor 6:12ff condemns fornication and all unchaste conduct, to which he opposes the chaste living incumbent upon followers of Christ especially.

Though among sins that exclude one from inheriting the kingdom of God are sins against chastity, we should not exaggerate their gravity at the expense of other sins. Violations of love of God and love of neighbor, or some sins against other Commandments (e.g., the Fourth and Fifth), can be just as great and greater. We should not go to either extreme, overstating sin of any kind on the one hand, or minimizing it on the other. In addition, some transgressions of chastity are more degrading than others, in particular unnatural vices like homosexuality. What our Lord said about keeping heart and mind clean applies not least in the area of sex. It is in the heart that both the chaste and the unchaste act are born.

328. *What natural means must we use to keep ourselves chaste?*

To keep ourselves chaste we must control our thoughts and desires, keep ourselves occupied, and as far as possible avoid anything that is a threat to chastity.

Threats to chastity are bad books, magazines, and pictures; certain movies, theatrical productions, and television programs; certain forms of dancing and other amusement; bad companions and company; immodest dress, liberties with the opposite sex, idleness, the influence of drink and "social" drugs.

329. *What supernatural means must we use to keep ourselves chaste?*

To keep ourselves chaste we must pray regularly and with fervor, be devoted to the Blessed Virgin Mary, to the Guardian Angel and Patron Saints of chastity, and frequent the Sacraments (Confession and Holy Communion).

When tempted against chastity we should think of God, Who sees all, and of death. We should invoke the holy names of Jesus and Mary, and remember to pray.

Prayer for chastity: O Mary, my Mother and Queen, I come to you, and in testimony of my devotion dedicate to you my eyes, my ears, my mouth, my heart, and my whole self. Because I am yours, keep me this day and watch over me as over your possession.

Among Patron Saints of chastity are: St. Aloysius, St. Stanislaus Kostka, St. John Berchmans, and St. Maria Goretti.

SEVENTH AND TENTH COMMANDMENTS OF GOD

"You shall not steal."
"You shall not covet your neighbor's goods."

330. *What does the Seventh Commandment forbid?*

The Seventh Commandment forbids harming others in regard to their goods and property.

Goods and property constitute everything that a person owns: house, household wares, clothing, tools, machinery, land, and much more. The supreme Lord and owner of all things is God, Who created them. But God gave humans the use of creation, the earth and all things in it. Every person has a right to ownership, which must however be exercised according to God's will, i.e., with due regard to justice and charity or consideration of others. We shall have to give God an account of what we did with what in His providence He permitted us to acquire and own. The rich have a duty to do good with their wealth and possessions. The poor ought not to be envious of the rich but do have a right to be helped when in need and unable to help themselves. Besides our own works of Christian charity, we help the poor by helping our government (through our taxes) to relieve the poor. Greed and covetousness, however, are wrong for rich and poor alike.

"Give alms. . . . If you have great wealth, give out of your abundance; if you have but little, distribute even some of that" (Tb 4:8).

In the Pastoral Constitution on the Church in the Modern World, *Vatican II says: "God intended the earth . . . for the use of all human beings and peoples. Thus, under the leadership of justice and in the company of charity, created goods should be in abundance for all in like manner. Whatever the forms of property may be, as adapted to the legitimate institutions of peoples, . . . attention must always be paid to this universal destination of earthly goods. In using them, therefore, human beings should regard the external things that they legitimately possess not only as their own but also as common in the sense that they should be able to benefit not only themselves but also others.*

"On the other hand, the right of having a share of earthly goods sufficient for oneself and one's family belongs to everyone. The Fathers and Doctors of the Church held this opinion, teaching that people are obliged to come to the relief of the poor and to do so not merely out of their super-

*fluous goods. . . . Since there are so many people prostrate
with hunger in the world, this sacred Council urges all to remember the aphorism of the Fathers, 'Feed those dying of
hunger, because if you have not fed them, you have killed
them.'*

*"According to their ability, let individuals and govern-
ments really share their earthly goods. Let them especially
use these goods to aid individuals and nations to help
develop themselves"* (no. 69).

331. *When do we harm others in regard to their
goods and property?*

**We harm others in regard to their goods and
property when**
1. **we rob or steal,**
2. **defraud or profiteer,**
3. **fail to return found or borrowed goods,**
4. **go into debt recklessly and neglect to pay our
debts,**
5. **or damage the property of others.**

We sin through *fraud,* when, for example, we use short
measure or short weight, pass counterfeit money, sell or
deliver imitation goods for the real thing, or engage in false
advertising. It is also fraudulent to submit a bill for more
hours of work than was done.

We sin through *profiteering* when we take advantage of
others by charging them too much interest on loans or in
any way exploit their need for the sake of excessive profits.

332. *Do only those persons sin who do the actual
harm to others in regard to their goods and
property?*

They also sin who
1. **advise or assist in doing the harm to others,**

2. **knowingly receive, buy, or deal in stolen goods and property,**
3. **or do not prevent the harm though they could and should have done so (e.g., the police or other public officials).**

Even when we are not charged by law to protect the goods and property of others, we still have an obligation in charity to forestall the stated harm to others if we are reasonably expected to do so. "It's none of my affair" may be a dereliction of Christian charity, to say the least. Circumstances will determine what we should or should not do in a given case.

333. *What must we do when we have harmed others in regard to their goods or property?*

When we have harmed others in regard to their goods or property we must do the following:

1. **in case of unjustly acquired goods, restore the goods as soon as possible;**
2. **in case of damage to goods or property, repair the damage as far as we are able.**

Sometimes stolen goods can be returned by arrangement with the confessor, who in this case also is bound by the seal of confession not to name the guilty party. Obviously, confessors are not eager to handle such transactions and do it only because no one is obligated to incriminate self if justice can be served in some other way. In the case of money, it could be returned by anonymous mail. The important thing is that stolen object or objects be restored to the rightful owner.

If the owner or heirs cannot be found, the unjustly acquired goods must be used for the poor or other pious purposes.

Restitution must be made without delay. If full restitution is not immediately possible, it must be made when and as possible, gradually or in periodic amounts.

If the actual perpetrators of harm to another (theft, property damage, fraud, etc.) fail to make restitution, the obligation devolves upon those who by word or deed were accessory to the harm, or upon those who did not prevent it even though they could have and were charged by law to do so.

334. What does the Tenth Commandment forbid?

The Tenth Commandment forbids the desire to take for our own the goods or property of others wrongfully.

Read 1 Tm 6:7-10, and for an example of a covetous person 2 Kgs 5:20-27 (Gehazi, servant of Elisha).

EIGHTH COMMANDMENT OF GOD

"You shall not bear false witness against your neighbor."

335. What does the Eighth Commandment forbid?

The Eighth Commandment forbids

1. **false witness,**
2. **lying,**
3. **and every sin against the character and good name of others.**

To bear false witness means: in a court of law, to give evidence which one knows to be untrue.

336. *What is a lie?*

A lie is saying what one knows to be untrue in order to deceive.

A direct lie is always wrong, even if uttered to prevent a presumed greater evil. There can be no greater evil than sin, and a good intention does not justify a sinful means.

However, not everything that is not literally true is necessarily a lie. Tall tales, intended for amusement, deceive no one and are not lies. Certain conventional greetings, compliments, and praises are commonly understood as being no more than polite address. In some circumstances (to keep a committed secret or maintain necessary privacy), one may have recourse to accepted forms of evasive speech. "Mr. Jones is not in" may mean that Mr. Jones is not prepared to see or speak with the caller. Everybody knows this, or should.

Evasive speech, however, must not be abused but be kept within the bounds of what is commonly accepted and understood. "Little white lies" are a contradiction. If they are lies they are not white and may not be little. Sometimes, on the other hand, what is called a little white lie falls into the category of legitimate evasive speech or legitimate convention.

Christians above all should be truthful: "See to it, then, that you put an end to lying; let everyone speak the truth to his neighbor" (Eph 4:25). — Related to lying is hypocrisy, because we pretend to be what we are not in order to deceive.

337. *Why should we guard against lying?*

We should guard against lying because lying comes from the devil and is an abomination to the Lord.

"He [the devil] is a liar and the father of lies" (Jn 8:44).
"Lying lips are an abomination to the Lord" (Prv 12:22).

338. How do we sin against the character of others?

We sin against the character of others
1. **through false suspicion and wrongful judgment,**
2. **and through slander and malicious gossip.**

We sin through *false suspicion* when without valid reason we suppose evil of others; and through *wrongful judgment* when without valid reason we deem a supposed evil to be true and certain. "Your verdict on others will be the verdict passed on you" (Mt 7:2).

339. What is slander?

Slander is to assert something evil of others which is not true, or to exaggerate an evil that is true.

Example: Potiphar's wife, against Joseph (Gn 39:7-20).

340. When do we sin through malicious gossip?

We sin through malicious gossip when we needlessly spread the faults of others (sin of detraction).

We may and should disclose the faults of others when it is necessary: (1) for correction of their faults, or (2) to forestall a greater evil, e.g., as a warning to someone else.

Akin to these sins of the tongue is *talebearing,* relating to others what (usually uncomplimentary) has been said about them: "Cursed be gossips and the double-tongued, for they destroy the peace of many" (Sir 28:13).

Also sinful is to encourage the slanderer or malicious gossiper: by a willing ear, by the remarks we make, the questions we interject, and other ways of spurring on. "The north wind brings rain, and a back-biting tongue an angry countenance" (Prv 25:23).

341. What must we do if we have damaged another's character or good name?

In case of slander, we must retract the slander. In case of needless spread of faults, we should try to find something good to say about the person. Both—slanderer and detractor—must as far as possible make good the harm done.

"The tongue . . . is a small member, yet it makes great pretensions. . . . It is a restless evil, full of deadly poison" (Jas 3:5, 8). — "Why look at the speck in your brother's eye when you miss the plank in your own?" (Mt 7:3).

A good name is a precious thing, "more desirable than great riches" (Prv 22:1). Shakespeare, in a famous line, echoes the sacred writer: "Who steals my purse, steals trash . . . but he that filches from me my good name. . . . " We should respect the good name of others not less than any of their possessions. The poorest person values his name, and we do wrong to besmirch it by sly insinuation or outright slander. The Christian prefers to think and speak well of people, and only talks of their faults when it must be done for their own good or the greater good of the community.

THE PRECEPTS OF THE CHURCH

342. *From whom does the Church have the right to make laws?*

The Church has the right to make laws from Christ Himself.

Christ gave this right to the Church in the words: "Whatever you declare bound on earth shall be bound in heaven" (Mt 18:18).

Included in this right of the Church is the authority to demand observance of her laws and to impose sanctions upon transgressors. The principal sanctions of the Church are: (1) denial of the Sacraments; (2) excommunication, by which the offender is deprived of many rights, graces, and blessings which members of the Church enjoy; and (3) denial of Church burial. — Example: Paul's exclusion of certain offenders from the Christian community in Corinth (1 Cor 5).

Is Church law an anachronism, something the Christian community has outlived? In particular, are the Precepts of the Church still necessary, and binding?

In recent years criticism of the Precepts of the Church has grown loud. The Church is a community of the redeemed, of the freed; therefore (it is charged) to tell someone how often to go to Mass or to receive the Sacraments is a reversion to the Pharisaic-Jewish worship of law and an encroachment upon the freedom of the children of God.

For a more correct evaluation of the Church's Precepts, perhaps the word "structure" or "regulation" may be helpful. Certainly the Church is the community of the redeemed, of faith, hope, and love, but nevertheless a community visibly established on earth. In the Dogmatic Constitution on the Church (no. 8), the Second Vatican Council stressed that the earthly Church and the Church enriched with heavenly things are not to be considered as distinct entities but as one complex reality in which a divine and a human element coalesce.

Because this human element also forms part of the Church, the Church needs regulation, as does every human community. In the Precepts of the Church this regulation finds expression. Their purpose is to assure at least the minimum of conformity among all the faithful of the community. No Precept of the Church was arbitrarily enacted but grew out of long experience, and was formulated not least in view of the weak and lukewarm.

All external requirements in the Church ultimately serve the life of grace. In question, therefore, is not mere external observance of law but free and inward acknowledgment of God and the things of God. Those who ignore or repudiate the Precepts of the Church ignore and repudiate the Church and lose contact with her. In doing that they also ignore what the Church was established to transmit to them —salvation.

No one can be compelled to join the community of the Church, but if we do join we may not regard as undue interference in our life the regulations of the community. Precepts and laws of the Church are not for the purpose of restricting our freedom but to show us how we can serve God and the world in freedom and so attain our own salvation.

343. *Why should we obey Church laws?*

We should obey Church laws

1. because the Church's power to make laws comes directly from Jesus,

2. and because the common good of the Church requires that her activity be regulated by law.

"Rulers of the Church and their appointed representatives have a right to obedience [of Church laws] on two counts. First, their power to command derives directly or indirectly from Jesus. Second, the common good of the

Church requires that the activity of the Church be regulated by law even in matters that are seemingly unimportant. The justice of law precludes arbitrariness and so ensures the necessary uniformity of treatment [of subjects]. . . .

"By its demands on members of the Church, Church law as such generally seeks no more than the minimum. Hence it is a perversion of its meaning and purpose to think that by satisfying it we have fulfilled all 'justice' or 'righteousness.' What God asks can at times go further than the law of the Church. The law determines what under normal circumstances is indispensable for the good of the community and the good of the individual. It fixes the lower limit. It cannot and does not express an upper limit. That is left to the Christ-formed conscience of the individual, who must determine what God here and now asks of it over and above the law.

"Between law and love there is no necessary contradiction. Love, at the very least and in its most basic expression, must strive for order and justice, for security and liberty. These are the very things for the sake of which law exists. As a general rule, therefore, love first must do what the law requires before it can think about doing something more and something else" (Karl Rahner in *Herders Theologisches Taschenlexikon*, 1972, vol. 4, p. 181).

The Protestant Church also recognizes that it cannot function without Church law. A distinguished member of the Protestant Synod of Zurich said in 1947: "Our Church exists in this terrestrial world, and so far as it exists in this world it needs order and regulation. More than that, Church law can help to give clear and pure expression to the life of the Church. . . . Church law contains not only duty and regulation but also profession of faith. It should be constructive and vitalizing. But above all one should see in it a reflection of the invisible world of heaven, which alone makes life worthwhile."

JESUS ENTRUSTED PETER WITH THE CARE OF HIS SHEEP
"Jesus said to Simon Peter, 'Simon, son of John, do you love me more than these?' 'Yes, Lord,' he said, 'you know that I love you.' At which Jesus said, 'Feed my lambs. . . . Feed my sheep' " (Jn 21:15ff).

344. *Which are the traditional Precepts of the Church?*

The traditional Precepts of the Church are:

1. To participate at Mass on all Sundays and Holydays of Obligation.
2. To fast and to abstain on the days appointed.
3. To confess our sins at least once a year.
4. To receive Holy Communion during the Easter time.
5. To contribute to the support of the Church.
6. To observe the laws of the Church concerning marriage.

The phrase "Precepts of the Church" refers primarily to laws that enable Catholics to carry out the Ten Commandments and are used in catechetical instruction and examination of conscience. Originally, in the 15th century, there were ten such laws in imitation of the Ten Commandments. In the 16th century, St. Peter Canisius listed five Precepts in his Catechism while St. Robert Bellarmine enumerated six.

This variation still holds from country to country. In the United States Catechisms followed the directive of the Third Council of Baltimore (1886) and listed the six Precepts given above. In 1975, the American Bishops published the *Basic Teachings for Catholic Religious Education* which gave the Precepts in an updated and fuller form and listed seven. (See next Question.)

The Church also has many other laws, contained for the most part in the Code of Canon Law. *As new circumstances arise, certain provisions of the Code are modified or replaced by others. Pope John XXIII (d. 1963) ordered a revision of the present Code, which was promulgated in 1918 and was itself the product of a long history of juridical development in the Church. The Pope wanted the new code to take into account the work of the Second Vatican Council and to lay greater stress on pastoral needs. The process of revision has been going on for about fifteen years. Cardinal Pericle Felici, president of the Pontifical Commission created for the purpose, recently expressed the hope that the revision will be finished and the new code ready for promulgation by the end of 1981. When it is promulgated, it will replace the one of 1918.*

345. Which are the updated Precepts of the Church?

The updated Precepts of the Church, set forth by the American Bishops in the *Basic Teachings for Catholic Religious Education* and the *National Catholic Directory,* are as follows:

From time to time the Church has listed certain specific duties of Catholics. Among those expected of Catholic Christians today are the following. (Those traditionally mentioned as Precepts of the Church are marked with an asterisk.)

1. To keep holy the day of the Lord's Resurrection: to worship God by participating in Mass every Sunday and Holy Day of Obligation;* to avoid those activities that would hinder renewal of soul and body on the Sabbath (e.g., needless work and business activities, unnecessary shopping, etc.).

2. To lead a Sacramental life: to receive Holy Communion frequently and the Sacrament of Reconciliation regularly —minimally, to receive the Sacrament of Reconciliation at least once a year (annual confession is obligatory only if serious sin is involved);* —minimally also, to receive Holy Communion at least once a year, between the First Sunday of Lent and Trinity Sunday.*

3. To study Catholic teaching in preparation for the Sacrament of Confirmation, to be confirmed, and then to continue to study and advance the cause of Christ.

4. To observe the marriage laws of the Church;* to give religious training, by example and word, to one's children; to use parish schools and catechetical programs.

5. To strengthen and support the Church*—one's own parish community and parish priests, the worldwide Church and the Pope.

6. To do penance, including abstaining from meat and fasting from food on the appointed days.*

7. To join in the missionary spirit and apostolate of the Church.

A comparison of the two lists of Precepts shows that the American Bishops, in addition to filling out the traditional Precepts, added two new ones: the study of Catholic teaching in order to advance the cause of Christ and the participation in the missionary spirit and apostolate of the Church. Both of these were dictated by the times in which we live, where much use is made of study and education in all fields and where the world has become a global village in which the lack of knowledge of Christ on the part of two-thirds of the world is most glaring.

FIRST PRECEPT OF THE CHURCH

"To keep holy the day of the Lord's Resurrection: to worship God by participating in Mass every Sunday and Holy Day of Obligation; to avoid those activities that would hinder renewal of soul and body on the Sabbath (e.g., needless work and business activities, unnecessary shopping, etc.)."

346. *What does the First Precept of the Church require?*

The First Precept of the Church requires that we be not only physically present at Mass but also

present in mind and heart by active participation in the celebration of the Eucharist.

As for unnecessary work, some people have to work on Sundays and/or holy days. If our employment requires us to work, we may hold ourselves excused from that part of the precept which forbids work on those days. But we are not automatically excused from participating in Holy Mass if we can do so without grave inconvenience. Nowadays employers generally are receptive to requests for time off for Sunday worship. Besides, the Saturday evening Mass can solve this problem for many people.

In the *Constitution on the Sacred Liturgy,* Vatican II says: "By a tradition handed down from the Apostles which took its origin from the very day of Christ's Resurrection, the Church celebrates the Paschal Mystery every eighth day; with good reason this, then, bears the name of the Lord's day or Sunday. For on this day Christ's faithful should come together into one place so that, by hearing the word of God and taking part in the Eucharist, they may call to mind the Passion, the Resurrection, and the Glorification of the Lord Jesus, and may thank God. . . . Hence the Lord's day is the original feast day, and it should be proposed to the piety of the faithful and taught to them so that it may become in fact a day of joy and of freedom from work" (no. 106).

Sunday should never be viewed as a gloomy day of obligation. It is a day of holy joy. It is a little Easter, when we celebrate Christ's glorious victory over sin and death and praise the Father for His wondrous salvation.

We proclaim our joy by our full participation in the Eucharist as well as by the way we live the rest of the day. All that we do should reflect the presence of God's Spirit, Who dwells in us and gives us His gift of joy.

Sunday should not be a time of turmoil and unceasing activity but a time of rest and re-creation. It should be a day of extra time spent with God in prayer, spiritual reading, Christian conversation, and self-giving. In this way, Sunday will become for us a day of reflection on God's work among us, on His Revelation, and on the Church's explanation and elaboration of God's truth.

See also Questions 303-307.

347. *Which are the Holy Days of Obligation?*

In the United States, the Holy Days of Obligation are:

New Year's Day	January 1
Ascension Thursday	40 days after Easter
Assumption of Mary into heaven .	August 15
All Saints Day	November 1
Immaculate Conception of Mary .	December 8
Christmas	December 25

Holy Days of Obligation are special feasts for Catholics. Formerly there were many more, but the industrial age led to a curtailment of the number. At the present time, there are ten Holy Days of Obligation listed for the Universal Church, but each Episcopal Conference is free to reduce these in view of the circumstances of its particular country and people. The ten include the six days listed above plus: Epiphany (January 6), Corpus Christi (Thursday after Trinity Sunday), Solemnity of St. Joseph (March 19), and Solemnity of Sts. Peter and Paul (June 29).

The Church in America celebrates two of the additional four Holy Days on Sundays (Epiphany and Corpus Christi). Thus, there are only two of the ten that are not Holy Days of Obligation in the United States (St. Joseph and Sts. Peter and Paul). However, the American Bishops recently gave some thought to a proposal to reduce the Holy Days for the reason, among others, that too many people must work and cannot observe them properly. Nevertheless, popular reaction was negative and the proposal was shelved.

348. *Who are bound by the precept to participate at Mass on Sundays and Holy Days of Obligation?*

Bound under pain of mortal sin by the precept to participate at Mass on Sundays and Holy Days of Obligation are all Catholics who have attained the use of reason and are not legitimately excused.

In the 1973, the Liturgical Commission of the Diocese of London, Canada, issued a leaflet intended as an aid to the deeper understanding of the Sunday Eucharist and its observance. Some of the pertinent parts are:

"Do Catholics still have an obligation to go to Mass on Sunday? Yes. Nothing has changed in this regard at all. You see, the obligation comes from the very nature of the Church. What is the Church? A Eucharistic community, a community whose very heart and center is the celebration of the Eucharist (as the Mass is commonly called today). This is what the Church does above all else. If we belong to the Church, it is first of all to celebrate the Eucharist. It is as simple as that.

"Of course, the question itself should not be necessary. There are many things in life that are real obligations, but which we rarely approach from this point of view. A mother has an obligation of love toward her children, but it is not for this reason that she loves them. It doesn't say much for our love of God if it is only out of obligation that we celebrate the sacrifice of Christ, the greatest act of God's love for mankind. . . .

"Why should I go to Mass? I don't get anything out of it. Good question. A better question is, 'What do you bring to Mass?' Do you bring faith? In the Liturgy of the Word, do you hear God? In the Liturgy of the Eucharist, do you make the great prayer of thanksgiving your own? Do you offer your life with Christ to God? Do you seal your love of God in the partaking of the Body and Blood of the Lord? Do you participate or do you just sit around putting in time?

"If you don't get anything out of it, if it doesn't turn you on, then perhaps what is missing is the one essential ingredient—faith. A dull Mass is inexcusable; but every Mass without faith is dull. We all need to pray for growth in faith. . . .

"*Is it a mortal sin to miss Mass on Sunday?* It most certainly can be. But first, what do we mean by mortal sin? The Christian life is centered upon a personal relationship —friendship with the living God. The 'state of mortal sin' is the condition of a man who has set aside his friendship with God. Sin is a breakdown in love between man and God.

"Now, what does the Sunday Eucharist have to do with all this? Everything; because the Sunday Eucharist is God's invitation to friendship—God's invitation to sit at His table, to share in His life, to be His friend. If, then, our departure from the Sunday Eucharist is taken at its face value, it means that we are setting our friendship with God aside, that we choose to keep Him out of our lives. We are talking about the complete breakdown of our friendship with God which, as we say, is called mortal sin.

"Often enough, of course, we don't think clearly about what we are doing. We miss Mass without careful thought —through weakness, carelessness, laziness, habit, or for some flimsy excuse. In the cold light of day, however, the fact remains that we neglect God's invitation to be His friend, we threaten our relationship with God. Despite our lack of thought, we play around with God's love, and we may slip away from it altogether.

"What is the degree of our guilt? We must consider before God and the Church, and in our own hearts, the extent of our realization and neglect, and, in short, the total picture.

"The Eucharist is a love-feast, and the Lord Himself understands that sometimes we simply can't be there. Attendance at Mass is not some cruel law with punishment hanging over us for any infringement, however involuntary. Practicing Catholics know the importance of Mass. They make it a point to be there. They know when they are excused."

Excusing Causes. *We have already seen that required work may be an excuse for failing to observe this precept. Illness, of course, excuses, and in general we are excused if we are bound by a prior obligation of justice or charity, e.g., taking care of a sick parent or helping out a neighbor struck by a tragedy or calamity. Every excuse assumes that going to Mass would pose an undue hardship.*

Radio and Television Mass. *The obligation to participate at Mass is not satisfied by hearing Mass on radio or television. As early as 1950 Pope Pius XII told an audience that radio does not supply for actual attendance—and the same is true of television. Nevertheless, for the sick and others unable to be present at Mass, a radio or television Mass offers an opportunity to do the next best thing by joining in spirit with the worshipers at church and following along as the celebration unfolds. When we are confined to bed or otherwise hampered from going out, we should try to find time for suitable prayer and Bible devotion at home. A radio or television Mass can help us to do this.*

349. *What is the Liturgical Year?*

The Liturgical Year is the succession of Seasons and Feasts of the Church celebrated annually from Advent to Advent.

As presently constituted, the Liturgical Year has the following Seasons (divisions):

Advent: This Season begins about four weeks before Christmas. It comprises four Sundays. The Sunday which falls on November 30, or is closest to it, is the First Sunday of Advent.

Christmas Time: This Season runs from the Solemnity of Christmas until the Sunday after Epiphany or after January 6, inclusive. The period from the end of Christmas Time until the beginning of Lent is included in the Ordinary Time of the year (see below).

CHRISTMAS CELEBRATES THE BIRTH OF JESUS
"(Mary] gave birth to her first-born son and wrapped him in swaddling clothes and laid him in a manger, because there was no room for them in the place where travelers lodged" (Lk 2:7).

Lent: The Penitential Season of Lent begins on Ash Wednesday and continues until Easter. The final week is called Holy Week, and its last three days are called the Paschal (Easter) Triduum.

Easter Time: This Season spans a 50-day period, from the Solemnity of Easter to Pentecost. Its central theme is the Resurrection of Christ together with our resurrection from sin to the new life of grace.

Ordinary Time: This Season comprises the other 33 or 34 weeks of the Liturgical Year. It includes not only the period between the end of Christmas Time and the beginning of Lent but all Sundays and weekdays after Pentecost until the beginning of Advent, It is "ordinary" only by comparison, because the great Feasts of our Lord are prepared for and specially celebrated other times of the year.

The first Christians knew only one Feast, Easter, the Feast of our Lord's Resurrection. But this they celebrated all the time, whenever they gathered for the Eucharist. In the Eucharistic celebration, every day and especially every Sunday became for them a little Easter. Easter, in fact, is the center in which all Mysteries of our Redemption merge. Eventually, however, the Church began to celebrate many of these mysteries in their own right, with feasts of their own, especially the Birth of our Lord, His Life and Death as well as His Resurrection and Glorification, and also the sending of the Holy Spirit and His work of grace in the soul. Gradually added were Feasts of the Blessed Mother Mary and the Saints. The Liturgical Year, therefore, has had a long history of development. As early as the year 700, however, the Roman Liturgical Year was essentially as it is today, with two major cycles, Christmas with its Advent and Easter with its Lent, plus the Sundays in between.

ADVENT - CHRISTMAS - EASTER

The Liturgical Year begins on the First Sunday of Advent. Literally, "advent" is a coming or arrival. Liturgically, it is a time of preparation for the feast of Christmas, which celebrates the Birth of Jesus, the first advent of the Son of God into the world. But we also focus our attention on the Second Coming, His glorious return at the end of the age, and on His coming to us in the interim in Word and Sacrament. Accordingly, the pervading mood of the Season of Advent is joy, joy over the past (the first coming), anticipated joy of the future (the Second Coming), and the present joy of His manifold presence even now in the Church and in the soul. Yet the violet color of the season tells us that Advent also is a quasi-penitential time, when festivities ought to be curbed and the spirit made ready for fruitful celebration of Christmas.

Liturgically, in the present calendar of the Church, the Feast of Christmas ranks with Easter. Historically, however, it came considerably later, Easter being the protofeast that goes back to the beginning. In some parts of the Christian world of antiquity Christmas was still not celebrated in the 4th and 5th century. Nor was December 25 always the day of the feast. Cyprus, Jerusalem, and Mesopotamia celebrated it on January 6. Constantinople, on the other hand, chose December 25, as did Rome. Why December 25? Primarily, it seems, as a countermeasure to the pagan feast of the Unconquerable Sun.

The sun reaches its lowest point below the equator on December 21 and then begins its annual climb, gathering strength each day. The pagans regarded this occurrence of nature as a rebirth or birthday of the sun and celebrated it on December 25. The Church was concerned about the lingering influence of the pagan feast on the newly-converted and so "Christianized" it by transforming it into a feast of the Birth of Christ, true Light and Sun of the world. St. Cyprian (d. 258) speaks of Christ as the true Sun, and St. Ambrose (d. 397) calls Christ our new Sun. — Though the birth of Christ is celebrated on December 25, the exact date is unknown. (See also Question 303.)

Because the Sunday on which it is celebrated depends on a variable, Easter is a so-called movable feast. The variable is the first new moon after the vernal equinox (March 21).

Easter is celebrated on the first Sunday following this new moon. Hence it "moves" from one year to the next. It can fall as early as March 22 and as late as April 25. The fiftieth day after Easter is the Feast of Pentecost (literally, fiftieth), when the Holy Spirit was sent to the Apostles and to the Church. With Pentecost the Church's founding was completed. Second Evening Prayer (Vespers) of the Feast terminates the Easter Season. The Easter candle, which burned at Mass during Easter, should be kept in a place of honor in the baptistery so that it can be used in Baptism and the candle of the baptized lit from it. It may also be brought out for burial services in church.

SECOND PRECEPT OF THE CHURCH

"To lead a Sacramental life; to receive Holy Communion frequently and the Sacrament of Reconciliation regularly—minimally, to receive the Sacrament of Reconciliation at least once a year (annual Confession is obligatory only if serious sin is involved); minimally also, to receive Holy Communion at least once a year, between the First Sunday of Lent and Trinity Sunday."

350. *What does the Second Precept of the Church require?*

The Second Precept of the Church requires that we lead a Sacramental life, that is, that we encounter Christ frequently through the Sacraments, and more specifically that we

1. **receive the Sacrament of Reconciliation (Confession) at least once a year (only if a serious sin is involved),**
2. **and receive Holy Communion at least once a year during the period prescribed loosely as Easter Time.**

Holy Communion is the means by which Jesus shares with His disciples His personal sacrifice and His personal victory over sin and death. By the bread and wine of the Eucharist, the ever-dedicated Redeemer, Who is the Holy One of God, sanctifies the lives of those who believe in Him.

At the same time, those who communicate in the Lord have their community in discipleship strengthened. Even more, their share in Jesus' sacrifice and victory is a pledge of its final fulfillment, with Him, in the world-to-come. The whole Church grows in holiness and hope by the Eucharist.

The Sacrament of Reconciliation enables Catholics who have lost their close unity with the Trinity to regain it and to once again attain communion with the Eucharistic Lord. It also gives restored communion with the Church and ease of conscience. Thus it is necessary for a truly Sacramental life when sin has intervened.

1) Obviously, an invalid Confession or unworthy Communion does not fulfill the precept; on the contrary it is a sacrilege. Nor is the precept fulfilled by taking part in a communal penance service without individual Sacramental Confession. Strictly speaking, persons who have not committed a grave sin are not bound to annual confession. But they are urged to do at least this much, for spiritual counsel and to receive the graces of the Sacrament.

2) For purposes of the Communion precept, Easter Time extends from the First Sunday of Lent to Trinity Sunday inclusive. Hence it covers more than the period called Easter Time in the liturgical calendar, which is the 50-day period from Easter to Pentecost.

351. *Why does the Second Precept of the Church say "at least" once a year?*

The Second Precept of the Church says "at least" once a year because the Church prescribes this as a minimum and strongly recommends more frequent Sacramental Confession.

Frequent confession is of great spiritual value. It makes us more responsive to God's grace and so helps us not only to persevere in the Catholic faith but to live our faith more completely.

352. What are the conditions for receiving Holy Communion?

The conditions for receiving Holy Communion are

1. the state of grace,
2. the right intention,
3. and the Eucharistic fast.

State of grace: freedom from mortal sin. But our Communions will bring more grace and blessing, and our spiritual growth in Christ will be greater, if we also strive to overcome venial sin in our life.

Right intention: not out of habit or human respect, but to please God and to live a better Catholic life.

Eucharistic fast: abstaining from food and drink (water excepted) one hour before Holy Communion. Plain water never breaks the fast. In addition, the sick and aged need fast only 15 minutes. The sick, moreover, if their condition requires, may take non-alcoholic beverages and solid or liquid medicine before Holy Communion without any time limit.

Nowadays, happily, faithful Catholics are receiving Holy Communion more than in the past, regularly on Sundays for many and also daily in goodly number. For such persons the Communion precept offers no problem. They will be receiving Holy Communion as a matter of course during Easter Time. Nor is it necessary for them to designate a particular Communion of that period as their Easter Communion.

Along with Questions 350-351, see again Questions 188ff (on the Holy Eucharist) and Questions 207ff (on the Sacrament of Penance).

THIRD PRECEPT OF THE CHURCH

"To study Catholic teaching in preparation for the Sacrament of Confirmation, to be confirmed, and then to continue to study and advance the cause of Christ."

353. *What does the Third Precept of the Church require?*

The Third Precept requires that Catholics

1. study the Faith both before and after their Confirmation

2. and advance the cause of Christ throughout their lives.

In an age when education and understanding are most highly prized, the Church wants the faithful to understand and practice their faith. She is, as it were, saying to all Catholics: "Believe what you receive; understand what you believe; and practice what you understand."

The Church gives us a faith that seeks understanding, and an understanding that seeks to be practiced. Then if we practice our faith, we well necessarily advance the cause of Christ throughout our lives.

The Church so prizes this understanding and practice on the part of her members that she grants a *partial indulgence* to all who take part in teaching or learning Christian doctrine *(Enchiridion of Indulgences,* no 20).

In the Declaration on Christian Education, *Vatican II declares: "Since all Christians have become a new creature by rebirth from water and the Holy Spirit, so that they may be called what they truly are, children of God, they are entitled to a Christian education. Such an education does not merely strive to foster in the human person the maturity already described [of responsible adulthood]. Rather its principal aims are the following: that as baptized persons are gradually introduced into a knowledge of the mystery of salvation, they may daily grow more conscious of the gift of faith which they have received; that they may learn to adore God the Father in spirit and truth (cf. Jn 4:23), especially through liturgical worship; and that they may be trained to conduct their personal life in the sanctity of truth, according to their new standard of maturity (Eph 4:22-24)" (no. 2).*

354. *What knowledge does the Church ultimately desire for her members?*

The knowledge that the Church ultimately desires for her members is the excelling knowledge of Jesus Christ, the incarnate Son of God, Who will in turn impart the saving knowledge of the Father.

"Eternal life is this: to know you, the only true God, and him whom you have sent, Jesus Christ" (Jn 17:3).

In the *Dogmatic Constitution on Divine Revelation,* Vatican II says: "This sacred Council earnestly and specifically urges all the Christian faithful . . . to learn by frequent reading of the divine Scriptures the 'excelling knowledge of Jesus Christ' (Phil 3:8). 'For ignorance of the Scriptures is ignorance of Christ' (St. Jerome)" (no. 25).

Thus one of the most important new aspects of Vatican II's treatment of religion is to speak of it in terms of "relationships" between persons. It places Christians not before formulas to be learned but before a Person, a Person Who is living and acting and Whose life and action consist in loving and saving human beings.

Divine Revelation is more than a doctrinal content—it is an event. It is an encounter that awaits a welcome. It is an action that requires a response. It is a sacred History of ancient time, of today, and of tomorrow. All of this is effected by the Father through Christ in the Holy Spirit.

Christians seek to learn not a theory but a Person, Jesus Christ. To believe is to come to Jesus. To believe is to listen to Jesus, for He speaks "the words of God" (Jn 3:34). To believe is to look at Jesus because the person who sees Him "sees the Father also" (Jn 14:9).

FOURTH PRECEPT OF THE CHURCH

"To observe the marriage laws of the Church; to give religious training, by example and word, to one's children; to use parish schools and catechetical programs."

355. *What does the Fourth Precept of the Church require?*

The Fourth Precept of the Church requires that Catholics

1. **abide by Christ's teaching on marriage and comply with the Church's requisites for getting married;**
2. **provide religious training and good example for their children;**
3. **and see that their children receive a formal Catholic education in the parish.**

1) The Church, in virtue of the commission received from Christ, teaches the law of God on marriage as well as on other things. The Church, moreover, is empowered to lay down certain conditions for a marriage for Catholics.

Many things can stand in the way of a marriage, the most obvious of which is a prior valid marriage of either partner. For more particulars, and especially when planning marriage, Catholics should consult a parish priest in sufficient time.

Two things ought to be kept in mind. First, the Church has no power to dispense from a divine impediment to marriage, in particular from the indissolubility of a valid Sacramental marriage. "Let no man separate what God has joined" (Mt 19:6). On the other hand, the Church can and sometimes does dispense from conditions that are purely of Church origin. For example, the Church prescribes that Catholics be married before a Catholic priest, but there is provision for this condition to be lifted in some cases and circumstances.

2) Pope John Paul II has called the family a "domestic church": "To visit the parishes, as part of the Diocese-Church, it is necessary to reach all the 'domestic churches,' that is, all the families. This, in fact, was the name given to all families by the Fathers of the Church. 'Make your home a Church,' St. John Chrysostom urged his faithful in one of his sermons" (December 3, 1978).

In a Homily during his Brazilian visit (July 5, 1980), the Pope explained what being a "domestic church" entailed for parents: "Catechesis in the family: Nothing can come before this. It lays the basis in the child's early years of life for what his future may be. Therefore parents ought to understand the importance of their mission in this regard. By virtue of their Baptism and Matrimony they are their children's first catechists. Educating the young is really a continuation of the act of begetting them. In our age God comes particularly 'through the part played by the family.'

"Children need to know and see that their parents love each other, that they respect God, that they know how to explain the first truths of the faith, (Catechesi Tradendae, no. 36), that they know how to present 'the Christian content' through testimony and perseverance in 'daily life lived according to the Gospel' (ibid., no. 68).

"Testimony is fundamental. God's word is efficacious in itself, but it takes on concrete meaning when it becomes reality in the person announcing it. To a child there is no distinction between a praying mother and prayer. Even more, such prayer has special value because it is the mother's prayer."

3) The Pope went on to stress that parents must also provide for formal Catholic education for their children: "Beloved parents listening to me, do not permit your children to come to individual, social, and professional maturity while remaining children in matters of religion. It is not true to say that faith is an option for adult age. True option presupposes knowledge. There can never be choice among things that have not been wisely and adequately expounded. . . .

"I would strongly recommend parish catechesis. The parish is where catechesis can deploy all its richness. There, associated with the hearing of the word, prayer, celebration of the Eucharist and the other Sacraments, fraternal communion, and the exercise of charity, the Christian mystery is announced and lived. . . .

"Then there is religious instruction in schools. A citizen is trained at school through cultural and professional education. Education of religious conscience is a right of the human person. The young demand to be set on the path to all dimensions of culture. They also wish to be able to find possibilities at school for getting to know the fundamental problems of existence. First place among these is taken by the problem of the response that they ought to give to God."

FIFTH PRECEPT OF THE CHURCH

"To strengthen and support the Church—one's own parish community and parish priests, the worldwide Church and the Pope."

356. *What does the Fifth Precept of the Church require?*

The Fifth Precept of the Church requires that each of us help to meet the temporal (as opposed to the spiritual) needs of the Church.

In these days, Church support usually is in the form of monetary contributions. Most parishes use envelopes for the purpose.

Church support, however, is not limited to money. We also help to meet the temporal needs of the Church by making available to the Church some of our time, some of our special talent or professional skills (e.g., as lawyer, doctor, accountant, plumber, mechanic, or whatever).

Our first obligation in this respect is to our local parish. But the true Christian does more, as individual circumstances permit. Christians from the beginning have assisted the Church far from the borders of the local community. St. Paul arranged for a collection from Gentile churches to help the poor Christians of Jerusalem (1 Cor 16:1). Our contributions to the home and foreign missions are a form of material support to the Church at large, which helps the universal Church to train missionaries, to send them to the mission field when they are ready, and to provide them with food and clothing after they arrive. Even better, though obviously not feasible for everybody, is volunteering a period of one's life (a few months, a year or two) for various kinds of work in mission lands.

Though we have an obligation to support the Church, let it be stated once for all that no one is expected to go without the necessities of life just to have something to give to the Church. Christ's Church is for the rich and the poor, and especially for the poorest of the poor who have nothing material to offer to the Church. No one should ever plead poverty for not participating in the Eucharist and entering into the mainstream of parish life. Christ's Church wants people more than it wants their money. Only those who are able are asked by our Lord to give. At the same time it must also be noted that there are those who are able who do not meet their obligation, or meet it only halfway. For them this Precept stands as a constant reminder.

SIXTH PRECEPT OF THE CHURCH

"To do penance, including abstaining from meat and fasting from food on the appointed days."

357. *What does the Sixth Precept of the Church require?*

The Sixth Precept of the Church requires that we practice the virtue of penitence which combines the inner conversion of the spirit with the voluntary exercise of external acts of penitence, such as fasting and abstinence, especially on the appointed days.

On February 17, 1966 Pope Paul VI issued a major statement on the revision of penitential discipline in the Church, the Apostolic Constitution *Poenitemini,* which went into effect on February 23 of that same year. After analyzing penitence in the Old and New Testaments, the Holy Father called for combining the inner conversion of the spirit with the voluntary exercise of external acts of penitence. In this way he retained the traditional triad of prayer, fasting, and charity but updated it, for example, by authorizing the substitution of other works of penitence for the customary and common observance of abstinence and fast on various days of the year.

"The preeminently interior and religious character of penitence and the new wondrous aspects which it assumes 'in Christ and in the Church'... prompts the Church—always attentive to the signs of the times—to seek, beyond fast and abstinence, new expressions more suitable for the realization, according to the character of various epochs, of the precise goal of penitence.

"True penitence, however, cannot ever prescind from physical asceticism as well. Our whole being, in fact, body and soul... must participate actively in this religious act whereby the creature recognizes divine holiness and majesty. The necessity of the mortification of the flesh also stands clearly revealed if we consider the fragility of our nature, in which, since Adam's sin, flesh and spirit have contrasting desires....

"Therefore the Church—while she reaffirms the primacy of the religious and supernatural values of penitence (values extremely suitable for restoring to the world today a sense of the presence of God and of his sovereignty over man and a sense of Christ and His salvation)—invites everyone to accompany the inner conversion of the spirit with the voluntary exercise of external acts of penitence

"She insists first of all that the virtue of penitence be exercised in persevering faithfulness to the duties of one's state in life, in the acceptance of the difficulties arising from one's work and from human coexistence, in a patient bearing of the trials of earthly life and of the utter insecurity which pervades it."

358. *What is required on days of fast?*

On the days of fast we must limit ourselves to one full meal.

In addition to one full meal, two lighter meals are allowed. But snacking between meals breaks the fast and the precept.

The law of fast is binding on Catholics from age to 21 to 59 inclusive. The sick (including pregnant women) are not bound by the precept. Other persons also may have sufficient grounds for being excused; e.g., if by fasting they cannot meet the demands of their regular work. In doubt, we may consult a priest, confessor, or any competent and trustworthy person.

In the United States, the days of fast prescribed by the Church are: Ash Wednesday and Good Friday.

359. *What is required on days of abstinence?*

On days of abstinence we must abstain from meat.

The law of abstinence is binding on Catholics from age 14; there is no upper limit. Conditions of health, unavailability of meatless fare, etc., may excuse a person.

In the United States, the days of abstinence are: Ash Wednesday and Good Friday *and* all other Fridays of Lent.

Days of fast and abstinence used to be more numerous. Older people can remember when every weekday of Lent was a fast day and all Fridays of the year were days of abstinence, not to mention the fast and abstinence on Ember Days and on the vigils of some holy days.

The American Bishops followed up Pope Paul VI's revision of the laws of fast and abstinence with a penitential message to American Catholics in which, like the Holy Father, they urged "love and imitation of Christ by special solicitude for the sick, the poor, the underprivileged, the imprisoned, the bedridden, the discouraged, the lowly, and persons of other color, nationalities, or backgrounds than our own" (Pastoral Statement on Penitential Observances, Nov. 18, 1966).

Children are not obligated to fast. Nevertheless, the spirit of penance and self-denial should be instilled by parents and teachers. Children can deny themselves tidbits of food and drink. For most of them if not all, a curb on television viewing would be a real and salutary penance. Children should also be introduced to the larger meaning of Christian penance by enlisting them in penitential programs designed to aid underprivileged children at home and abroad, particularly in what is called the Third World.

Sometimes one hears the charge that Catholics, or Christians generally, must think the body is evil or they would not mortify and bring it into subjection. The charge of course is untrue. As Paul VI stated: *"This exercise of bodily mortification—far removed from any form of stoicism—does not imply a condemnation of the flesh which children of God deign to assume. On the contrary, mortification aims at the 'liberation' of human beings, who often find themselves, because of concupiscence, almost chained by their own senses. Through 'corporal fasting' we regain strength and the 'wound inflicted on the dignity of our nature by intemperance is cured by the medicine of a salutary abstinence.'*

"Nevertheless, in the New Testament and in the history of the Church—although the duty of doing penance is motivated above all by participation in the sufferings of Christ—the necessity of an asceticism which chastises the body and brings it into subjection is affirmed with special insistence by the example of Christ Himself."

The Bible has many examples of men and women who fasted: Moses (Ex 24:18), King David, in reparation for his sin (2 Sm 12:16ff), Daniel and his companions (Dn 1:8ff), Judith (Jdt 8:6), Esther (Est 7:16), and the Ninevites, in response to the preaching of the prophet Jonah (Jon 3:5ff).

Jesus Himself fasted (Mt 4:2). Many Saints are known for their fasting, at times to such an extent that they seem to have been miraculously sustained.

Other religions also practice fasting. The Mohammedans have a month every year of daily fasting during which they do not eat or drink anything at all entil evening.

SEVENTH PRECEPT OF THE CHURCH

"To join in the missionary spirit and apostolate of the Church."

360. *What does the Seventh Precept of the Church require?*

The Seventh Precept of the Church requires that all Catholics take part in the missionary spirit and apostolate of the Church, through prayer, the witness of a good life, or active practice of evangelization.

In the *Decree on the Apostolate of the Laity,* Vatican II states: "The mission of the Church pertains to the salvation of human beings, which is to be achieved by belief in Christ and by His grace. The apostolate of the Church and of all her members is primarily designed to manifest Christ's message by words and deeds and to communicate His grace to the world. This is done mainly through the ministry of the Word and the Sacraments, entrusted in a special way to the clergy, wherein the laity also have their very important roles to fulfill if they are to be 'fellow workers of the truth' (3 Jn 8). It is especially on this level that the apostolate of the laity and the pastoral ministry are mutually complementary.

"There are innumerable opportunities open to the laity for the exercise of their apostolate of evangelization and sanctification. The very testimony of their Christian life and good works done in a supernatural spirit have the power to draw people to the belief and to God; for the Lord says, 'Your light must shine before men so that they may see goodness in your acts and give praise to your heavenly Father' (Mt 5:16).

"However, an apostolate of this kind does not consist only in the witness of one's way of life; a true apostle looks for opportunities to announce Christ by words addressed either to non-believers with a view to leading them to faith, or to the faithful with a view to instructing, strengthening, and encouraging them to a more fervent life. 'The love of Christ impels us' (2 Cor 5:14). The words of the Apostle should echo in all hearts, 'I am ruined if I do not preach [the Gospel]' (1 Cor 9:16).

"Since, in our own times, new problems are arising and very serious errors are circulating which tend to undermine the foundations of religion, the moral order, and human society itself, this sacred Council earnestly exhorts lay people—each according to individual gifts of intelligence and learning—to be more diligent in doing what they can to explain, defend, and properly apply Christian principles to the problems of our era in accordance with the mind of the Church" (no. 6).

VIOLATION OF COMMANDMENTS AND PRECEPTS

I. SIN

361. *When do we sin?*

We sin when we knowingly and intentionally break a Commandment of God or a Precept of the Church.

God permits us to be tempted to sin in order to: (1) keep us humble, (2) prove our faithfulness, and (3) increase our merits. "Happy the man who holds out to the end through trial. Once he has been proved, he will receive the crown of life" (Jas 1:12).

Temptation becomes sin only when we consent, i.e., consciously let it go on or encourage it.

Things to do to overcome temptation:
—avoid the occasion,
—pray fervently,
—invoke the holy names of Jesus and Mary,
—make the Sign of the Cross,
—remember God's presence and the last things (death, judgment, heaven, hell,
—bend the mind to wholesome thoughts.

In the Pastoral Constitution on the Church in the Modern World, *Vatican II says: "What divine revelation makes known to us agrees with experience. Examining their hearts, human beings find that they have inclinations toward evil too, and are engulfed by manifold ills which cannot come from their good Creator. Often refusing to acknowledge God as their beginning, human beings have disrupted also their proper relationship to their own ultimate goal as well as their whole relationship toward themselves and others and all created things" (no. 13).*

362. *How are we inwardly warned against sinning?*

We are inwardly warned against sinning by our conscience, which prods us to do what is good and steer clear of what is evil.

When we have done something good, conscience approves (good conscience). When we have done something evil, conscience accuses (bad conscience).

See earlier Questions 272, 273.

363. *What are the ways of sinning?*

In general, the ways of sinning are:
1. **thoughts, desires, words, and deeds,**
2. **neglect or omission of a good that is one's duty.**

We sin in thought when we consciously keep sinful thoughts in the mind and delight in them (fantasize about sinful things). We sin by desire when we long to see, hear, or do something evil.

Desire in itself is not evil. What makes it evil is when the desire is for something evil and is approved by the will. Approval by the will means having the intention to satisfy the desire.

II. THE GRAVITY OF SIN

364. *Are all sins equally grave?*

Not all sins are equally grave; there are sins of such gravity that they are mortal sins, and lesser ones that are called venial.

In Sacred Scripture some sins are compared to a plank, others to a speck (Mt 7:3).

365. *When do we commit mortal sin?*

We commit mortal sin when we
1. **have a grave matter,**
2. **understand the gravity,**
3. **and act voluntarily.**

1) *Grave matter:* Not all the things we do, not all our duties and responsibilities have the same moral ramification. A grave matter affects the core of our relationship to God or

neighbor. A lesser matter leaves our basic orientation untouched. Some of the things that come under grave matter are: marital fidelity, sacredness of human life, Christian love of enemies, apostasy from Christ or the Church, the duty to worship God. In general, a grave matter is any serious violation of the Commandments of God or the Precepts of the Church.

2) *Knowledge of the gravity:* Mortal sin presupposes that people realize the moral gravity of their acts. Without this awareness the sin is not mortal.

3) *Voluntary action:* This means that we are not under emotional or physical compulsion but knowingly and willingly act against the will of God as we understand it.

If there is any doubt about even one of these conditions, there is no mortal sin in what we do. But if all three conditions are verified, the act is gravely culpable and the sin is called mortal (deadly) because it robs the soul of its supernatural life through the loss of sanctifying grace. — "I know your conduct; I know the reputation you have of being alive, when in fact you are dead" (Rv 3:1).

Catholic teaching on mortal sin is not designed to frighten us but to keep us mindful of its possibility and the spiritual ruin it leaves behind. Through mortal sin we renounce our inheritance as children of God. We turn our back on His love and friendship. We run the risk that our "no" to His love will be our last word, which would close the door to His everlasting love in heaven.

While mortal sin may not be as frequent as one is sometimes led to believe, there is no justification for the suggestion that no one would commit mortal sin knowingly. This flies in the face of Sacred Scripture and human experience alike. At the same time, however, there is room for discriminating between an "isolated" mortal sin and sinning mortally habitually. But more to the point is that the Lord "wants none to perish but all to come to repentance" (2 Pt 3:9). A humble and contrite heart He never turns away (Ps 51:19).

366. *When do we commit venial sin?*

We commit venial sin when we have
1. a lesser matter,
2. or a grave matter but are not sufficiently aware of the gravity of the act or do not give full consent.

Venial means "more easily forgiven," because this sin does not result in spiritual death, i.e., the loss of sanctifying grace. No sin, however, should be taken lightly. Though less serious, venial sin disposes one toward mortal sin and in fact is the greatest evil next to it. If, spiritually speaking, mortal sin kills, habitual venial sin paves the way.

The Christian's life is motivated by love of God. If we truly love God, we will not want deliberately to offend Him even venially, in the slightest.

367. *Which are the seven capital sins?*

The seven capital sins are: (1) pride, (2) covetousness, (3) lust, (4) envy, (5) gluttony, (6) anger, and (7) sloth.

They are called capital sins because each is the source of many others.

368. *When do we sin by pride?*

We sin by pride when we have an inflated opinion of ourselves, glory in ourselves instead of God, and despise others.

"Name something you have that you have not received. If, then, you have received it, why are you boasting as if it were your own" (1 Cor 4:7). "If anyone thinks he amounts to something, when in fact he is nothing, he is only deceiving himself" (Gal 6:3).

"God resists the proud but bestows his favor on the lowly" (Jas 4:6). — Example: the Pharisee in the temple.

The opposite of pride is *humility*.

369.   *When do we sin by covetousness?*

We sin by covetousness when we set our heart on money and possessions but are cold and indifferent to the needy.

"Those who want to be rich are falling into temptation and a trap. They are letting themselves be captured by foolish and harmful desires which drag men down to ruin and destruction" (1 Tm 6:9).

The opposite of covetousness is *charitableness*.

370.   *When do we sin by lust (sins of sex)?*

For the answer, see under Sixth and Ninth Commandments, Questions 326ff.

The opposite of lust is *chastity*.

371.   *When do we sin by envy?*

We sin by envy when we are unhappy because of the good fortune of others, or happy because of their misfortune.

"By the envy of the devil, death entered the world, and they who are in his possession experience it" (Wis 2:24). — Examples: Cain (Gn 4:5f); the brothers of Joseph (Gn 37:4f).

The opposite of envy is *kindly love.*

372.   *When do we sin by gluttony?*

We sin by gluttony when we eat or drink too much or too greedily.

"Be on guard lest your spirits become bloated with indulgence and drunkenness and worldly cares. The great day [of judgment] will suddenly close in on you like a trap" (Lk 21:34). — Example: the rich man of the Gospel (Lk 16:19ff).

The opposite of gluttony is *moderation*.

373. When do we sin by anger?

We sin by anger when we become provoked without good reasons or beyond measure, indulge in swearing and vituperation and want revenge.

"Let every man be ... slow to anger; for a man's anger does not fulfill God's justice" (Jas 1:20).

The opposite of anger is *gentleness*.

374. When do we sin by sloth?

We sin by sloth when we neglect our duties because of a distaste for the work or the exertion required.

The worst kind of sloth is indifference to the worship of God and the needs of the soul.

"How I wish you were one or the other—hot or cold! But because you are lukewarm, neither hot nor cold, I will spew you out of my mouth!" (Rv 3:15-16). — "Idleness is an apt teacher of mischief" (Sir 33:28). — Example: the lazy servant (Mt 25:18ff).

The opposite of sloth is *diligence* in work, and *zeal* for what is right and good.

375. Which sins are called sins against the Holy Spirit?

Sins against the Holy Spirit are those which hinder God's grace more grievously and therefore make repentance or conversion of life more difficult.

Among these are:

1) Tempting God's mercy, e.g., the people facing the imminent Flood.

2) Doubting God's grace and forgiveness, e.g., Cain, Judas.

3) Contradicting Christ's known truth, e.g., the Pharisees.

4) Resenting God's favor toward another, e.g., Cain.

5) Stubbornly ignoring salutary warnings or admonitions, e.g., Pharaoh, the city of Jerusalem.

6) Deliberately disregarding calls to repentance, e.g., the Pharisees.

"You stiff-necked people, uncircumcised in heart and ears, you are always opposing the Holy Spirit" (Acts 7:51).

376. *Which sins are called shared sins?*

Shared sins are those committed by others but which also are imputed to us as accomplices.

We share in the sins of others by: (1) advising sin, (2) commanding others to sin, (3) approving their sin, (4) provoking them to sin, (5) praising their sin, (6) keeping silent about their sin, (7) not punishing sin, (8) sharing in wrongful goods, or (9) defending the sin of others.

Children as well as adults can become party to sins of others when, for example, they have secret knowledge of a brother or sister's wrongdoing and fail to report it to parents. In the Old Testament, Joseph told his father Jacob about the misdeeds of his brothers even though he had good reason to fear that they would make him suffer for it (Gn 37:2ff).

"Through all your days, my son, keep the Lord in mind, and suppress every desire to sin or to break his commandments" (Tb 4:5).

CHRISTIAN VIRTUES AND PERFECTION

377. *Is it enough to avoid sin?*

It is not enough to avoid sin; we must also grow in virtue and strive for Christian perfection or holiness.

Virtuous persons are those who have habituated themselves to living as pleases God. "The virtuous must live on in their virtue and the holy ones in their holiness!" (Rv 22:11). — "You must be made perfect as your heavenly Father is perfect" (Mt 5:38).

378. *How are the virtues classified?*

The virtues are classified as
1. theological virtues: faith, hope, and love;
2. and moral virtues.

1) Faith, hope, and love are called theological virtues because along with sanctifying grace they are infused in the soul by God, and refer directly to God. "The love of God has been poured out in our hearts through the Holy Spirit who has been given to us" (Rom 5:5).

"There are in the end three things that last: faith, hope, and love, and the greatest of these is love. Seek eagerly after love" (1 Cor 13:13—14:1).

2) The other virtues are called moral virtues because they regulate our moral life in a manner pleasing to God.

379. *Which moral virtues are the four basic ones?*

The four basic virtues are:
(1) prudence, (2) temperance, (3) justice, and (4) fortitude.

These are named cardinal virtues, because all other moral virtues hinge on them, are contained in them, and flow from them.

Prudence helps us to take the right means to a good end, specifically the means to our spiritual good and salvation. *Temperance* masters our unruly desires. *Justice* gives each his due. *Fortitude* ennobles us to do what is right in the face of difficulties and opposition.

Some people seem to think that the life of virtue and Christian perfection or holiness is not for them but only for priests and people in the religious life, in monasteries and convents. This is a misconception. In the *Dogmatic Constitution on the Church,* the Second Vatican Council reiterates that the call to holiness in the Church is universal: "The Lord Jesus, the divine Teacher and Model of all perfection, preached holiness of life to each and every one of His disciples of every condition. He Himself stands as the author and consummator of this holiness of life: 'Be you therefore perfect, even as your heavenly Father is perfect'.... Thus it is evident ... that all the faithful of Christ, of whatever rank or status, are called to the fullness of the Christian life and to the perfection of charity.... In the various classes and differing duties of life, one and the same holiness is cultivated by all, who are moved by the Spirit of God, and who obey the voice of the Father and worship God the Father in spirit and truth" (nos. 40, 41).

Also to the point is St. John Chrysostom (d. 407), speaking to his congregation: "Some say that it is impossible to live in the city [substitute: in the world] and at the same time lead a virtuous life—for that, you must flee to the hills, and be a hermit—but anyone with a home to keep up and who is married and has children and people to look after, cannot possibly keep himself virtuous. Such persons should take a look at the righteous Lot, who with wife and children and servants lived in the city, in the midst of wicked men, yet shone like a harbor light in the dark and was not quenched but rather let his light shine more brightly.

"I do not say this to dissuade anyone from withdrawing into solitude. I only want to point out that none of this is a hindrance to those who exercise self-control and watchfulness. To the worldly-minded solitude would be no help, since it is not where we live that makes us virtuous but having the right will and mind and doing the right deeds; in which case we cannot be harmed though living in the city" (Homilies on Genesis, 43:1).

380. *Which virtues are especially praised in the Gospel?*

Especially praised in the Gospel are the virtues contained in the Beatitudes (Mt 5:3-11).

The Beatitudes are:

1. **How blest are the poor in spirit: the reign of God is theirs.**
2. **Blest too are the sorrowing; they shall be consoled.**
3. **Blest are the lowly; they shall inherit the land.**
4. **Blest are they who hunger and thirst for holiness; they shall have their fill.**
5. **Blest are they who show mercy; mercy shall be theirs.**
6. **Blest are the single-hearted, for they shall see God.**
7. **Blest too the peacemakers; they shall be called sons of God.**
8. **Blest are those persecuted for holiness' sake; the reign of God is theirs** (Mt 5:3-10).

381. *Which is the way to Christian perfection?*

The way to Christian perfection is imitation of Jesus Christ.

JESUS GAVE THE BEATITUDES IN THE SERMON ON THE MOUNT
"When [Jesus] saw the crowds he went up on the mountain-
side. After he had sat down his disciples gathered around him,
and he began to teach them: 'How blest are . . . ' " (Mt 5:1ff).

"I am the light of the world. No follower of mine shall ever walk in darkness; no, he shall possess the light of life" (Jn 8:12).

382. In particular, what should we do to attain Christian perfection?

To attain Christian perfection, we should

1. love to pray, be eager for the word of God and devoted to the Sacraments;
2. practice self-denial and strive to overcome even venial sin;
3. perform our daily work in the state of grace and for good intentions.

"Whoever wishes to be my follower must deny his very self, take up his cross each day, and follow in my steps" (Lk 9:23).

Self-denial means we do without some things we like and at times abstain even from what is permitted so that we can more readily reject what is not permitted.

383. Which are the special means of Christian perfection?

The special means of Christian perfection are the three Evangelical Counsels, namely: (1) voluntary poverty, (2) perpetual virginal chastity, and (3) total obedience.

The Evangelical Counsels are assumed by vow by members of religious orders or congregations after their period of testing (postulancy and/or novitiate). Secular priests also are bound to perpetual virginal chastity (celibacy) and obedience, not by vow in the strict sense but still by sacred promise to God and their bishop. They also strive to maintain at least the spirit of the Counsel of poverty.

The Counsels, as Counsels, differ from the Commandments, which are not optional but necessary for salvation. The Counsels we are free to embrace or not, but having embraced and vowed them in a religious community (or as individuals living in the world), we are bound in conscience to observe them.

Young people should pray regularly to find their true vocation in life, asking themselves whether God has called them to a life of virginity in the world, to establishing and bringing up a family, to the priesthood or religious life, or to the work of spreading the faith as missionaries.

On October 28, 1965, the Second Vatican Council promulgated the *Decree on the Adaptation and Renewal of Religious Life,* i.e., the life professed by members of religious orders and congregations. Herewith some excerpts:

"From the very beginning of the Church men and women have set about following Christ with greater freedom and imitating Him more closely through the practice of the Evangelical Counsels. . . . Many of them, under the inspiration of the Holy Spirit, lived as hermits or founded religious families. . . . So it is that in accordance with the Divine Plan a wonderful variety of religious communities has grown up which has made it easier for the Church . . . to be equipped for every good work (2 Tm 3:17) and ready for the work of the ministry—the building up of the Body of Christ (Eph 3:10)" (no. 1).

"The adaptation and renewal of the religious life includes both the constant return to the sources of all Christian life and to the original spirit of the institutes and their adaptation to the changed conditions of our time. . . . The purpose of the religious life is to help the members follow Christ and be united to God through the profession of the Evangelical Counsels. It should be constantly kept in mind, therefore, that even the best adjustments made in accordance with the needs of our age will be ineffectual unless they are animated by a renewal of spirit. This must take precedence over even the active ministry" (no. 2).

"Members of each institute should recall first of all that by professing the Evangelical Counsels they responded to a divine call so that by being not only dead to sin (Rom 6:11) but also renouncing the world they may live for God alone.... This constitutes a special consecration, which is deeply rooted in that of Baptism and expresses it more fully" (no. 5).

"Members of those communities which are entirely dedicated to contemplation give themselves to God alone in solitude and silence, through constant prayer and penance willingly undertaken. No matter how pressing the needs of the active apostolate may be, such communities will always have an honorable place in the Mystical Body of Christ...." (no. 7).

"The chastity 'for the sake of the kingdom of heaven' (Mt 19:12) which religious profess should be counted an outstanding gift of grace. It frees the human heart in a unique fashion (1 Cor 7:32-35) so that it may be more inflamed with love for God and for all people. Thus it not only symbolizes in a singular way the heavenly goods but also the most suitable means by which religious dedicate themselves with undivided heart to the service of God and the works of the apostolate" (no. 12).

"Religious should diligently practice and if need be express also in new forms that voluntary poverty which is recognized and highly esteemed especially today as an expression of the following of Christ. By it they share in the poverty of Christ Who for our sakes became poor, even though He was rich, so that by His poverty we might become rich (2 Cor 8:9; Mt 8:20). With regard to religious poverty it is not enough to use goods in a way subject to the superior's will, but members must be poor both in fact and in spirit, their treasures being in heaven (Mt 6:20)" (no. 13).

"In professing religious obedience, religious offer the full surrender of their own will as a sacrifice of themselves to God.... Under the motion of the Holy Spirit [they] subject themselves in faith to their superiors who hold the place of God" (no. 14).

Religious and the religious life are also treated in the Dogmatic Constitution on the Church, *Among other things, the Council says: "All should take note that the profession of the Evangelical Counsels, though entailing the renunciation of certain values which are to be undoubtedly esteemed, does not detract from a genuine development of the human person, but rather by its very nature is most beneficial to that development. Indeed the Counsels . . . contribute a great deal to the purification of heart and spiritual liberty. They continually stir up the fervor of charity. But especially they are able to more fully mold the Christian to that type of chaste and detached life which Christ the Lord chose for Himself and which His Mother also embraced. . . .*

"Let no one think that religious have become strangers to their fellow human beings or useless citizens of this earthly city by their consecration. For even though it sometimes happens that religious do not directly mingle with their contemporaries, yet in a more profound sense these same religious are united with them in the heart of Christ and spiritually cooperate with them. In this way the building up of the earthly city may have its foundation in the Lord and may tend toward Him, lest perhaps those who build this city shall have labored in vain" (no. 46).

The Religious Life: An Historical Perspective

In the history of Christianity, the eremitic life preceded the monastic and convent life. Christian hermits literally dotted Upper Egypt until St. Pachomius, himself a hermit (d. 346), instituted a common life that brought hermits together for common prayer and worship and other community activity. But the real founder of Eastern monachism was St. Basil (d. 379), who later became archbishop of Caesarea. He wrote a monastic rule, and his monks were and still are called Basilians.

In the West, St. Martin of Tours established the first monastery about the year 360, in the vicinity of Poitiers. The title of founder and patriarch of Western monachism, however, goes to St. Benedict of Nursia (d. 547). The rule he wrote for his monks—the Rule of St. Benedict—virtually supplanted every other rule and maintained its hegemony until the 13th century. That was the century of the rise and development of the so-called Mendicant Orders (Franciscans, Dominicans).

With the founding of the Jesuits in 1534, religious life took a new turn but without prejudice to the older traditions. Subsequently, other orders and congregations sprang up. In general, the more recent communities, like the Jesuits, put less emphasis on common recitation of the Divine Office and also are more engaged in extramural and independent activity.

Religious orders and congregations of women are as varied as those for men. Among them, some represent the female counterpart of a religious order, e.g., Sisters of St. Benedict, St. Francis, St. Dominic, etc.

Despite new directions in activity, the basic purpose of the religious remains what it always has been: to praise and glorify God. To this end, religious continue to be occupied in multitudinous work, some traditional and, especially after Vatican II, some innovative, to meet special needs of the time. Whatever the work, the heart of the religious life is prayer and worship. When that cools or wanes, a community is in spiritual recession and unless conditions improve its days are numbered.

If ours is not the religious vocation, there are many other ways that we can contribute to the growth and attraction of the religious life, not least by regular prayer for vocations together with the spiritual tone we set in our homes and our parishes.

THE CHRISTIAN'S DAY

1. Every morning, offer morning prayer. Never neglect it. Give thanks to God for the night's rest. Offer Him the new day, with its demands, its cares, its trials. Ask God to bless the day. — Count it a special blessing if you can participate

in Holy Mass even on weekdays. Do not let a little discomfort or inconvenience keep you away. Now and then, through the day, turn your thoughts to Jesus in the tabernacle.

2. Be a good worker, whether as a school child or as holding down a job in the world. Work so as to transform it into a service of God, for His greater honor and glory. At opportune moments, renew the morning offering.

3. Pray at mealtime, before and after. Pray thoughtfully, remembering that it is God Who provides the daily bread. Eat moderately; be content with that.

4. Recreation is necessary. But recreation, too, should be wholesome and holy. Shun pastimes that offend God.

5. In association with others, be friendly and courteous. Guard against improper speech of any kind. Take care in whom you place confidence.

6. When vexed or distressed, be patient and resigned to God's will. Think of our Lord's suffering for us. Try to follow His example.

7. Sanctifying grace is the supernatural life of the soul, the bond of filial love and friendship with our heavenly Father. Preserve it at all cost. Go to Confession regularly, and to Holy Communion whenever possible. Should you fall into grave sin, make an act of perfect contrition without delay and go to Confession at an early opportunity.

8. Keep Sunday holy, and observe the Holy Days of Obligation to the extent possible. Never miss Mass on Sundays or Holy Days through your own fault. Try also to attend other parish services, as in Lent, or for funerals, or on parish renewal days. Bear in mind that Sunday observance includes Sunday afternoon and evening.

9. At night, say night prayers. Give thanks to God for the blessings of the day. Examine your conscience. Make an act of perfect contrition for all your sins, past and present. Ask God to watch over you through the night.

———————

THE ECUMENICAL COUNCILS

This illustration shows the bishops gathered in St. Peter's Basilica in Rome for the Second Vatican Council. This Council, which is quoted extensively throughout the present Catechism, was the twenty-first (and latest) Council of the Church. The following pages give a handy summary of the principal teaching of all the Councils.

THE ECUMENICAL COUNCILS

THE COUNCILS	RELIGIOUS AUTHORITIES	CIVIL POWERS	THE CIRCUMSTANCES AND WORK ACCOMPLISHED
1. NICAEA I May 20 July 25, 325 318 bishops, a majority of them Eastern: only 5 Western.	St. Sylvester I Pope (314-335)	*Constantine the Great* (306-337)	Convoked by the Emperor. Condemns and deposes Arius; proclaims that the Word is consubstantial with the Father and draws up a formula of faith that will become the *Nicene Creed* (June 19, 325). Fixes the date for Easter. The order of precedence of the patriarchal sees is also established: Rome Alexandria, Antioch, Jerusalem. Confirmation by St. Sylvester.
2. CONSTANTINOPLE May July 30, 381 150 bishops Eastern only.	**Rome** St. Damasus I (366-384) **Constantinople** St. Gregory I of Nazianzus (379-381)	*Theodosius I* (379-395)	Convoked by the Emperor, with the Pope neither invited nor present nor represented. Condemns the Macedonians (or Pneumatomachi), who denied the divinity and consubstantiality of the Holy Spirit; as well as the Subordinationists and the Modalists. Publishes the *Creed of Nicaea-Constantinople*. The Arian patriarch of Constantinople, Demophilus, is replaced by St. Gregory of Nazianzus. The 3rd canon, reviewing the decisions of Nicaea, places Constantinople on the second rank of patriarchal sees.
3. EPHESUS June 22 Sept. 431 200 Eastern bishops	**Rome** St. Celestine I (422-432) **Constantinople** Nestorius (428-431) **Alexandria** St. Cyril (412-444)	Theodosius II (408-450)	Convoked by the Emperor. Presided over by St. Cyril, representing the Pope. St. Augustine was invited, but died before the Council. Condemns and deposes Nestorius, patriarch of Constantinople, who denied that Mary was the Mother of God *(Theotokos)*. Does not formulate any dogmatic formula, but approves the second letter of St. Cyril to Nestorius. Condemnations of Messalianism and Palagianism. Confirmation by St. Celestine I.

NOTE: This section on the Ecumenical Councils (pp. 398-411) is translated and reproduced with permission from the French **Dictionnaire Chrétienne de la Foi** (2 vol.) published by Les Editions du Cerf (Paris) under the editorship of Olivier de la Brosse, Antonin-Marie Henry, and Philippe Rouillard. The material on the Councils was authored by Olivier de la Brosse and appeared on pages 125-143 of the second volume ("L'Histoire"). C 1968 by Editions du Cerf. All rights reserved.

THE ECUMENICAL COUNCILS

THE COUNCILS	RELIGIOUS AUTHORITIES	CIVIL POWERS	THE CIRCUMSTANCES AND WORK ACCOMPLISHED
4. CHALCEDON Oct 8 Nov. 451 500 to 600 Eastern bishops; 5 Western, legates of the Pope, and 2 Africans	**Rome** St. Leo I (440-461) **Constantinople** Anatolius (449-458)	*Marcian* (450-457)	Convoked by the Emperor, approved later by Pope. Condemned Eutyches and Monophysitism and defined the existence of two perfect natures, divine and human, in Christ. Deposed Dioscorus, leader of the "Robber Synod" of Ephesus of 449. Publishes the *Creed of Chalcedon*. Condemns simony, mixed marriages, and heretic baptisms. Forbids "absolute" ordination, namely, those without specific pastoral functions. Constantinople affirms her power by claiming the second place after Rome within the order of patriarchal sees (28th canon).
5. CONSTAN- TINOPLE II May 5 June 2, 553 160 bishops mostly Eastern; 6 Western	**Rome** Vigilius (537-555) **Constantinople** Eutyches (552-565)	*Justinian I* (527-565)	Convoked by the Emperor, in spite of the opposition from Pope Vigilius, who was kidnapped by Justinian in order to secure an assembly, and who refused to take part in it and did not and did not recognize the Council until a later date. Condemns the three Chapters, writings by Theodore of Mopsuestia, Theodoret, and Ibas of Edessa, suspected of Nestorianism. Confirmation by Gregory I in 591.
6. CONSTAN- TINOPLE III Nov. 7, 680 Sept. 16, 681 174 Eastern bishops	**Rome** St. Agatho (687-681) St. Leo II (682-683) **Constantinople** George I (679-686)	*Constantine IV* (668-685)	Approved by Pope St. Agatho and St. Leo II. Condemns Monothelitism and defines the existence of two wills and two activities in Christ.

THE ECUMENICAL COUNCILS

THE COUNCILS	RELIGIOUS AUTHORITIES	CIVIL POWERS	THE CIRCUMSTANCES AND WORK ACCOMPLISHED
7. NICAEA II Sept. 24 Oct. 23, 787 263 Eastern bishops and numerous prelates	**Rome** Hadrian I (772-795) **Constantinople** Tarasius (784-806)	*Irenaeus* (780-790) and *Constantine VI* (780-797) *Charlemagne* (768-814) Emperor after 800	Against the Iconoclasts, it defines, authorizes and regulates the cult of images. The patriarch Nicephorus and St. Theodore the Studite are the soul of this resistance against Iconoclasm.
8. CONSTANTINOPLE IV Oct. 5, 869 Feb. 28, 870 102 Eastern bishops	**Rome** Hadrian II (867-872) **Constantinople** Photius (858-867) Ignatius (867-877)	East: *Basil I* *the Macedonian* West: *Louis II* (850-875) France: *Charles the Bald* (843-877)	Assembled to judge the cause of Photius, who provoked the schism after 859; it deposes this patriarch. Affirms that Tradition is a rule of faith. Reaffirms the legitimacy of the cult of images. Proclaims the unity of the human soul. Confirms Rome's primacy among the patriarchal sees. The 21st canon sets forth the order of precedence: Rome, Constantinople, Alexandria, Antioch, Jerusalem. Confirmed by Hadrian II.
9. LATERAN I March 18 April 16, 1123 300 Western bishops and abbots	**Rome** Callistus II (1119-1124) Honorius II (1104-1130) **Constantinople** John IX Hieromnemus (1111-1134)	East: *John II* *Comnenus* (1118-1143) West: *Henry V* (1106-1125) France: *Louis VI* (1108-1137)	First ecumenical council celebrated in the West. Regulates the administration of the Sacrament of Holy Orders; opposes simony and Nicolaitism (marriage of priests). Confirms the Concordat of Worms and resolves the *Dispute over Lay Investiture*. Confirmation by Callistus II.
10. LATERAN II April 4-30, 1139 More than 500 participants (Western)	**Rome** Innocent II (1130-1143) **Constantinople** Leo the Stypiotite (1134-1143)	East *John II Comnenus* (1118-1143) West: *Conrad III* (1138-1152) France: *Louis VII* (1137-1180)	Renews the condemnation of simony, usury, tournaments, and marriage of clerics, who are also forbidden to practice law and medicine. Strengthens the law of ecclesiastical celibacy (Canon 7). Decides the schism of Anacletus II; condemns the errors of Bruys and Arnold of Brescia. Confirmation by Innocent II.

THE ECUMENICAL COUNCILS

THE COUNCILS	RELIGIOUS AUTHORITIES	CIVIL POWERS	THE CIRCUMSTANCES AND WORK ACCOMPLISHED
11. LATE-RAN III March 5-19, 1179 300 Western bishops, 400 prelates	**Rome** Alexander III (1159-1181) **Constantinople** Theodosius I Boradiotes (1178-1183)	East: *Manuel I Comnenus* (1143-1180) West: *Frederick I* (1152-1190) France: *Louis VII* (1137-1180)	Condemnation of the Cathari and other heresies of the time. Legislation against the numerous offices and prebends and in favor of education (appointment of school directors in cathedrals). Establishes the rules for the election of popes (a majority of 2/3). Confirmation by Alexander III.
12. LATE-RAN IV Nov. 11-30, 1215 404 bishops, 800 abbots and superiors of Orders (Cistercians, Premonstratensians, Hospitallers, Templars). Absence of Greeks	**Rome** Innocent III (1198-1216) **Constantinople** Theodosius II Irenicus (1213-1215) Maximus II (1215) Charitopoulos (1215-1222)	Constantinople is in the hands of the Crusaders from 1204-1261. West: *Otho IV* (1198-1215) *Frederick II* (1215-1250) France: *Philip Augustus* (1180-1223)	Condemns the Waldensians and Albigensians and the errors of Joachim of Fiore. Encourages the Crusades for the liberation of the Holy Land. Regulates many matters of discipline: sacraments, marriage, and organization of preaching. Annual confession and communion are made obligatory. Publishes a eucharistic confession of faith using the term "transubstantiation." Confirms the hierarchy of the patriarchal sees: Rome, Constantinople, Alexandria, Antioch, Jerusalem. Confirmation by Innocent III.
13. LYONS I June 28 July 17, 1245 3 Patriarchs, 150 bishops, numerous prelates or abbots.	**Rome** Innocent IV (1243-1254) **Constantinople** Manuel II (1244-1255)	West: *Frederick II* (1215-1250) France: *St. Louis* (1226-1270)	Convoked against Frederick II, it institutes proceedings to depose this emperor. Gives help to Christian minorities in the East; supports the crusades against the Sarracens, and in the recovery of the Holy Land. Reorganizes the canonical procedure. Confirmation by Innocent IV.

THE ECUMENICAL COUNCILS

THE COUNCILS	RELIGIOUS AUTHORITIES	CIVIL POWERS	THE CIRCUMSTANCES AND WORK ACCOMPLISHED
14. **LYONS II** May 7 July 17, 1274 500 bishops, 570 prelates, abbots, numerous theologians. Attendance of Greeks	**Rome** St. Gregory X (1271-1276) **Constantinople** Joseph I (1267-1275)	East: *Michael VIII Paleologus* West: *Rudolph of Hapsburg* (1273-1291) France: *Philip III, the Bold.* (1270-1285)	Accomplishes a brief union with the Greeks (Joseph I attends the Council and Emperor Michael Paleologus signs a profession of faith). Confirms the privilege of religious (Dominicans. Franciscans, Carmelites, Augustinians). Issues decree *Ubi periculum*, regulating the election of popes. Confirmation by Gregory X.
15. **VIENNE** Oct. 16, 1311 May 6, 1312 231 Fathers (20 Cardinals, 4 patriarchs, 100 archbishops and bishops, numerous abbots, priors, and superiors of Orders).	**Rome** Clement V (1305-1314) **Constantinople** Niphon I (1311-1315)	East: *Andronicus II* (1282-1328) West: *Henry VII* (1308-1313) France: *Philip IV, the Fair* (1285-1314)	Condemnation of the Knights Templar: Bull *Vox clamantis in excelso* (April 4, 1312). Condemnation of the fallacies of the Béghards and the Béguines. Reforms ecclesiastical discipline, especially with respect to the poverty of the Mendicant Orders. Rejects in this regard the dogmatic fallacies of John Olivi and the Spiritual Franciscans. Confirmation by Clement V.
16. **CON-STANCE** Dec. 5, 1414 April 22, 1418 32 Cardinals, 183 bishops, 100 abbots, 350 prelates.	Three rival Popes: **Rome** Gregory XII (1406-1415) **Avignon** Benedict XIII (1389-1424) **Pisa** John XXIII (1410-1415) then elected at **Constance** Martin V (1417-1431) **Constantinople** Euthymius II (1410-1416)	East: *Manuel II Paleologus* (1291-1415) West: *Sigismund of Hungary* (1410-1437) who convoked it. France: *Charles VI* (1380-1422)	Puts an end to the Great Schism. Reform of ecclesiastical practices. Condemnation of John Wycliffe, John Huss, and Jerome of Prague. Affirms the legitimacy of the Eucharistic communion under the sole species of bread. Theological and practical triumph of the conciliar theories: Decrees *Haec Sancta* (5th Session, April 6, 1415), and *Frequens* (39th Session, Oct. 9, 1417), on the relations of the Pope and Council and on the frequency of the General Councils. Confirmation by Martin V.

THE ECUMENICAL COUNCILS

THE COUNCILS	RELIGIOUS AUTHORITIES	CIVIL POWERS	THE CIRCUMSTANCES AND WORK ACCOMPLISHED
17. **BASLE, FERRARA, FLORENCE, ROME** BASLE: July 23, 1431 FERRARA: 1438 FLORENCE: 1439-1443 ROME: 1443-1445 115 Fathers. Many Greeks attended.	**Rome** Eugenius IV (1431-1447) Felix V antipope (1439-1449) **Constantinople** Joseph II (1416-1439)	East: *John VII Paleologus* West: *Albert II* (1438-1493) *Frederick III* (1440-1493) France: *Charles VII* (1422-1461) Fall of the Byzantine Empire in 1453. *(Constantine XIII)*	Basle: Council convoked by Martin V, who died before it opened; it reaffirms the Conciliarist theses of Constance. Ferrara: Disavows the theses of Basle. Transfers the Council to Florence. Florence: Brings about unity with the East; Greeks: Bull *Laetentur coeli* (July 6, 1493); Armenians: Bull *Exultate Deo* (Nov. 22, 1439); Copts: (Jacobites) and Ethiopians: Bull *Cantate Domino* (Feb. 4, 1442). Transferred to Rome. Rome: Continues the work begun at Florence. Syrians: Bull *Multa ed admirabilia* (Nov. 30, 1444); Chaldeans and Maronites: Bull *Benedictus* (August 7, 1445). Confirmation by Eugene IV.
18. **LATERAN V** May 3, 1512 March 16, 1517 15 Cardinals, 79 bishops.	**Rome** Julius II (1503-1513) Leo X (1513-1521) **Constantinople** Pachomius I (1504-1513) Theoleptus I (1513-1522)	Germany: *Maximilian I* (1493-1519) France: *Louis XII* (1498-1515) *Francis I* (1515-1547) Spain: *Charles V* (1516-1556)	Condemnation of the Conciliarist theses on the primacy of Councils over Popes. Attempts to reform the clergy and the Roman Curia. Condemnation of simony in the election of Popes. Revocation of the Pragmatic Sanction of Bourges and establishment of the Concordat of 1516 with France. Legislation concerning the printing of books and preaching. Confirmation by Leo X.
19. **TRENT** 1545-1563 From 70 to 252 Fathers	From Paul III to Pius IV	France: *From Henry II to Charles IX* Spain: *From Charles V to Philip II*	See Table p. 404.
20. **VATICAN I** 1869-1870 774 Fathers (50 Eastern)	Pius IX (1846-1878)		See Table, p. 407.
21. **VATICAN II** 1962-1965 2500 Fathers	John XXIII (1958-1963) Paul VI (1963-1979)		See Table, p. 408.

THE DECREES OF THE COUNCIL OF TRENT

CHRONOLOGY	THE DOCUMENTS	CONTENTS AND COMMENTARIES
FIRST PERIOD (1545-1547) **Paul III** (1534-1549) **IV Session** April 8, 1546	Decree on the reception of the sacred books and the tradition of the Apostles. Decree on the edition of the *Vulgate*	Determination of the Canon of the Scriptures. The *Vulgate* is declared the "authentic text" of the Bible.
V Session June 17, 1546	Decree on original sin: *Ut fides nostra.* An introduction and six paragraphs in form of canons.	The Sin of Adam. Its transmission to all mankind. Its redemption by the grace of baptism. It aims at the ties established by Lutheran theology between concupiscence and sin, and also against the practices of the Anabaptists.
VI Session Jan. 13, 1547	Decree on justification: *Cum hoc tempore.* An introduction, 16 chapters, 33 canons. 7 months of preparation. Decree on the residence of bishops. 5 chapters.	God's plan of salvation for mankind: sin, redemption, justification by Christ, life of grace, reconciliation, good deeds, and merits. A look at the doctrine of the grace as a whole, it is directed partly against Luther and Calvin (predestination), and partly against Jovinian and Pelagius. The obligation of residence is aimed at increasing the work of the reform of the clergy and dioceses.
VII Session March 3, 1547	Decree on the sacraments: *Ad consummationem.* An introduction, 30 canons.	The sacraments in general. Baptism. Confirmation. Directed against sacramentological theses of Luther *(De captivitate babylonica)* and Melanchthon.
VIII Session March 11, 1547	Transfer of the Council to Bologna. Discussions. Suspended on September 13, 1549.	

THE DECREES OF THE COUNCIL OF TRENT

CHRONOLOGY	THE DOCUMENTS	CONTENTS AND COMMENTARIES
SECOND PERIOD (1551-1552) **Julius III** (1550-1555) **XIII Session** Oct. 11, 1551	Decree on the Eucharist: *Sacrosancta.* Introduction, 8 chapters, 11 canons.	The Eucharist: fact, possibility, proofs of the Real Presence. Transubstantiation. Cult and use of the Sacrament. Against the Eucharistic theses of Calvin, Oecolampius and Zwingli.
XIV Session Nov. 25, 1551	Teaching on the Sacrament of Penance and Anointing of the Sick: Penance: introduction, 9 chapters, 15 canons. Anointing of the Sick: introduction 3 chapters, 4 canons.	Penance: necessity, character of the Sacrament; essential parts, contrition, confession, absolution; reserved cases, satisfaction. Anointing of the Sick: origins of the Sacrament, its effects, its administration, its subject. Against the theses of Wycliffe and Luther.
XVI Session **April 28, 1552** **Marcellus II** (1555) **Paul IV** (1555) **Pius IV** (1559-1565)	New suspension of the Council.	
THIRD PERIOD (1562-1563) **XXI Session** July 16, 1562	Teaching concerning Communion under both species and Communion of little children. Introduction, 9 chapters, 9 canons.	The problem started by John Huss and his followers in Hungary and Bohemia. The Church affirms her right to legislate on this matter.
XXII Session Sept. 17, 1562	Teaching on the Holy Sacrifice of the Mass. Introduction, 9 chapters, 9 canons.	The Mass is truly the sacrifice of Christ. It recalls and makes present the redeeming sacrifice of the Cross. The rites. The use of the vernacular. Against the Protestants' theses of the Eucharist as simple memorial of the Last Supper.

THE DECREES OF THE COUNCIL OF TRENT

CHRONOLOGY	THE DOCUMENTS	CONTENTS AND COMMENTARIES
XXIII Session July 15, 1563	Teaching on the Sacrament of Holy Orders: *Sacrificium et sacerdotium.* 4 chapters, 8 canons.	Against the Protestant denial of a priestly state, a magisterium, and a hierarchy, it affirms that the priesthood established by the New Law is an Order and a Sacrament, and that the priestly state is an aggregation to the Hierarchy.
XXIV Session Nov. 11, 1563	Teaching on the Sacrament of Marriage: *Matrimonii perpetuum.* Introduction, 12 canons. Canons on reform of Marriage: Decree *Tametsi.* 10 chapters.	The divine institution of Marriage and its sacramental character. Supernatural grace perfects the natural bond. Monogamy. Indissolubility. Right of the Church to legislate in this matter. Dignity of celibacy. Against Luther, Melanchthon, Philip of Hesse (bigamist), and the tendency to reduce marriage to a simple contract of natural law. The Church abandons the practice of clandestine marriages (aimed at insuring its freedom), and sets down conditions of publicity.
XXV Session Dec. 3-4, 1563 Jan. 26, 1564	Decree on purgatory: *Cum catholica ecclesia.* Decree on the invocation and veneration of relics of Saints, on holy images and indulgences. Decree on religious persons and nuns. 22 chapters. Bull *Benedictus Deus.*	There is a purgatory. The souls of the faithful may be helped by prayers and the Mass. It is permitted and recommended to pray and invoke the Saints. One may render them a cult of honor and veneration. Religious life. The law of the monasteries. Religious vows. Measures of reform. Pius IV confirms the body of Conciliar texts.

THE WORK OF VATICAN COUNCIL I

(1869-1870)

CHRONOLOGY	THE DOCUMENTS	CONTENTS AND COMMENTARIES
Pius IX (1846-1878) **III Session** April 24, 1870	Dogmatic Constitution on the Catholic Faith: *Dei Filius* Introduction, 4 chapters, 18 canons.	God, creator of all things, reveals Himself in His creation and through His Son. He may be known through human intelligence and through faith, which cannot be in disagreement. Against fideism, traditionalism, deism, and rationalism, especially directed against Gunther, Hermes, and Bautain.
IV Session July 18, 1870	Dogmatic Constitution on the Church of Christ *Pastor aeternus.* Introduction and 4 chapters, each containing a canon.	The Church is founded upon Peter and the Apostles. Peter and his successors have a perpetual primacy in the apostolate and the power of jurisdiction. The Pope, supreme judge in Church matters, has an infallible magisterium when he speaks *ex cathedra.* Interrupted by the Franco-Prussian war, the Council resolved only the first part of its reflections on the Church, concerning the Pope. Therefore, the role of the bishops was not sufficiently defined.

THE WORK OF VATICAN COUNCIL II
(1962-1965)

CHRONOLOGY	THE DOCUMENTS	CONTENTS AND COMMENTARIES
John XXIII Oct. 28, 1958- June 3, 1963		
Jan. 25, 1959	Discourse announcing the Council. Bull *Humanae Salutis,* convoking Vatican Council II.	The term "aggiornamento" is used for the first time. Enumeration of the great purposes of the Council: the renewal of the Church, its role in the world, and ecumenism.
Paul VI June 21, 1963		
II Session Dec. 4, 1963 (N.B.-In Vatican Council II the terms session designates a period and not an isolated seating.	Constitution on the Sacred Liturgy: *Sacrosanctum Concilium.* Introduction, 7 chapters. Decree on the Means of Social Communication: *Inter mirifica.* An introduction, 2 chapters.	General principles for the restoration and progress of the liturgy. The Eucharist, the other Sacraments and Sacramentals, the Divine Office, the Liturgical Year, sacred art and music, and the materials for worship. Media of information (radio, film, television), in themselves and in their relations with the pastoral functions of the Church. Voted upon too hastily, this decree is lacking with reference to the science of social communication and the later atmosphere of the Conciliar declarations.
III Session Nov. 21, 1964	Dogmatic Constitition on the Church: *Lumen gentium.* 8 chapters. Decree on the Eastern Catholic Churches: *Orientalium Ecclerum.* Introduction and 6 paragraphs.	The Mystery of the Church, the People of God, the episcopate, the laity, holiness within the Church, religious life, eschatology, the Virgin Mary in the Mystery of Christ and of the Church. Unity of the Church and diversity of local Churches. Dignity and riches of the Eastern Churches. The Patriarchate. The right to absolute freedom, within the Church, of Eastern traditions. *Communicatio in sacris.*

408

THE WORK OF VATICAN COUNCIL II
(1962-1965)

CHRONOLOGY	THE DOCUMENTS	CONTENTS AND COMMENTARIES
III Session Nov. 21, 1964	Decree on Ecumenism: *Unitatis redintegratio* Introduction and 5 chapters.	Catholic principles of ecumenism: its exercise, relations between separated brethren, the ecclesiological status of communities separated from the Roman See.
	Decree on the Pastoral Office of Bishops in the Church: *Christus Dominus.* Introduction, and 3 chapters.	Bishops and the universal Church (episcopal collegiality, relations with the Apostolic See); bishops and particular Churches or dioceses; their cooperation for the common good of several Churches
	Decree on the Renewal and Adaptation of the Religious life: *Perfectae caritatis.* Introduction and 27 paragraphs.	Principles for the renewal of religious life, forms of contemplative and apostolic life; lay religious life, secular institutions, vows, communl life, organisms created to bring about reform.
	Decree on Formation of Priests: *Optatam totius Ecclesiae renovationem.* Introduction and 22 paragraphs.	Priestly vocations, organization of seminaries, spiritual, intellectual, and pastoral formation of priests, programs of studies; formation continued within the ministry.
	Declaration on Christian Education: *Gravissimum educationis momentum.* Introduction and 12 paragraphs.	Universal right to an education; Christian education, those responsible for it, its means. Duties and rights of parents. Catholic schools, faculties and universities. School coordination. This text is a renewal of the perspectives given in 1929 by *Divini illius magistri,* although not in great depth.
IV Session Oct. 28, 1965	Declaration on the Relationship of the Church with Non-Christian Religions: *Nostra Aetate.* Introduction and 5 chapters.	The community of peoples. The different Non-Christian religions: Hinduism, Buddhism, Islamism, Judaism, The universal fraternity, which excludes all discrimination.

THE WORK OF VATICAN COUNCIL II

(1962-1965)

CHRONOLOGY	THE DOCUMENTS	CONTENTS AND COMMENTARIES
	Dogmatic Constitution on Divine Revelation: *Dei Verbum.* Introduction and 6 chapters.	Nature of Revelation. Its transmission (Tradition, Scriptures, People of God, Magisterium). Interpretation of Sacred Scripture and its role in the life of the Church.
		Text intended as a general preface to all the Conciliar documents, a meditation upon God's Word. After the rejection of an overly narrow treatment of the "sources" of revelation *(De fontibus revelationis),* it is an encouragement to the work of the exegetes and a contribution to the problem of the relations between Scripture and Tradition.
Nov. 18, 1965	Decree on the Apostolate of the Laity: *Apostolicam actuositatem.* Introduction and 6 chapters.	The vocation of the laity to the apostolate, the goals to be achieved, the fields of the apostolate, the methods, and the formation of apostles. First text of a Council on this subject. No lay people were among the members of the commission that worked on it.
	Pastoral Constitution on the Church in the Modern World: *Gaudium et spes.* Lengthy introduction and 9 chapters.	The Human condition in today's world. Human dignity, community, and activity in the universe. Role of the Church. Marriage and family, culture, economic and social life, politics, peace.
		First known under the name of Schema XVII, and later as Schema XIII, this text was not included in the initial program and was introduced later under the influence of the encyclicals *Mater et Magistra, Pacem in Terris,* and *Ecclesiam suam,* as an element of dialogue between the Church and the modern world.

THE WORK OF VATICAN COUNCIL II

(1962-1965)

CHRONOLOGY	THE DOCUMENTS	CONTENTS AND COMMENTARIES
	Declaration on Religious Freedom: *Dignitatis humanae.* Introduction and 2 chapters.	The object and bases of religious freedom, individual and collective. Its exercise and limits. Its roots in Revelation. Role of the Church in this sphere. Separated from a projected schema on ecumenism and at first centered on the "rights of conscience," the redaction of the text evolved toward the affirmation of "the rights of human beings" based on the dignity of the human person.
	Decree on the Church's Missionary Activity: *Ad Gentes.* Introduction and 6 chapters.	Doctrinal principles of mission: the Father's design, sending of the Son and the Spirit. Missionary nature of the Church. The work of the missions: testimony, preaching, formation of communities. Particular Churches. Organization of life and activities of missionaries. After 7 preparatory redactions and 3 total revisions this schema benefited from numerous interventions by missionary bishops. Great theological unity, homogeneous to other ecclesiastical texts of the Council.
	Decree on the Ministry and Life of Priests: *Presbyterorum Ordinis.* Introduction and 3 chapters.	The presbyterium in the mission of the Church. The ministry of priests: their functions (Word and Sacraments), relations to the world, kind of life (vocation to holiness, spiritual demands, celibacy, obedience, poverty), material conditions of existence. Fruit of the Conciliar work itself, this text joins in one single perspective several scattered propositions on the discipline of the clergy: priestly unity, in the mystery of Christ, the service of the Gospel, and
Dec. 7, 1965		the worship of the New Covenant.

Analytical Index

Altar, 181
Amen, 142
Angels: fallen, 64; Guardian, in New Testament, 64; perfect spiritual beings, 63; worship God, 63
Anointing of the Sick: administration, 234; communal anointing, 235; preparation for, 236; recipients, 236; helps sick, 233
Apostles, 113f
Apostles' Creed, 55
Baptism: administered, 153; of blood, 156; of desire, 156; effects, 156; forgives sins, 157; godparents, 157; incorporation into Christ, 157; made members of Church, 152; necessity, 154
Blessed: happiness of, 134
Blessed Sacrament: adoration of, 211; Corpus Christi, 212; vigil lamp, 210; where kept, 209
Blessings: given by laity, 258; obtains spiritual effects, 257; praise God, 257; purpose, 258f; Sacramentals, 257
Bible: abbreviations of Books, 16; Acts of the Apostles, 41, 47; Apocrypha, 24; Books total 73, 15; canon, 22; chapters and verses, 29; citations of, 15; contains Revelation, 12; Dead Sea Scrolls, 25; Deuterocanonical Books, 23, 25; Deuteronomic tradition, 32-34; differences, 29-31; early translations, 26; Elohist tradition, 32; English translations, 28; God's Word to us, 52; Gospel, 41ff; how to read, 50; human authors, 17, 19; incomparable, 13; inerrancy, 19; inspiration, 18; interpretation of, 21; interpreted by Church, 51; language of,

24; library of books, 13; literacy forms, 20; main parts, 14; manuscripts, 25; New Testament, 23, 40; Old Testament,23; other names, 14; Pauline Epistles, 45; Pentateuch, 18, 31; Priestly tradition, 32; principal author, 17; principles of interpretation, 20; Prophetic Books, 29, 37f; Protocanonical Books, 23; senses of, 51f; Septuagint, 26; Targums, 26; Torah, 29; and truth, 21; use in Liturgy, 49f; and veneration of images, 129; vernacular versions, 28; Vulgate, 26; what it is, 13; Wisdom Books, 35; Writers, sacred, 18; Writings, 18, 29; Yahwist tradition, 32
Bishops: duties, 103; empowered to consecrate, 164; forgive sins, 221; office of teaching, sanctifying, governing, 103; shepherd a diocese, 102; successor of Apostles, 102; Synod, 101
Candles, 184
Cardinals: college of, 101; counselors to Pope, 101
Christian Initiation of Adults: preparation for Baptism, 158; stages, 158; and Vatican II, 159
Christian's Day: prayer, 395; recreation, 396; work, 396
Church: ceremonies, 280; Eucharistic teaching, 166; founded by Christ, 95; grants God's forgiveness, 221; honors relics, 128; infallible pronouncements, 115; invisible head is Christ, 96; is apostolic, 113; is catholic, 112; is holy, 109, 111f; is one, 109f; marks, 108; missionaris of, 120; missionary work, 121; Mystical Body, 93f; needs reg-

ulation, 351; People of God; 93f; pilgrimages, 281; Pope is visible head, 96; power to bless, consecrate, and perform exorcisms, 258; Precepts of, 350ff [See Precepts of Church]; prepared in Old Testament, 92; preserved from error, 115; processions, 279; relations with Jews, 79; Roman Catholic has four marks, 109; church of salvation, 118; societies, 281; sodalities, 281; soul of, 118; teaches veneration of Saints, 125; teaches what God has revealed, 53; those who do not know her, 119; threefold office, 114; truly present in diocese, 102; universal sacrament of salvation, 94; use of Bible in worship, 49; visible society, 350; visible kingdom of Christ, 93; vivified by Spirit, 94; who belongs to? 95
Commandments, Ten: Fulfilled by Christ, 296; greatest, 288; list, 295; violation of, 379 [See individual Commandments]
Communion: bodily preparation, 207; demeanor for, 208; effects, 204; under both kinds, 200; in the hand, 202; under one form suffices, 199; prayers after, 208; what we receive, 198; worthy reception, 199; worthy and unworthy reception, 204f
Communion of Saints, 124
Confirmation: administration, 161; definition, 159; effects, 160; instituted by Christ, 161
Conscience: obliged to follow, 287; points to God, 57; voice of God, 286
Conscientious objection, 331.

177f; Prayer of the Faithful, 50; Preparation of the Gifts, 192; Roman Missal, 181; Sacramentary, 182; Sacrifice of New Covenant, 170; special garments, 187; stipends, 176f; use of candles, 184; to whom offered? 175; [See also Communion; Eucharist]

Matrimony: administered by couple, 248; dissolution of, 250; duties of, 249; graces of, 249; impediments to, 252; instituted by Christ, 247; mixed marriages, 252; requirements for, 251; sharers in mystery of Christ and Church, 248

Missionaries, 121

National Catechetical Directory, 49, 213

Ninth Commandment [See Sixth and Ninth Commandments]

Parish: family of God, 105

Penance: absolution, 220; Act of Contrition, 227; Christ commands us to confess, 228; confession of sins, 219; contrition, 218; effects of, 216; examination of conscience, 226; forgives sins, 215; general confession, 224f; how Church grants God's forgiveness, 221; how God forgives, 221; instituted by Christ, 215; penitential celebrations, 226; penitents participate in, 218; principal parts, 218; reasons for, 216; reception of, 222; reconciliation with God and Church, 217; role of priest, 222; satisfaction, 219; Seal of Confession, 230; sins to confess, 227; where to confess, 229; who can absolve? 221; who forgives sins? 221

People of God: missionary duty, 123; royal priesthood of, 108 [See also Laity]

Pope: bishop of Rome, 98;

encyclicals, 100; is infallible, 116; nationality of, 100; summary history of, 99

Prayer: effects, 264; features, 263; need, 9; reasons for, 261; time for, 264; for what? 261; for whom? 255; what it is, 261

Prayers: Acts of Virtues, 278; Angelus, 270; Canticle of Mary (Magnificat), 274; Canticle of Simeon (Nunc Dimittis), 276; Canticle of Zechariah (Benedictus), 275; Glory to the Father, 268; Hail, Holy Queen, 269; Hail Mary, 268; at Meals, 276; Morning and Evening, 277; Our Father, 266; Regina Caeli, 271; Rosary, 271; Sign of the Cross, 267; Te Deum, 273; We Fly to Your Patronage, 269

Precepts of the Church: difference between know and love, 352; reason for obeying, 351; right to make laws, 350; traditional, 341; updated, 355; violation, 379 [See also individual Precepts]

Priesthood: of Christ, 108; common of the faithful, 244; ministerial, 237ff, 108

Priests: anointed, 104; celibate life, 241; empowered to consecrate, 164; entrusted with spiritual care of people, 105; forgive sins, 221; may be assistant pastor or pastor of a parish, 105; permanency of, 240; representatives of Christ, 239; secular or religious, 104; take place of bishop, 105

Purgatory: place of purgation, 135; the poor souls, 136; who go there? 134

Religious Life: history, 394; purpose, 395

Roman Curia: helps Pope to govern, 101; nine congregations, 101

Revelation: began with first man, 11; contained in Bible and in Sacred Tradition, 12; event, encounter, action, History, 369; twofold source, 12; sources of, 48; taught us by Church, 53; truths revealed by God, 17

Sacramentals: chief benefits, 256; chief kinds, 257; differ from Sacraments, 255; make Christ's saving power accessible, 259; sacred signs, 250; use of, 260

Sacraments: instituted by Christ, 149ff; third part of Catechism, 9; seven, 150 [See also individual Sacraments]

Sacred Heart: devotion to, 213; feast of, 214

Sacrifice: of the Cross, 170ff; of the faithful, 169; of the Mass, 170ff; offered to God, 169

Saints: beatification of, 130; canonization of, 130; help our prayers, 127; intercession, of, 126; mirror God's goodness, 125; Patron, 158; relics of, 128; veneration of, 125, 127

Salvation: faith necessary for, 53; plan for, 40

Second Commandment: forbids taking God's name, 311; oaths, 312; perjury, 313; blasphemy, 312; taking vows, 314

Second Precept: Communion, 366; conditions for Communion, 367; sacramental life, 365

Seventh and Tenth Commandments: aiding and abetting, 344; forbids harming others in their goods, 342; reparation, 345; stealing, 344

Seventh Precept: help missionary apostolate, 378; practice of evangelization, 378

Sin: against Holy Spirit,